T0371384

Heuertz is the most compassionate, fresh, and thoughtful voice in the Enneagram. A true luminary. *The Enneagram of Belonging*, his finest work to date, so beautifully reminds us that the Enneagram, at its very best, is a map to better loving ourselves and others. What a gift.

– **Ryan O'Neal,** Sleeping At Last

Chris has lived with the teachings and traditional language of the Enneagram long enough to integrate and embody its insights, and he has found creative new ways to explain them to newcomers and to those familiar with the system. *The Enneagram of Belonging* is essential reading!

– **Russ Hudson,** coauthor of *The Wisdom of the Enneagram*

In his earlier bestselling *The Sacred Enneagram*, Chris showed us that the Enneagram is not just a map of personality but a map of the archetypes of soul. In *The Enneagram of Belonging*, Chris reveals his gifts not just as a mapmaker but as a soul-archaeologist. If you long to more deeply belong—first and foremost to yourself— you will want to grab a figurative shovel and let Chris compassionately companion you as you dig up the buried parts of your True Self.

– **Nhiên Vương, JD, MDiv,** founder of Evolving Enneagram

I have found the Enneagram a helpful tool in enabling me to better understand not only my own strengths and weaknesses but those of others' as well. Chris Heuertz's new book invites us to use the Enneagram to grow in compassion for our own complicated selves and, therefore, love ourselves more and allow God to encounter us in our limitless complexity.

– **James Martin, SJ,** author of *The Jesuit Guide to (Almost) Everything* and *Becoming Who You Are*

The Enneagram of Belonging is a book that was everything I didn't know I needed to accept myself wholly and to "live into my own goodness." Chris's voice comes through as a dear friend, chatting over coffee and guiding me through my own walls, uncovering places I needed to see to better hope for the best in myself and those around me.

– **Sally Kang,** musician in Run River North

In *The Enneagram of Belonging* Chris Heuertz has successfully distilled the essence, research, and finding of all schools of the Enneagram into a highly readable and balanced book. Bravo! If I had to name one book that offers a most complete and thorough portrait on the subject of the Enneagram of Personality, I would choose this one.

– **Jack Labanauskas,** editor and publisher of *Enneagram Monthly*

The
ENNEAGRAM
of BELONGING

OTHER BOOKS BY
CHRISTOPHER L. HEUERTZ

Simple Spirituality:
Learning to See God in a Broken World

Friendship at the Margins:
Discovering Mutuality in Service and Mission

Unexpected Gifts:
Discovering the Way of Community

The Sacred Enneagram:
Finding Your Unique Path to Spiritual Growth

The Sacred Enneagram Workbook:
Mapping Your Unique Path to Spiritual Growth

The Enneagram of Belonging Workbook:
Mapping Your Unique Path to Self-Acceptance

The
ENNEAGRAM
of BELONGING

A Compassionate Journey of Self-Acceptance

CHRISTOPHER L. HEUERTZ

ZONDERVAN
THRIVE

ZONDERVAN THRIVE

The Enneagram of Belonging
Copyright © 2020 by Christopher L. Heuertz

Requests for information should be addressed to:
Zondervan, 3900 Sparks Dr. SE, Grand Rapids, Michigan 49546

Zondervan titles may be purchased in bulk for educational, business, fundraising, or sales promotional use. For information, please email SpecialMarkets@Zondervan.com.

ISBN 978-0-310-35781-0 (audio)

Library of Congress Cataloging-in-Publication Data

Names: Heuertz, Christopher L., 1971- author.
Title: The enneagram of belonging : a compassionate journey of self-acceptance / Christopher L. Heuertz.
Description: Grand Rapids : Zondervan, 2020. | Includes bibliographical references. | Summary: "While most contemporary Enneagram books stop at the descriptions of the nine types, Enneagram teacher and bestselling author Chris Heuertz uncovers the missing link in our journey of living into our true self: radical self-compassion that can bring us back to belonging. The Enneagram of Belonging is your guide to this essential journey"-- Provided by publisher.
Identifiers: LCCN 2020000395 (print) | LCCN 2020000396 (ebook) | ISBN 9780310357780 (trade paperback) | ISBN 9780310357803 (ebook)
Subjects: LCSH: Enneagram.
Classification: LCC BF698.35.E54 H48 2020 (print) | LCC BF698.35.E54 (ebook) | DDC 155.2/64--dc23
LC record available at https://lccn.loc.gov/2020000395 LC ebook record available at https://lccn.loc.gov/2020000396

Author is represented by The Christopher Ferebee Agency, www.christopherferebee.com.

Zondervan Thrive, an imprint of Zondervan, publishes books that empower readers with insightful, expert-driven ideas for a life of thriving in today's world.

Cover and interior illustrations: Elnora Turner
Author photo: PS Drickey
Interior design: Kait Lamphere

To the EnneaCurious, may you continue wading through the murky waters of this tradition to bring forth its mysteries.

Contents

Introduction

A Compassionate Guidebook for Belonging

This is a book about dragons. Dragons that deliver messages, dragons that protect treasures, and dragons that need to be slain. While working on this book I've had to face my own dragons. It has not been an easy journey but one well worth it. And I imagine if you're searching for the courage to welcome and face your own dragons, then a little volume like this serves as the perfect guide.

I've faced these dragons during late nights and early mornings; at writing retreats in Berlin, México City, and Santa Fe; and while being warmed by more pots of Ethiopian pour-over coffee than I would want to count. I've encountered these dragons during battle after battle of wills with my sweet dog Basil, as if he were trying to Jedi-Mind-Trick me into a walk to the park where he likes to chase bunnies instead of letting me slug away at my own inner work in peace. Facing these dragons has been one of the most enthralling inner journeys I've undertaken. It's also been one of the most demanding.

In being introduced and reintroduced to the dragons, I've become a reluctant Enneagram mapmaker, charting the unexplored interior landscape of my ego. And my ego hasn't made this easy. It's taken (as it always has) more from me than I'd consciously or willingly surrender. Like all egos do, mine has superimposed itself on my sense of self like a disproportionately large rendering of Greenland on a flat, 2-D map. My ego has presented itself as much heftier than it actually is; an oversized projection of what it wants me to believe it has become—and subsequently who I've become.

So, what's the source of all this tension?

If I'm honest, it's been a journey in learning to like myself. And that's the punchline here: if there's any part of ourselves that we can't or won't make room for—*if any part doesn't belong*—then the truth is, *no part fully belongs*.

This should sound like good news, especially for those of us familiar with the Enneagram. But awareness of our type is not enough to change everything. True and sustainable transformation requires an *honest* relationship with ourselves that is rooted in deep compassion. And compassion then leads the way to the belonging we crave most.

Seems simple enough. But as we've learned, our fragmented self fights against our truest, purest self (what I will refer to as our Essence) to make this experience of belonging seem impossible.

Accepting our Essence as the truest, purest core of ourselves allows us to remember what Howard Thurman remarked at his Baccalaureate address at Spelman College on May 4, 1980: "There is something in every one of you that waits and listens for the sound of the genuine in yourself. It is the only true guide you will ever have. And if you cannot hear it, you will all of your life spend your days on the ends of strings that somebody else pulls."

This *sound of the genuine* within us is the melody of our Essence, affirming our soul's created reason for being. You can't get much truer than that.

Thankfully we have a teaching like the Enneagram to unscramble all these crossed wires and find a pathway back to the core of who we are, the most beautiful aspects of our self that many of us have forgotten. And once we can embrace the wholeness of who we are, a portal for compassion opens up—for ourselves and for others.

So that's the journey in this book. What you hold in your hand is a compassionate guidebook for belonging.

We'll start with a simple stroll through the very basics of the Enneagram, a kind of throwback to the original building blocks of the Enneagram of Personality. However, this probably shouldn't be the first Enneagram book you read. Before diving in, it would be helpful for you to know your type, and it would be important to have a grasp on the key components of type structure.

Even though I know better, I still read the comments from the reviews of my last book, *The Sacred Enneagram*. So, to help manage your expectations, let me make the implicit explicit.

- First, there is not an Enneagram type test in this book. The Enneagram is not "a test" and many of the tests are actually unhelpful.
- Second, I have not organized the content so that you can simply turn to the chapter on your type. Why? Because the system is much more complex than that, plus you deserve better than isolated type descriptions that don't honor their connection to the whole.
- Finally, there are spiritual undertones to this book, but I have written it with accessible interspiritual language hoping that no matter what outlook or tradition you subscribe to, you will find something of value here.

Together, we will explore what it means to let our whole self belong. We'll review the first four Enneagons—Holy Ideas, Fixations, Virtues, and Passions—that Óscar Ichazo initially introduced in the deserts of Chile back in 1969, and that make up the key components of the Enneagram of Personality as most know it. I'll offer fresh language and a rejuvenated approach to incorporating the gifts of these original Enneagons as we learn to make peace with the whole of ourselves. We'll also dip our toes into the deep end of the conversations happening around the Instincts and Subtypes, attempting to harmonize some of the disparate and contradictory ideas out there.

Through this deep dive into *The Enneagram of Belonging*, you will recover the parts of yourself you once thought couldn't possibly be essential aspects of the whole. Like a diamond with rough edges and hairline fractures, you'll realize how even seemingly unattractive parts of yourself make you not only who you are, but are crucial to the unique beauty that is you.

Before we get much further, let me remind us, we all have a shadow—the part of ourselves hidden from awareness. This is a great place for dragons to hang out but a pretty poor strategy for belonging. So, let's examine what happens when we dare to bring it all into view, encounter honestly the whole of who we are, and thereby remember who we are. This journey to belonging requires all of you—your body, heart, and head. What was once a fragmented and disconnected expression of you now beckons you toward alignment. This is a journey toward wholeness. It's a challenging sojourn for sure. It requires great fortitude, for it will cost you everything you think you are. But engaging undaunted risks will be rewarded with meaning and realization like you've never known.

It's also important to remember that belonging is about integration: bringing our body, heart, and mind into alignment with our unshakeable belovedness, and realizing that *all* the complexities of ourselves belong. You see, when we abandon parts of ourselves in an effort to make a break from our desired identity, we further our own fragmentation. What if we discovered it *all* belonged? That we could actually learn from the scrappiest, most broken, and deepest wounded parts of ourselves, alongside the most beautiful, perfect, and strongest aspects of ourselves? What if all of who we are is a gift, intended for our whole belonging and becoming? What if we came to believe that we aren't fundamentally flawed, bad people hoping to be good, but good people hoping to be better—wanting to accept ourselves for who we've always been?

Because the truth is, if we can't self-observe, then we can't self-correct. We are doing ourselves great harm by rejecting and refusing to learn from the parts of ourselves we dislike the most—even the parts we perceive are flawed. It all belongs.

Tragically, life is painful. We suffer. We suffer even more when we reject parts of our true identity and when we refuse to love and practice compassion toward the whole of who we are. But we can stop the cycle of suffering when we come home to ourselves. And we come home to our Essence by bringing our body, heart, and mind into alignment with all-encompassing love. *The Enneagram of Belonging* is for the lifelong sojourner willing to engage the idea that the process of *becoming* the person we're made to be demands that we must first learn how to authentically *belong*.

Our journey together will begin in the head where we'll find fresh language and clarification for the Enneagram's Holy Ideas—the tradition's most convoluted and most misunderstood teaching. We'll learn that the Holy Idea is the first truth we tell ourselves when the mind is centered in its true self. We'll discover that the Fixations are the lies our mind attaches to which keep us distanced from our Holy Idea or divine mind. Simultaneously, we'll learn how to hold our Fixation with compassion, and why this even needs to belong.

From there we'll make passage into our heart, where we'll remember that our Virtue is simply the unconditioned fruit of a centered heart that is present to love. Here we'll include the unexpected gift of our Passions, our type's pattern of emotional suffering. We'll realize that our Passion, which has sometimes been framed as sin, is in truth how our heart suffers disconnect from Essence.

Finally, we'll travel perhaps to the most unchartered territory of the body and explore the impact our unobserved and unconditioned Instincts make on our whole sense of self. Here, we will let our lack of self-awareness shift to mindful self-observation.

So, pour yourself a fresh cup of hot coffee and let's get ready to meet some dragons.

PART I

GOING DEEPER
into the
ENNEAGRAM OF PERSONALITY

1

Show Me *a* Dragon

Finding the Courage to Face Our Shadow

I was at a hip little farm-to-table spot in Minneapolis, just having finished facilitating an Enneagram workshop. The team that helped host the event had set up the reservation for this lovely meal, and the dinner conversation we shared complemented the spread fabulously.

One of the people who had tirelessly led the efforts in pulling off the successful event happened to be the head children's minister at a fairly large suburban church. A young parent herself, she told one of the funniest stories I'd heard in a long time.

Apparently, her five-year-old daughter Janae had recently determined that she was an atheist.

As you can imagine, her mother, tasked with spiritual formation for hundreds of other children, rightly expressed concern. Wanting to figure out how this early existential restlessness had emerged, this distressed mother attempted to investigate the "why" behind Janae's decision.

It turns out, one fine morning at church, a Sunday school teacher told a classroom full of little kids, "God will give you *whatever* you ask for in prayer." Seems no-nonsense enough for most religious people who understand prayer as a transactional exchange of human requests and divine responses. And so, little Janae took this adult's word to heart and later that night as she lay in bed she asked God to show her a dragon.

Pretty awesome prayer actually.

Over the course of the next several days Janae eagerly awaited the arrival of her dragon, but to no avail. And so, she quite sensibly determined God must not be real.

I love this story so much because, in a sense, it's all of our stories.

Why? This girl's prayer was a plea for courage. And courage is always the first step in the journey of belonging.

BELONGING TAKES COURAGE

For whatever reason, every one of us feels in some way that we don't belong. Perhaps we hold on to memories of failures and regrets, or maybe the experiences of disappointments or unmet expectations. It might be the doubts and fears we wrestle with, or simply the guilt or shame that plagues our notions of who we think we are.

These fragmented aspects of self are introduced in the constant replayed scripts that circle through our thought lives—"Why am I always so worried?" or "I overdid it again . . ." or "I wish I could keep my emotions under control." They appear in the familiar mental commentary that fill in all the quiet spaces of our hearts and minds. They also surface when we are confronted with what we understand to be the "worst" features of our Enneagram type or personality structure, that we'd rather ignore or skip over, if we're being honest.

Conversely, these fragments of our identity may be the best, truest, or most innocent parts of who we are. At their most authentic and vulnerable, these splintered aspects of self have so much to say to us about who we really are. Yet too often we are quick to push them away—out of anger, shame, fear, or otherwise—rather than listen to them and learn from them. This may especially be true for those of us who were socialized in more conservative religious traditions where we were taught that our souls are fundamentally sinful and in urgent need of a redeemer—as if there's nothing intrinsically good, true, and beautiful hardwired to our Essence. Sadly, there are amazing parts of ourselves we sometimes have difficulty accepting. But learning to own the fabulous parts of self is also part of this journey because, after all, it's not bragging if it's true. We have to learn to live into all our goodness.

Whatever these fragments of our identity might be, we've cut ourselves off from them—the bad *and* the good. Then these fragments haunt or control us; fundamentally they end up becoming the forgotten parts of self. And in losing awareness of them, in a sense they become little monsters, or even dragons, that we don't want to see.

Sure, we know these forgotten fragments of self are still there. In fact, most of us spend quite a bit of egoic[1] energy running from

---

1. The "ego" is one's identity construct rooted in our sense of awareness (or lack thereof) that vacillates between our conscious sense of self and the subconscious influences

them. It's as if we believe that *hiding* from these perceived flaws will keep us *pure* from them.

What ends up happening is the undesirable fragments of our identity get parked in the silhouette of our consciousness—in our shadow, the unobserved aspect of our nature. This is where we try to hide the least-tidied-up bits of what we don't want or feel incapable of bringing into our psycho-spiritual awareness. But of course, these fragments of our psyche don't fall asleep or disappear in our shadow. Rather they grow up, becoming stronger than we ever could have anticipated.

In a sense, these fragments become the dragons of our subconscious and unconscious that protect the treasure of our hidden Essence—our most authentic and truest selves. You see, long ago our Essence was bruised, wounded, maybe even traumatized. And so, we adapted these other parts of self in an attempt to protect our conditioned self from being hurt again. Here we find the plot twist: the dragons are not our enemy; rather, they were called upon at an early age to protect our inmost treasure. So, it makes sense why we get ourselves into trouble when we reject the very force of protection we most need.

---

that fortify our notions of who we are: a substantial construction of who we think we are (identity) and what we think we are worth (dignity). In large part our ego is the illusion diverting us from who we can become when awakened through self-awareness and committed mindfulness, meditation, or contemplative practices. The truth of self is rooted in the instinctive unconscious, the part of us that is almost never uncovered or recognized except when touched by deep love, awakened through deep spiritual practice, or drawn forward through psychoanalysis. Though conscious awareness is required to observe our ego, fundamentally our ego is how our character structure emerges through (but not limited to) nature, preferences and affinities, religious and existential beliefs, talents, abilities, our so-called Enneagram Childhood Wound (or Kidlife Crisis from here forward), relationships, and connections to institutions and communities. Within religious traditions the idea of our False Self or "sinful nature" has sometimes been misidentified as the ego (even co-opted as the ego), but I use egoic language in a neutral or indifferent aspect, not making judgment about the possible flawedness of the ego but drawing attention to the ego's tendency toward a lack of awareness.

DRAGONS: Monsters and Messengers

Throughout history, dragons have been a universal symbol of what connects the earth and sky—symbolically the unconscious and conscious mind.

In mythology and folklore, dragons have come to epitomize the power of hidden knowledge and instinctual strength and are depicted as protectors of priceless treasure. Many of the stories that portray dragons illustrate a s/heroic conflict requiring the dragon be slain in order to take possession of whatever it may be guarding—often a maiden (as a totem of purity) or a pile of gold (as a symbol of the treasure of our own inner resources).

In Western traditions they are perceived to be a larger-than-life enemy that must be destroyed. In the aftermath of their demise some buried treasure, mysterious fortune, or even immortality may be claimed by its *vainqueur*.

In the iconography of philosophical and religious traditions from the East, dragons are ambivalent if not helpful omens of prosperity or the tension of unity. In Eastern traditions, dragons are often welcomed message-bearers of wisdom and truth—in some stories even spiritual guides.

Around the mid-1200s, Song Dynasty politician and painter Cheng Rong (陈容) brilliantly splashed black ink (actually spitting it from his mouth much like a dragon spurting billowing flames) across a fifty-foot-long handscroll. This masterpiece, *Nine Dragons* (wait for it . . . wait for it . . .), may be the most illustrious and well-known portrayal of these monsters. In it, Chen Rong illustrates the fluidity of Tao, the water-like nature of the universal philosophy that teaches the flow of aligning *knowing* with *being*—a rejection of duality, harmonizing will with Essence; essentially, the way of aligning what is hidden in our shadow with that which has been brought into our field of awareness. Another way of understanding this might be *integrating our three levels of consciousness*.[2]

Here we'll consider how we've allowed our own dragons, arguably *both* monsters *and* messengers, to be a symbol of our Enneagram type, if not our lost Essence. This suggests that type is simultaneously a messenger of grace by reminding us what has been forgotten and what can be hoped for, while also carrying the potential of becoming a monster that takes over the emptiness created by this loss. (And once it takes over, it becomes the guardian of the cave, or our shadow.)

The dragons can be monsters—if we allow them to grow unobserved in our shadow, rather than dealing with them directly. But they can also be messengers, if we welcome them into awareness and seek to understand them as authentic parts of ourselves. Simply put, they really are what we allow them to become.

Sure, little Janae probably wasn't aware of all the iconographic, philosophical, or religious symbolism of the dragon she was asking to see, but I can't help but imagine that on an unconscious level, her humanity was aching to be seen and ultimately known.

It's daunting to ask to face our dragons. It's a request that summons our deepest courage.

That awesome little prayer needs to become our prayer in our journey of belonging.

---

2. When referring to the three levels of consciousness, I carefully delineate the conscious mind, the subconscious, and the unconscious. I characterize the notion of the "three minds" as three of the basic spaces that hold our ego. The *conscious* (most clearly contained in the Mind or Head Center) is what we experience as awareness of the present, most attainable through thoughts and the intellect. A layer below our conscious mind lies the *subconscious* (most clearly contained in the Heart or Feeling Center), our awareness and memories that we are not attentive to in the present but that are still accessible through triggers, familiar sensations, or intentional recall—in this way, most attainable through our feelings and emotions. At the base of all the levels of consciousness is the *unconscious* (most clearly contained in the Body or Instinctive Center) as that which is largely consciously inaccessible on an instinctual level yet still drives attitudes and behaviors, often felt more in the body than in the mind or emotions.

BELONG → BEHAVE → BELIEVE → BECOME

How many of us really want to see our own dragon? How many of us want to face the very parts of ourselves that keep our Essence, our soul's purpose for being, hidden? How many of us as grownups have the same courage as that little girl to explore our shadow and excavate our Essence—unearth the buried treasure within?

You see, the treasures that most dragons protect are actually resources they can't possess or consume. That's the tragedy here. The aspects of our human nature that limit and prevent us from living into our destiny have little-to-no concern with whether we live faithfully into our purposed calling. So why do we give our shadow, these dragons (or our personalities as we'll come to understand), so much power over who we are and who we can become? Why do we feel they must be destroyed rather than welcomed and accepted?

Could it be that we've failed to grasp what it means to belong, fully belong, to ourselves so that, ultimately, we can belong to one another and inevitably belong to divine love?

Many of us who were socialized in religious communities have a conflicted relationship with what it means to belong because our religions and spiritual traditions have failed us. Congregations and worshiping communities unfortunately misappropriated concepts of belonging by co-opting the imagery of family, suggesting that the faith communities we grew up in were a spiritual form of a surrogate family.

But let's stop right here and recalibrate all this.

When my mother gave birth to me way back in 1971 I *belonged* to her and my father. It didn't matter how goofy I looked (the medical staff actually needed to use obstetrical forceps to aid in my birthing process, temporarily leaving a couple of slightly impressed dents on both sides of my wee baby head); they thought I was beautiful and I was part of them. I belonged to my parents and we were a family.

As I grew up, secure in my awareness of belonging to my family, I learned to adapt and adhere to the rules and expectations of my parents and figured out how to *behave* appropriately to avoid punishment. But even when I misbehaved, I still belonged.

That's a mark of true family.

Today as a full-grown man, though still the child of my mother and father, I don't worship or vote the same ways they do—fundamentally we *believe* very different things on quite a few very significant issues, but I still belong to them and they belong to me. And freedom to trust my belonging regardless of behavior or beliefs has contributed to the flourishing of my *becoming*—the path of being the best I can, given access to the resources and opportunities made available to me.

That's what the best of family looks like . . . whether it's a biological family we're born into or a surrogate family we're adopted by, a dynamic set of friends or a community that becomes our chosen family. The flow of belonging allows behavior and beliefs to contribute to the blossoming of becoming.

However, many so-called religious "families" jumble this up by reordering this path and arresting our ongoing psycho-spiritual development, our becoming.

Beliefs are usually the entry point for joining most religious communities, and in many cases, strict adherence to the sophisticated nuances of these beliefs is required for ongoing participation. But that's not enough: how could it be if religious notions of belonging are conditional on what a person believes? So then, to prove one has sufficiently changed their mind through alignment with a right set of beliefs, there has to be evidence of that through right behavior.

And now, if you believe the right things, you will be forced to prove that by demonstrating right behavior that falls in line with your right beliefs. As long as you don't misbehave, you still might "belong"—just as long as you also keep believing the right things.

When belonging is contingent on beliefs and behavior, it suspends the necessary step of becoming, which prevents the fruit of transformation that is inevitable when we absolutely know and trust that we belong.

This is why we have houses of worship full of people who have *changed* their minds about what they believe but remain *untransformed* in how they live. This is how so many of us grew up in faith communities of converted people who are still racists or don't recycle.

The flow from believe to behave to belong was never true belonging but conditional belonging, despite how many of our religious communities tried to communicate that they were a kind of "family." And if that's how so many of us grew up, confused by the source of our belonging, then it's no wonder so many of us maintain a perplexing relationship to what it means to belong.

Thankfully, we have the Enneagram to help bring much of this back into balance and help reset this twisted journey back to our true selves. Because the truth is, we have always belonged. Our belonging is intrinsic and inherent and has been so from the beginning. We are also always becoming—sometimes in the direction of our soul's created purpose, and sometimes away from it. To tell the difference, we need compassionate self-awareness, and that's exactly what the Enneagram provides us with.

WHAT IS THIS ENNEAGRAM?

The Enneagram may be best known today as a personality profiling system, but to truly understand it, we have to look beyond this to its roots.

Originally, the Enneagram wasn't a personality profile system[3] but,

---

3. Many sources would have you believe otherwise, but when someone states, "The Enneagram is an ancient personality system . . ." they are only partially right in that there are

as its modern midwife George Ivanovitch Gurdjieff (c. 1866–1949) attested to, the Enneagram was a symbol that expressed a tradition for understanding *any* and *every* true system. He also suggested that if left alone in a desert, one could draw the Enneagram in the sand over and over to see into it all that had been taught and all that 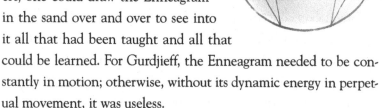 could be learned. For Gurdjieff, the Enneagram needed to be constantly in motion; otherwise, without its dynamic energy in perpetual movement, it was useless.

Today the popularization of the Enneagram of Personality has contributed to the organization of patterns around how people act, feel, and think into nine archetypes for human character structure. In the early 1970s these nine ways of being were originally called *Enneatypes* by the late Chilean Gestalt psychoanalyst, the grandfather of typology as we understand it today, Dr. Claudio Naranjo.

What Naranjo and his students were codifying way back then has now taken over Instagram meme accounts, coffee shop conversations, corporate team-building retreats, and contemplative spirituality practices in what's quickly becoming shorthand psycho-slang. "Oh, that's sooooo *Two-ish* of you," or "Why do you have to be such an *Eight-hole?*" or "Stop *Nine-ing* so hard."

Sadly, the Enneagram mugs and memes culture, though popular, have thinned out something that's ultimately sacred.

But even the Enneagram of Personality describes much, much more than mere fixed or conditioned personality, as if we are who we are, and this cannot be changed.

---

ancient roots of the Enneagram, though none of them specifically address personality styles. Further, the Enneagram is not a "test," though there *are* tests you can take to determine your type.

The Enneagram's nine types offer us roadmaps detailing *how* we got lost or disconnected from our soul's purpose for being. They also show how we *stay* lost, and each type's specific set of addictive patterns that keep us lost. This cycle of patterns eventually forms our personality structure. Grasping our Enneagram type can be a *start* to understanding who we are, yet it's far from the whole of who we are.

Different Enneagram schools have suggested different names for these nine types, hoping theirs would stick. By the mid-1990s, the claiming of the nine types with handles had gotten so out of hand that there were over a dozen competing labels tagged to the types. Luckily for us, in the natural consolidation process, just a couple of them seemed to stick: the names given by Helen Palmer and her professional partner, the late Dr. David Daniels, as well as the names attributed to the Enneagram by the late Don Riso and his professional partner, Russ Hudson. Let's review them here.

	Don Riso and Russ Hudson The Enneagram Institute	Helen Palmer and David Daniels Enneagram in the Narrative Tradition
Type One	The Reformer	Perfectionist
Type Two	The Helper	Giver
Type Three	The Achiever/Status Seeker	Performer
Type Four	The Individualist/Artist	Tragic Romantic
Type Five	The Investigator/Thinker	Observer
Type Six	The Loyalist	Trooper/Devils' Advocate
Type Seven	The Enthusiast/Generalist	Epicure
Type Eight	The Challenger/Leader	Boss
Type Nine	The Peacemaker	Mediator

Before we fall too far down this rabbit hole, let's step back to evaluate the broader design in how these types were formed.

THE INTELLIGENCE CENTERS
AND BELONGING

Most people are familiar with the Enneagram's nine-type structure, but the types are merely predictable patterns rooted in the foundations of the three Intelligence Centers. So, let's take a step back and consider these.

Intelligo or *intelligere* are Latin for "understanding," derived from the Latin root words *inter*, which means "between," and *lego*, which means "to collect." Essentially to understand something means you read between the lines or grasp into the empty spaces between the words, concepts, or ideas to really gather everything you can about something you want to learn.

This is where our English word "intelligence" comes from. To have intelligence suggests understanding, but even more than that, it's about understanding *connections*.

The Intelligence Centers of the Enneagram are the three ways we distinctly perceive and process reality: through the body, heart, and head. If you can understand the three Centers of Intelligence, then the entire system makes complete sense. Everything put into and taken out of the Enneagram builds off these three foundational elements.

Gurdjieff taught that we are all three-storied (as in the levels of buildings, not stories as told in books or parables) or three-brained beings. These three aspects of self are the rudimentary ways we perceive and process reality. In fact, Gurdjieff suggested that only a true spiritual experience could only be possible when all three centers were accessed simultaneously. Three-centered awareness allows for a deep level of compassion and integration through embodied experience, heartfulness, and mindfulness.

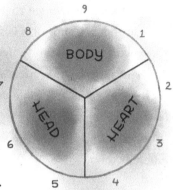

INTELLIGENCE CENTERS

The Centers are naturally and physiologically hardwired to our brains and thus form the basis of *preconscious* cognition. Though we have a principal or preferred Center that steers our primary perception, all three of the aspects of self are constantly at play, configured into nine unique expressions.

These Centers are called:

- The Instinctive Center for the Body Types: Enneagram types Eight, Nine, and One
- The Emotional Center for the Heart Types: types Two, Three, and Four
- The Intellectual or Mind Center for the Head Types: types Five, Six, and Seven

The Instinctive Center

The Instinctive Center is what gives the Body Types effortless access to their innate intuitive awareness. Maybe you've found yourself dropping off your child at child care only to have an arresting concern about one of the employees. That gut sense is so disturbing that you decide not to leave your little one after all, but instead take them

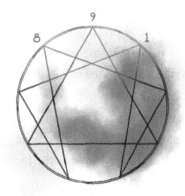

BODY~GUT~INSTINCTIVE

to work with you. In effect you've read the "energy" of someone you don't know, nor ever conversed with, but there was something in you that just *knew in your gut* that individual was a little off.

Our natural intuition is an actual intelligence that is difficult to explain but profoundly real and felt in our bodies. The Body Types experience the visceral toomuchness of life which triggers their type's most accessible emotion, often expressed as a form of frustration or anger. The Body Types also have a conflicted relationship with control and, when not in control, act out in three very different ways.

The Emotional Center

The Emotional Center is what gives the Heart Types genuine sensitivity and attunement to the emotional well-being of those in their communities. The Heart Types just seem to be able to feel what everyone feels. This allows for the gift of their validation— confirming and endorsing the validity of our feelings, especially when we

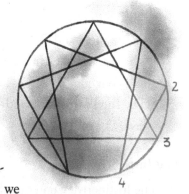

HEART~FEELING~EMOTION

2

3

4

don't have words for them. These types easily build trust through their natural warmth of presence, sympathetic understanding, and sincere kindness flowing out from their hearts into ours. However, swimming through the sea of emotions can be overwhelming. Coupled with their drive to make deep connections, they are subtly preoccupied with comparisons, which awakens their most accessible emotion of guilt or shame. But because they are less concerned with control than the Body Types, the Heart Types really do prioritize their need for connections.

The Intellectual Center

The Intellectual Center is what gives the Head Types their clever cerebral abilities, which are supported through analysis, conjecture, speculation, and their exceptional knack for forecasting and planning. The determination of the Head Types to suss out all that can be mentally sorted is the basis for their assimilation of every

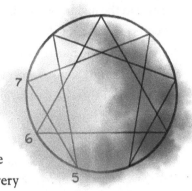

HEAD~INTELLECTUAL~THINKING

aspect of what they collect—be it information, safety measures, or experiences. But living within the confines of the mind can offer challenges: over-thinking things, causing a form of mental paralysis; obsessive worrying; or preoccupation through aggressive anticipation. These imbalances activate the Head Types' most accessible emotion of anxiety or distress, constantly keeping them alert and cerebrally restless. And substantially less concerned with control or connections, the Head Types consider competency to be their social currency.

Clearly differentiated among themselves, the three types within each Center follow a pattern of how they relate to the bias of their Center. This is why it's unfair to suggest that all Body Types experience anger in the same way, or that all Heart Types feel their emotions similarly, or that all Head Types practice cerebral understanding with comparable patterns.

Flowing clockwise within each Intelligence Center, the first of

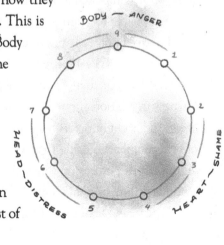

BODY — ANGER
HEAD~DISTRESS
HEART~SHAME

the types on the left edge (Eight, Two, and Five) express the force of their energy by exaggerating it; the second set of types, sitting squarely in the middle of their Center (Nine, Three, and Six) suppress or repress the core of their Center by unconsciously disconnecting from it and losing touch with it; while the third set of types on the right edge of the Centers (One, Four, and Seven) idealize the flow of energy within their Center by giving over to its momentum.

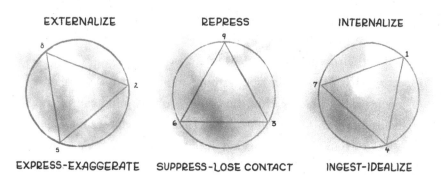

EXTERNALIZE	REPRESS	INTERNALIZE
EXPRESS-EXAGGERATE	SUPPRESS-LOSE CONTACT	INGEST-IDEALIZE

This is why Eights, Twos, and Fives appear to amplify instinctive anger, emotional shame, and mental anxiety. There's a true force driving these types from the external edge of their Center as if they were being catapulted around the entire circle of the Enneagram in an unstoppable rotation.

The mid-points (sometimes called the Anchor Points or the Revolutionary Types) Three, Six, and Nine lose contact with the essential basis of their Center, subsequently causing a void or hollowness in relationship to it. Because they don't have a wing (wings are the adjacent numbers to each type, the types to the left and right of each number) outside their Center, they experience a figurative loss of depth perception, limited by lack of immediate access to a secondary dimensional Center.

Types One, Four, and Seven ingest the extremes of their

Centers by idealizing what they effortlessly pull forward from within them. These types make the accessing of their Center's gifts seem uncomplicated and natural; the movement is a kind of soul-cursive they gift to the world.

It's important to start with the Intelligence Centers because they become the primal lens for perceiving ourselves, others, and the world around us. If we fail to understand how we process our environments, we run the risk of believing our Center's bias is the preferred, if not the only, way of observing the world. As Anaïs Nin popularized the notion, "We don't see things as they are, we see them as we are."[4]

REPRESSED INTELLIGENCE CENTERS

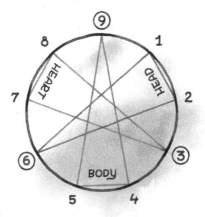

This also requires being aware of our most restrained (repressed) Center. Of course, each of us has access to our intuition, feelings, and thoughts, and just as it's good for us to practice awareness of our primary Center, it's likewise good for us to be aware of our most neglected Center.

---

4. This famous quote appears in her 1961 autobiographical novel *Seduction of the Minotaur* (Swallow Press, 1961), while citing this line's original source as Rabbi Shmuel ben Nachmani in בְּרָכוֹת the Talmud Tractate Berakhot (55b).

Since these three Centers are always present, though not always integrated, they are situated into nine patterns that produce the rails for the nine Enneagram types. Our type is formed by the stacking of our dominant or preferred Center to our secondary or supplemental Center to our tertiary or repressed Center.

Making room for the repressed Center is the first interior path to incorporating a key aspect of our ego that is fundamental to our sense of self that's out of line. This is the primordial work of belonging.

Flowing from the Anchor points (types Three, Six, and Nine), those types most naturally disconnected from their Centers, three isosceles triangles form in the triads of the repressed Intelligence Centers connecting:

> types Nine, Four, and Five as those with a repressed
> Instinctive Center
> types Three, Seven, and Eight as those with a repressed
> Emotional Center
> types Six, One, and Two as those with a repressed
> Thinking Center[5]

REPRESSED BODY CENTER   REPRESSED HEART CENTER   REPRESSED HEAD CENTER

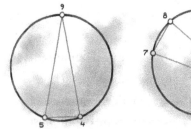 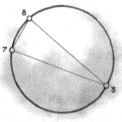 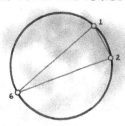

5. Coincidentally, these triadic groupings also detail each of the types' relationship to time: types Nine, Four, and Five are past oriented; types Three, Seven, Eight are future oriented; and types Six, One, and Two are present oriented. For an excellent summary of this, see Dr. Drew Moser's brilliant article, "Discernment and Time: Dominant and Repressed Perspectives within the Hornevian Groups" in the June/July 2018 issue of *Enneagram Monthly*, 1, 13–16.

In Greek mythology, the Graeae sisters offer us an illustration of the interplay of these three Centers. These old sorceresses, according to the myths, were three blind sisters whose parents were sea deities. Deino, Enyo, and Pemphredo never saw the sun or the moon and were so epically ancient (it's said they were born old) they could hardly comprehend a newborn. Throughout their stories their old age represents wisdom; their gray garments represent neutrality; and, as siblings, they represent the law of three.

Most memorably, these three sages shared an eye, a wig, and a tooth. That single eye, however, was their most unforgettable feature. For any of the sisters to gain temporary sight, they had to practice deference to one another and common partnership to share the resource needed to perceive the world they inhabited. In the same way, if we want to see the world as it is, our three Centers must find cooperative alignment in sharing the gift of perception. Partnership, rather than competition, is required. Yet challenges arise when we subconsciously overemploy the Center that comes most naturally to us, at the expense of the others.

Sadly, when we overuse any one of our Intelligence Centers, something is lost. We miss experiencing the fullness of any experience or relationship. This is why the hard work of learning to bring them all into awareness is the compassionate path to integration.

IDENTIFYING YOUR PRIMARY, SECONDARY, AND REPRESSED CENTERS

Once we've identified our dominant Center and repressed Center, we can bring our attention to our secondary Center right in the middle. This secondary Center works both to fortify our governing Center and to bring forward our most underdeveloped Center. These stacked combinations reveal a bias of perception, holding us back from the integration of our whole selves. In our journey into belonging, it becomes our task to understand these biases so that we can bring them into greater harmony.

Essentially, the jumbling of these Centers creates the preconscious rails for our Enneagram type long before personality forms. How these Centers are ordered shapes one's perception, how we observe the world, and this sets the foundation for a person's Enneagram type. In fact, the Centers reveal the physiological basis at work behind each of the types. They show how our brain chemistry informs how we perceive and process the world.

In Kathleen Hurley and her late partner Theodore Dobson's[6]

---

6. As the story goes, Theodore E. Dobson's professional visibility in the field of personality studies was on the rise concurrent with another Colorado psychologist, who though unrelated, shared his surname. Attempting to avoid all unintended complicity with the controversial positions of this other Dobson who was gaining notoriety for his politicized fundamentalist religious views on family values, Theodore changed his name (while continuing to write and teach) to *Theodorre Donson*—but not until after coauthoring his first two published books on the Enneagram.

fabulous work, *My Best Self: Using the Enneagram to Free the Soul,* they develop the theory that personality is a compulsive pattern of overusing or preferring one of these Centers.[7] (They use *Creative* for the Instinctual Center, *Relational* for the Emotional Center, and *Intellectual* for the Thinking or Head Center.)

REPRESSED INTELLIGENCE CENTERS

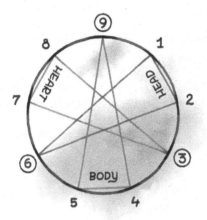

I find this an important correction to the unfortunate and misinformed type descriptions that simply describe how people externally present temperament and disposition. The idea that type is fundamentally an intelligent design of how these three brains relate shows us something much more meaningful and mysterious, dare I say spiritual, than merely the latest, hippest Enneagram listicle on where to travel, what book you should read, how to decorate your apartment, or how to choose the best workout based on your type.

When we take a more complex view of what crafts type, we can recognize how our intuitive, feeling, and thinking Centers layer our view of the world.

---

7. Kathleen Hurley and Theodore Dobson, *My Best Self: Using the Enneagram to Free the Soul* (New York: HarperOne, 1993).

Type One	Emotionally reinforces their intuition while containing reasoning.
Type Two	Instinctively supports their emotional awareness while stifling rational faculties.
Type Three	Fuses their intuitive awareness with impartial objectivity while suspending their feelings.
Type Four	Objectively braces their affecting emotions while quelling their body intelligence.
Type Five	Acknowledges their sensitivities to confirm their analytical reasoning while cautioning their instincts.
Type Six	Vacillates between intuitive instincts and their heightened sensitiveness while maintaining suspicion toward their reasoning.
Type Seven	Intuitively confirms their logic while rejecting access to their emotions.
Type Eight	Rationally justifies their intuition while denying access to their feelings.
Type Nine	Merges their emotional sensitivities with a grounded objectivity while abnegating their gut reactions.

I believe this is why the Enneagram has been compared to the eighteenth camel.[8] The reference is derived from a Sufi parable of three grief-stricken Bedouin brothers whose father had unexpectedly passed away. In the tale, these siblings are fighting over their inheritance, the caravan of camels left behind by their dad. In his will, their father clearly directed how his herd was to be divided among his sons: to his firstborn, half of the caravan; to the middle son, a third of the camels; and to the youngest of the brothers, a ninth of the herd. But when they counted the camels there were seventeen, making the math impossible to sort out what they thought could be an equitable distribution.

---

8. Torrey Wagg, "What Is the Enneagram?" *Enneagram Monthly 1, no.* 6 (August 1995): 8.

In the midst of their grieving, the boys found themselves wrapped up in a conflict that they feared would destroy their family. After days of journeying deep into the desert, they brought this dilemma to one of their community's wise leaders and explained the quandary. Offering her condolences, she gifted to these grieving, though querulous, young men a camel from her own herd and then urged the sons to return to the will to consider if they had overlooked something.

Now, with eighteen camels the math suddenly worked. The oldest son claimed half of the herd (nine camels) and the second son took a third (six camels), which allowed the youngest son to take possession of a ninth (two camels) of the caravan. When they counted out their inheritance it totaled seventeen camels, the original size of their father's herd—and so with gratitude the brothers returned the eighteenth camel to the wise elder who had gifted them.

The intelligence of these three Centers offers us the ability to grasp what we've already had, what we already know, and what we've always been able to access. The problem is that we don't trust our own inner wisdom, nor do we know how to work with it, and so we appeal to other tools, teachers, resources, or trainings to try to help us make the very decisions we're inherently capable of making ourselves.

As the eighteenth camel, the Enneagram helps us solve the complex quagmires we keep ourselves stuck in—illuminating for us that we already have what we need to solve the problems that keep us tethered to the worst of our type structure.

With remarkable fluency, our Intelligence Centers have the capability to reach beyond the observable to the spiritual resources that reside within but are often left untapped. For example, when a heart-centered person is listening to someone speak, they are listening in between the spaces of the words to get a sense of how the person feels. Each of the Intelligence Centers reads between the lines, picking up on implicit cues.

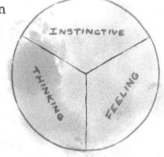

THE ENNEAGRAM WE WANT AND
THE ENNEAGRAM WE NEED

Healing our experience of belonging isn't a process that can be done for us, or even outside us for that matter. Aligning the best and worst of ourselves; integrating the good, the bad, and the ugly; and allowing for every aspect of who we've become to belong is the beginning of this journey.

Because if *any part of ourselves can't belong, then no part of ourselves will truly belong.*

How I wish I had learned this years ago. While there are parts of myself that I have come to love and hold with compassion, there are parts of myself that are very, very difficult for me to accept.

The space in between these fragments is filled with fears and resentments, doubts and regrets, wounds and misunderstandings. In an age of social media cluttered with friends, fans, and followers, I'm still learning how to like myself, how to find the compassion to truly love myself—how to belong to myself.

Thankfully, this way to belonging is hidden in a sacred map charted against nine energy points known as the Enneagram.

However, to reduce the Enneagram to nine personality styles misses the depth and richness of this tradition which is rooted in transformation. The Enneagram is not meant to peg us in our fixed personalities but *invites* us into rich and meaningful growth. But that's the inevitability of all great wisdom. Once it becomes popularized, it necessarily has to be thinned out to its most relatable elements so it can be brought to the masses.

What the general population *wants* is an accessible Enneagram that describes quirks and caricatures of individuality plotted against temperaments and dispositions. But what we *need* is a map showing us how to knit together the fragments of our identities that we've allowed to lay claim to the whole of who we think we are. What we are desperately yearning for is an Enneagram of Belonging, pointing us back to an integrated experience of radical self-acceptance. The Enneagram backfires entirely when we use it to box ourselves or others in. Rather, when we practice radical self-acceptance, we find our path to personal growth.

WHERE WE'VE COME FROM, WHERE WE'LL GO FROM HERE

Here we will unpack some of the more underexamined and underinterrogated facets of this tradition by locating its evolving expressions of efficacy. This, however, requires at the least a basic understanding of the trajectory of this teaching on its elusive timeline. I find this to be some of the most urgent work for professionals in the Enneagram community, because without a proper understanding of where this has come from, there can't be the needed clarity of where it can go.

It reminds me of that overlooked line from George Orwell's classic novel *1984*, ". . . if all others accepted the lie which the Party imposed—if all records told the same tale—then the lie passed into history and became truth. 'Who controls the past,' ran the Party slogan, 'controls the future: who controls the present controls the past.' And yet, the past, though of its nature alterable, never had been altered."[9]

Sadly, this distortion of the Enneagram's past (and its ensuing future) is paraded by the carelessness of many in the present who fail to trace the roots of the Enneagram of Personality beyond what has been published about Enneagram types since the first book written in English was published (coincidentally) in 1984. Further, surface treatments of the Enneagram's nine personality types do not do justice to the complexity of a system that actually reveals 108 renderings of type. When thrown into a kaleidoscope of compulsions supported by one of the Enneagram's three Instincts, twenty-seven Subtypes are subsequently revealed. Type is even more intricately styled by layering these three Instincts in order to shape the fifty-four Instinctual Variants. With even more distinction, observing the influence of these fifty-four variants' dominant wing brings forward 108 forms of Enneagram types.[10] Wait, what? There are 108 Enneagram types!? Yep. There are 108 types.

---

9. George Orwell, *1984* (London: Penguin Books, 1989), 37.

10. The sacredness of the number 108 shows up throughout history and religion. Surprisingly in ancient times early astronomers calculated (with near accuracy) the stretch between the earth and sun to essentially be 108 times the sun's diameter and the stretch between the earth and the moon to be more or less 108 times the moon's diameter. Further, the sun's diameter is just about 108 times that of the earth's own diameter. Vedic astrologers have mapped twenty-seven *nakshatras* (Lunar Mansions) each with four *padas* (rooms or quarters) equaling 108. In addition they've named nine *navagrahas* (planets) in each of twelve *rashis* (zodiacs) equaling 108. Most Japmala prayer beads used by Buddhists, Hindus, Jains, and

LOOKING BACK, LOOKING FORWARD:
A Brief Modern History

Though an ancient tradition that's potentially thousands and thousands of years old, the modern history of the Enneagram is still loaded with controversy and conflict, something that in recent years has undergone a much-needed mending.

George Gurdjieff

The Russian wisdom teacher George Gurdjieff (born in Alexandropol, Armenia) is pivotal to understanding a so-called rediscovery of this tradition.

Brought forward in Paris in 1916 at his Institute for the Harmonious Development of Mankind, Gurdjieff introduced the Enneagram to his students through dance and body movement. He himself a tangle of contradictions, Gurdjieff seemed larger than life and used his presence viscerally to embody his teachings. When it came to the Enneagram, it's clear Gurdjieff never taught it as a personality profile nor did he ever teach Enneagram types; he only taught the tradition on an energetic and esoteric level.

He did however weave into his school the idea that our psyches are all piloted by a mental chief feature (perhaps the undeveloped concept that would later become Ichazo's idea of Fixation). It was this aspect of the personality which Gurdjieff would ridicule, provoking his students to expose their own chief feature through elaborate dinner parties where Gurdjieff would taunt and humiliate his disciples after serving them inordinate amounts of alcohol. He would also enlist provocateurs, especially difficult personalities, to secretly enroll

---

Sikhs have 108 beads. There are 108 defilements or impure thoughts in Buddhism. Ayurveda, an ancient medical system developed in South Asia, teaches there are 108 emotions (a third pointing to the past, a third rooted in the present, and a third of them focused on the future) as well as 108 pressure points in the human body.

in his school whose sole purpose was to agitate fellow disciples as a way of jarring loose the characteristics of these chief features.

The Enneagram was just a small part of his larger legacy, one marked by problematic controversies as well as significant contributions, and to this day Gurdjieffian students and the Gurdjieff schools around the world generally dismiss the modern Enneagram of Personality as a degeneration of how he had introduced the Enneagram. Regardless, all students of the Enneagram of Personality are indebted to him for reinvigorating this teaching through his school.

Curiously, he kept the origins of his own introduction to the Enneagram a secret, sometimes offering elusive hints of where he learned about it that often contradicted prior hints he had already shared. Until recently it was speculated he had obtained his knowledge of the Enneagram from a Sufi sect, and now we have some plausible evidence of that.[11] *The Naqshbandi Sufi Way: History and Guidebook of the Saints of the Golden Chain* tells the story of Gurdjieff paying a visit to Shaykh Abdullah Allah ag-Daghestani, one of the leaders of the Naqshbandi order. Despite hundreds of pilgrims arriving daily to visit with the Shaykh, he agreed to meet with Gurdjieff, who was interested in learning from him the teaching of the knowledge of the nine points. Remarkably, this sect of Sufis had mapped nine spiritual energy centers on the human torso that represented the nine Sufi saints who were traced back to the Prophet Muhammad. During their visit the Shaykh said to Gurdjieff, "You are interested in the knowledge of the nine points. We can speak on it in the morning after the dawn prayer."[12] But during the prayers Gurdjieff received a vision of the Shaykh transporting Gurdjieff to a beautiful rose garden where the fragrance of the flowers contained secret teachings.

11. Mike MacLeod, "The Sufi Connection," *Enneagram Monthly* 1, no. 8 (October 1995): 8.

12. Shaykh Muhammad Hisham, *The Naqshbandi Sufi Way: History and Guidebook of the Saints of the Golden Chain* (Chicago, IL: Kazi Publications, Inc., 1995), 360.

Gurdjieff explained in his vision that he had smelled an opened rose which carried him into the consciousness of the teacher: "I found myself entering into your heart and becoming part of you. Through your spiritual power I was able to ascend to the knowledge of the power of the nine points."[13]

Never admitted by Gurdjieff, this account validates his claim that no one explicitly taught him the Enneagram while simultaneously confirming the role Sufism had in advancing aspects of the tradition.

Only after multiple fallings out among he and his students and his death in 1949 did the symbol of the Enneagram show up that same year—almost 300 pages deep in P. D. Ouspensky's book, *In Search of the Miraculous*. There the Enneagram is introduced in its process overlays with some pretty trippy renderings that, apart from basic Gurdjieffian understanding, is more confusing than helpful for those who only know the Enneagram of Personality.

Óscar Ichazo

Right about this time, in 1950, a nineteen-year-old Bolivian man, Óscar Ichazo, was welcomed into a clandestine group of wisdom teachers who met "to share their knowledge of various esoteric consciousness-altering techniques. . . . They were trying to implement the idea that it was possible to synthesize all mysticism, that it was the time to do it and to present it."[14] The teachers of the group were from all the world's great spiritual traditions and had traveled to Buenos Aires, Argentina, where Ichazo's date with destiny materialized.

The story of his inclusion in this small assembly has changed over the years. In a 1973 interview with Sam Keen for *Psychology Today*, Ichazo recounted, "I became the coffee boy for this group. I would get up at four a.m. to make their coffee and breakfast and would

13. Ibid., 361.
14. Dick Myers, "The Worlds of Óscar Ichazo," *The Gurdjieff Journal* 16, no. 1 (#61): 4.

stay around as inconspicuously as possible. Gradually they got used
to my presence and started using me as a guinea pig to demonstrate
techniques to each other. To settle arguments about whether some
particular kind of meditation or mantra worked, they would have me
try it and report what I experienced."[15]

In that same interview Ichazo goes on to report, "One day when
I was serving coffee, an argument arose between two members of the
group. I turned to one and said, 'You are not right. He is right.' Just like
that. Then I explained the point until both of them understood. This
incident changed everything. They asked me to leave and I thought
I was being kicked out for being pretentious. But after about a week,
they called me back and told me they had all decided to teach me.
They worked with me for two more years and then opened doors for
me in the Orient."[16] From there Ichazo traveled to Kashmir, Kabul,
remote locations in Tibet, Hong Kong, and throughout other parts
of Asia learning from master teachers and gurus. "After working
alone for a year, I went into a divine coma for seven days. When I
came out of it, I knew that I should teach; it was impossible that all
my good luck should be only for myself."[17]

Another account details that his initiation into this secret group
required that he meditate for three days in lotus position while sitting
on a fence post; afterward his body was so stiff he needed assistance
to get off the post.[18]

Regardless of how he began his path as a wisdom teacher in his
own right, his accounts of how he came to know of the Enneagram
also have changed over the years. Was it during that (hallucinogenic

15. Sam Keen, "We Have No Desire to Strengthen the Ego or Make It Happy": A conversation about Ego Destruction with Óscar Ichazo, *Psychology Today*, July 1973, 64.
16. Ibid.
17. Ibid.
18. "The Worlds of Óscar Ichazo," *The Gurdjieff Journal* (Number 61, Volume 16,
Issue 1), 4.

induced, as some versions of the story report) "divine coma" that Ichazo received 108 *Enneagons* from the Archangel Gabriel or the Archangel Metatron (an archetypal figure of the higher mind or mental states) or the Green Qu Tub (a symbol of evolving spiritual consciousness), all of whom he, at one time or another, attested to attaining the Enneagons?

Later his story would change. In one of his last public interviews (the same conversation where he contradicted his earlier asserta-tions that he was the group's coffee boy), "I started visualizing the Enneagons in front of me. They didn't just appear."[19] This suggests he materialized the Enneagons and then spent fifteen years developing them before introducing the Enneagons of Holy Ideas, Fixations, Virtues, and Passions during a ten-month-long cohort of sixty Jesuits and mental health practitioners in the deserts of Arica, Chile.

Claudio Naranjo

It was a Chilean Gestalt psychoanalyst, Dr. Claudio Naranjo, who organized this group. In his *Gnosis* interview "The Distorted Enneagram," it's recounted that Ichazo originally "claimed that the enneagram was passed on to him orally by the Sarmouni, a Sufi brotherhood,"[20] which he also would later deny.

Shortly before meeting Ichazo, Naranjo had lost his ten-year-old son in a car accident. Naranjo grieved the death of his child with unimaginable agony. This suffering opened his heart to new ways of being with himself, eventually leading him to Ichazo and the training in the Chilean desert.

These ten months were the critical incubator for what would become the Enneagram of Personality. Naranjo had always honored

---

19. Michael J. Goldberg, "Inside the Enneagram Wars," *LA Weekly* (October 15–21, 1993), 24.
20. OM C. Parkin and Boris Fittkau, "The Distorted Enneagram: The Gnosis Interview with Claudio Naranjo," *Gnosis: A Journal of the Western Inner Traditions* 41 (Fall 1996): 22.

Ichazo as the proverbial *grandfather* of the Enneagram of Personality while maintaining, "Though I am the unintentional father of the enneagram movement, I feel prompted to call it my bastard child."[21]

His unintentional relationship with the Enneagram was aggravated by the tensions experienced in his relationship with Ichazo. On one hand, Ichazo was all but repulsed by what he perceived to be Naranjo's over inflated egocentricity, even going so far as sending him away to meditate in the wilderness for forty days, while on the other hand choosing him to be the sole student to whom Ichazo would "download" the Enneagons. And that first introduction was clumsy at best; as Naranjo would later write, "he [Ichazo] drew an enneagram with the names of the passions at the corresponding points and asked me to situate myself on the map. I suggested two hypotheses, and got it wrong both times."[22]

According to various accounts Naranjo was dismissed, sent away early from the cohort in Arica, but he had learned enough to begin developing *Enneatypes*, by triangulating what he had picked up from Ouspensky's Gurdjieffian Process Enneagram teachings, Ichazo's first four Enneagons, and observations of pathologies mapped against the DSM-III.

It seems Ichazo wanted to claim more authorship for what Naranjo was developing, but according to Naranjo there were only two hours of those ten months in the Chilean desert that Ichazo even presented Enneagons.[23] And for years the two maintained a cantankerous relationship at best; even going twenty-plus years without speaking to each other.

---

21. Ibid., 21.

22. Claudio Naranjo, *The Enneagram of Society: Healing the Soul to Heal the World* (Nevada City, CA: Gateway Books and Tapes, 2004), 33.

23. Naranjo, Claudio, "A Report to the 'First International Enneagram Conference' at Stanford University, 1994 [Transcript of the Video-taped Presentation]." *Enneagram Monthly* 2, no. 2 (February 1996): 16.

From Arica, Chile, to Berkeley, California, Naranjo spent the next three years codifying the *Enneatypes* with small groups of graduate students, some of whom would become the Enneagram's most notable authorities (including Hameed Ali, Sandra Maitri, and Kathleen Riordan Speeth). Even Helen Palmer showed up for a couple of Naranjo's public sessions, and at one of them he introduced panels as a pedagogy for teaching the Enneagram. As he worked through the intricacies of the nine types, he realized the powerful potential of this tool and so, to avoid it being misused, he required all students to sign a contract of reserve (similar to an agreement he had with Ichazo) requiring explicit permission before any of them could share what they were learning.

The Jesuits, Don Riso, and Helen Palmer

Of course, one of the participants, Bob Ochs, a Jesuit, just couldn't keep the secret and sent hand-scribbled notes back to his community at Loyola University in Chicago. This betrayal of the confidentiality agreement so angered Naranjo that he stopped teaching in the US for more than two decades and cynically suggested the Enneagram had come "to the streets a little prematurely."[24]

The Enneagram took off within the Jesuit community (an order of men known for intellectualizing a deep spirituality rooted in discernment) because it provided a framework for supporting spiritual development. But even the Jesuits knew that what they were working with needed to be kept under wraps, and so they promised to study and integrate the Enneagram for two years before teaching it to others. Eventually even that agreement was broken.

By 1984, the first Enneagram book with a personality overlay was published: *The Enneagram: A Journey of Self Discovery*, by Sister

---

24. Ibid.

Maria Beesing, OP; Robert J. Nogosek, CSD; and Father Patrick O'Leary, SJ.

In 1987, Don Riso, a former Jesuit himself, had been tirelessly working out his own theories on the Enneagram. Observing the litigious climate developing around the new field, he spent considerable time ensuring that his own work maintained a high level of originality and authenticity.[25]

In 1988, Helen Palmer's ovarial work, *The Enneagram: Understanding Yourself and the Others in Your Life*, was published. It wasn't long before The Arica Institute, Ichazo's school, sued the authors of these works, citing intellectual property right infringement. Beesing, Nogosek, and O'Leary settled with the Aricans, but Helen Palmer fought them in court and won the case. Palmer noted that the material was already in the public domain, as Naranjo's ex-girlfriend (Dr. Kathleen Riordan Speeth) had published a chapter on Gurdjieff's Enneagram in Charles Tart's 1975 work, *Transpersonal Psychologies*.

With all the enthusiasm and new thought leaders emerging on the Enneagram landscape, Naranjo was still displeased with the teaching's growing popularity. With biting cynicism, he leveled disparaging critiques of the two most visible leaders of the movement, both of whom would prove to be among the most durable given the lasting impact of their contributions. Toward one's work he commented, "[it's] the most informative, though I would have expected a greater original contribution"; toward the other's work he said, "[it's] more original, but less accurate."[26] Naranjo would also continue to throw shade at another beloved author and teacher whom he'd simply refer to as "the Friar." None of this endeared him to the larger community, while he still held a revered place within it.

25. Andrea Isaacs and Jack Labanauskas, "Conversation with Don Riso," *Enneagram Monthly* 2, no. 9, (September 1996, issue 19): 20.
26. Claudio Naranjo, *Character and Neurosis: An Integrative View* (Nevada City, CA: Gateways/Idhhb, Inc. Publishers, 1994), xxxi.

The History of the Enneagram Tradition Goes On

There is much, much more to the unfolding modern history of the tradition, but I at least wanted to highlight these aspects of it to illustrate a few invitations for the larger Enneagram community's continued growth.

1. Recognizing the modern forbearers of this movement are Russian-Armenian, Bolivian, and Chilean reminds us that the forerunners offer a snapshot of ethnic diversity that is often lacking in the contemporary, professional, and, specifically, Western religious Enneagram communities. We must do better in making a collective commitment to decolonize a teaching that is quickly being overrun by Western Christian biases that are diluting the natural diversity of this tradition.

2. The painful fallouts between Gurdjieff and his students, between Ichazo and Naranjo, between Naranjo and the Jesuits, and even some of the divisions present in today's Enneagram community are some of the strongest *disproofs* of the teaching. If there is a wake of broken and fractured relationships following those who give themselves over to working with the Enneagram, then something is clearly missing. If the Enneagram doesn't lead to community and unity, then perhaps one has failed to internalize its gifts. It's yet another reason we so urgently and desperately need the Enneagram of Belonging.

3. As in all great mentoring relationships, you can only take someone else as far as you've gone yourself. This is precisely why over the years there has been caution in allowing students of the Enneagram to teach the tradition before they've internalized and integrated it themselves. Rather than giving in to the compulsions to type everyone in your own life, take this

teaching inward first and metabolize all that you can for your own compassionate belonging.

4. It's often said the Enneagram is a psycho-spiritual tool which highlights the psychological contributions of Naranjo's work supported by the spiritual development added by the Jesuits, but this description fails to connect the head and heart with the body. If Gurdjieff primarily taught the Enneagram through dance and body work, then we need teachers who can facilitate this lost layer of transmitting the fullness of a teaching that is psycho-spiritual-AND-somatic.

5. The Enneagram of Personality is a young teaching, not even fifty years old, which makes it an exciting time to advance what has yet to be revealed with this new overlay. Where it goes from here is largely dependent on those of us who would make the commitment to curate authentic diversity and inclusion within a growing community of curious practitioners who want a transformed world, but realize transformation begins inside each and every one of us.

6. Finally, as Brené Brown suggests, "True belonging doesn't require you to change who you are; it requires you to be who you are."[27] This is the human journey—to show up with all the good and bad, the sacred and profane, and the celebrated and tragic aspects of ourselves—allowing everything to belong. That's why learning to make peace with our type is part of our urgent journey of integrating the whole. You see, the human flawedness of Gurdjieff, Ichazo, Naranjo, and all who've followed them (ourselves included) allows for the flawedness of each of us to belong in the ongoing development of the Enneagram as a living tradition embodied in our perfectly imperfect souls.

27. Brené Brown, *Braving the Wilderness: The Quest for True Belonging and the Courage to Stand Alone* (New York, NY: Random House, 2017), 40.

The Enneagram's history is instructive for its future. As we recall the divisions and misunderstandings, it's obvious that even the legacy teachers were attempting to make peace with their own dragons. And as they've learned to recognize these monsters as messengers, may we too take heed of their message and allow it to lead us to a compassionate, present, and hope-filled future for where this teaching will take us.

2

Transcending Type

*The Nature of Type, the Limits of Type,
and Living in True Freedom*

Several of my friends are extremely talented musicians who, when touring a new record, always have to contend with that exuberant superfan in the crowd who hollers out uninvited requests: "Play the hits! Play the hits! Play the hits!"

I'm guilty myself. Weezer recently played a festival in Omaha, and though I'm not a hardcore fan, I do love some of their older stuff. When they came through town, I didn't have the energy to catch up with the current canon of their discography, and so I intended to skip the show. But the possibility of them playing some of the classics from the glory days got the best of me, and I went to hear them. It was spectacular, and they were hospitable enough to weave into their set list plenty of their greatest hits.

That "play the hits!" tendency in all of us shows up while digging into the Enneagram when we pick up a book and immediately turn to the chapter on our own type.

The bummer is, even though type descriptions really are the "hits" of the Enneagram material, they've been done over and over ad nauseum. And, if we're honest about it, the vast majority of type descriptions are simply triangulated regurgitations of what Claudio Naranjo tricked out in the early '70s, blended with Helen Palmer's ovarial work of developing thorough type renderings in the '80s, and then kneaded into Don Riso's elaborate contributions to the delicate nuances of type from his work in the '80s and '90s.

Yet, somehow, we always hope there's something fresh or new in how the next teacher or author frames our type. And so many of us keep buying the next book or listening to yet another podcast only to experience disappointment fatigue from our ever-growing hunger to know ourselves better. Sure, pursuits in self-awareness are necessary, because if we can't self-observe we can't self-correct. The intentions behind prioritizing our personal journeys back to our truest self are admirable. But we can't export this important work to a teacher or author; we have to own the process.

So, let's consider the nature of the type, the limits of type, and why living beyond type is essential for our freedom.

WHAT IS TYPE?

The various assumptions on what is meant by "type" have led to quite a bit of confusion in Enneagram conversations.

Since coming to terms with our own type can be such a precious journey of self-discovery and inner liberation, it's imperative that we have as firm a footing as possible when unpacking a compassionate representation of what type tells us about ourselves. In fact, this is the first step in establishing an honest relationship with our Enneagram type.

What do I mean by *an honest relationship with our type?*

There's not a lot of middle ground when it comes to relating to one's Enneagram type—we either love our type (proudly posting it on our social media profile, rocking type-specific T-shirts, or referencing our type regularly in casual conversation) or we feel a great bit of unease with the more unfavorable aspects of what our type confirms for us.

Doting over your type doesn't always mean you have a healthy relationship with it. On the contrary, what enamors you about your type could simply keep you fixated on its addictive patterns. *Loving* yourself requires you hold *all* aspects of yourself, including your type, with honest compassion, making room for the positive as well as the negative aspects to belong.

On the other hand, quite a few of us came into awareness of our type because of how uncomfortable we felt after reading a description of our Enneagram number. That discomfort actually reveals something important. The aspects of self that I feel ashamed or embarrassed by are often exposed by the Enneagram. But what feels like a sudden disclosure is of no surprise to those around me. It's nearly impossible to hide what is woven into our personality structure. Though it may feel devastating to me, it's of no news or consequence to those who know me.

Our selective relationship with type, both in affirming and denying certain qualities, usually leads to added inner fragmentation. Having an honest relationship with our type, on the other hand, means we avoid letting any fragment of our type lay claim to the whole of who we are. We recognize that type is simply one aspect of self, maybe the most formidable aspect, yet it is still just a piece of the puzzle. Like my friend and teacher Russ Hudson frequently says, "You're not your type. You *have* a type, but you're *not* your type."

In the same way, I have a body, I have a mind, and I have

emotions. But I am not the body that houses my soul, I am not the feelings that drive my heart, nor am I the thoughts that inhabit my mind. These elements are merely a silhouette, a featureless outline of the image of who we can become. This is the good news for us all: we are never restricted to our type, as a fixed, immovable script for our life. Rather, we are always becoming. When we transcend type we refuse to let it constrain us and open ourselves up to a world of possibilities of who the growth journey might make of us.

While we are always *more* than our type, let's examine a few theories of what type may actually represent.

Type as Personality

The Enneagram is much more than a personality profile system. In fact, reducing it to how personality presents itself shortchanges the core of what is contained within this tradition. When the prevalent misunderstanding of type solely focuses on personality, then so much is lost.

Certainly, Enneagram types describe patterns that present as personality. But we have to understand that this is a *conditioned* personality structure—patterned evidence that we are suffering our loss of innocence, as experienced through our Kidlife Crisis (to be described below). These patterns are highly developed skill sets that take an entire lifetime to perfect. These structured skill sets are conditioned year after year to react and respond to whatever life throws at us. The conditioning leads to a *personality structure* that is fortified by a point of view.[1] And as Óscar Ichazo says about

---

1. Ichazo suggests that a point of view (maybe the foundation for personality) is actually the ninth basic structure in human experience, "The first basic structure is *Distance*. An infant does not know about distance. If [one] sees a light far away, [it] will try to grasp it. [It] does not yet have the first structure. The second structure is *Volume*. The third is the structure of *Weight*. The fourth is the structure of *Movement*. The fifth is the comprehension that this is *Time*. It is impossible to have time without the prior structures of *Distance*, *Volume*, *Weight*, and *Movement*. After the development of the structure of *Time*, the structure of the *Past* emerges.

structures, they "are an accumulation of repeated experiences that finally make a pattern inside us."[2]

To cope with suffering our loss of innocence, evidenced as the confirmation bias of our Kidlife Crisis, we brilliantly wear masks (conditioned patterns) to hide the pain. These masks help us survive the initial wound of separation and then serve to project who we wish we were or hope to be seen as.

But as we will come to understand, we're not our personality. Rather, we are the Essence that we've lost contact with. Our personality type is the mask that we cover up our Essence with, keeping us distracted from who we really are. The Zen saying expresses this perfectly: "Your Essence is the Original Face, the face you had before your parents were born." Understanding your type is the first step of self-awareness in the journey of becoming who you really are. Working with your type, which is what the Enneagram of Belonging is helping you do, is the way to break through the prison of personality to discover your Original Face.

Type as Passion

Second, type can be understood as our ego's patterned addiction to the coping mechanisms we use to fill the void of what has been lost. Now, the truth is, our Essence was never lost, but experiencing a degree of disconnection from it creates a profound *sense* of loss within each of us. In Enneagram language, this emotional suffering that fills the void of what was lost is the Passion of our type—our heart's emotional coping habits to deal with this deep pain. The Passion emerges

---

The next structure is the *Future*. *Anticipation* is the next structure. At this point, reasoning begins. The final basic structure is the structure of the *Idea of Self*. There are eight basic structures that have to emerge one after another before the child makes the first statement, 'I am'—the ninth structure. In that very movement the child acquires a *point of view*." (*The Human Process for Enlightenment and Freedom* (New York, NY: Arica Institute, Inc., 1972), 29).

2. Óscar Ichazo, *The Human Process for Enlightenment and Freedom* (New York, NY: Arica Institute, Inc., 1972), 28–29.

from the heart and, as such, colors our emotional intelligence. You can understand how something so deeply affecting inevitably shapes type, and the Passion offers itself as a living demonstration of *how we suffer* this perceived loss.

PASSIONS

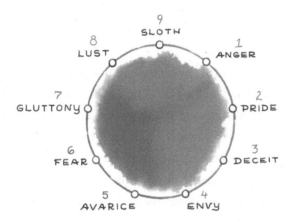

Though it suggests desire, the word *passion* is etymologically derived from the notion *to suffer*, and our Enneagram Passion is how our type contends with the unbearable ache of having lost contact with our soul's purposed reason for existing, our Essence. Naranjo suggested that the Passions "reveal themselves to be a thirst for Being [Essence], ultimately based on a loss of contact with [our Essence]."[3]

The invitation is to move from passion to *compassion*, from how we suffer to how we can be gentle with our pain. Compassion, *suffering with*, is both conscious sympathy and mindful empathy for one's own inner agony. It allows for the heartache to exist without having to fix it. Because our Passion is an inextricable part of who we are, compassion allows for the agonizing pain of our Passion to remain.

---

3. Claudio Naranjo, *The Enneagram of Society: Healing the Soul to Heal the World* (Nevada City, CA: Gateways Books and Tapes, 2004), 23.

Moving from passion to compassion also fosters honest accountability. Compassion holds the pain in tender embrace, mitigating its entitled attempts to control and define us. It's in the holding of the pain, rather than fixing it, that our Essence can shine through.

Type as a Prison

In addition to the evidence of our suffering (personality) and how we suffer (our Passion), type confirms the inevitability of what we do with that suffering.

Most of us are incapable of handling the profound anguish of our human condition. We don't know how to embrace our goodness, especially the inherent aspects of it that seem lost. So, we must find people or experiences to blame for that loss. And blame is toxic; it requires someone or something to punish. Tragically, the noxiousness of blame castigates the easiest target, which almost always ends up being the most unprotected elements of ourselves—our unsophisticated goodness which by its nature is blameless.

I like how one of my teachers used to compare type to a prison cell, as if it's the way we incarcerate our Essence. Because we don't know what to do with our suffering, we have to hide it, or lock it up, but what ends up imprisoned is the freest part of who we've always been.

Sandra Maitri echoes this when she writes, "Variations in prison walls do not make them any less confining."[4] As if to say describing the thickness of my prison walls doesn't help take them down. Maitri goes on to affirm that the work is to "move beyond these constraints, rather than making [people] more complacent about their captivity."[5]

Sadly, most of us think our type-confined prison term is a life

---

4. Sandra Maitri, *The Spiritual Dimensions of the Enneagram: Nine Faces of the Soul* (New York, NY: Jeremy P Tarcher/Putnam, 2000) 16.
5. Ibid.

sentence and so we spend considerable effort decorating our cell. Others of us are so infatuated with our type that we brand it across our chests on T-shirts, as if to proudly announce the incarceration of our Essence that keeps us stuck in these type structure prisons.

Our type can certainly expose us to the prison in which we live, but living *beyond type* is embracing our true freedom. It's knowing that our suffering is the delicate thread that must be pulled to find our way back home to our truest, most authentic selves. Resisting the temptation to penalize our suffering wakes us up to the message it has always been sending: there are beautiful aspects of ourselves that want to be remembered. Freeing our suffering frees our souls to reconnect to our Essence.

A NEW WAY TO UNDERSTAND
THE FORMATION OF TYPE

Over the years, my approach in teaching type has been framed by two things: how our imperfect early holding environments shaped our sense of self, and why self-compassion is essential in the journey of self-understanding. I've attempted to redefine the Enneagram's so-called Childhood Wounds less as actual trauma and more in line with an experience of confirmation bias—confirming to the tenderness of our young egos that our true Essence has dissipated and been replaced with our type. This loss of innocence is actually a necessary part of our story. It's the figurative doorway that we pass through as we are welcoming in the tragic pain of being human.

I call this our *Kidlife Crisis*.

Perhaps rehabilitating the Original Wound, Childhood Wound, and the Lost/Unconscious Childhood Messages language by substituting it with Kidlife Crisis offers a more compassionate approach to understanding why we are the way we are.

Perhaps reframing these so-called Childhood Wounds as the inevitable Kidlife Crisis allows for us to understand this integral passage as one of the most crucial stages of our earliest experiences of *becoming*.

Perhaps embracing our Kidlife Crisis is the very thing we need to help heal the brokenness in some of our relationships with a parent or caregiver. Honest awareness of our Kidlife Crisis and how it has fortified type as a kind of confirmation bias is one of the most crucial steps in belonging. We have to understand *why* we are the way we are if we are to practice compassion toward every aspect of ourselves, even the parts we'd rather not identify with.

Could this be yet another way then to answer the question, "What do we mean by 'type'?". Could this be found in the struggle to organize a sense of self on the other side of this Kidlife Crisis? Let's explore in the next chapter.

3

Introducing *the* Kidlife Crisis

How Compassion Helps Us Reimagine
the Childhood Wounds

It was more than twenty years ago when I first learned the Enneagram. I was visiting friends in the slums of Cambodia when they asked if I had ever heard of the teaching. At that point it was all new to me, and though I found the Enneagram fascinating, I resisted being typed as if there are *only* nine kinds of people.

My friends clearly had a sense of my type (it seems like our types are always showing), but they didn't type me. Instead of telling me what type they had (correctly) assumed, they asked me some questions about my relationship with my mom. Those questions shook me. I remember being stunned about how accurately they guessed at how our relationship has played out even into my adulthood.

In those first moments of being confronted with my type's so-called Childhood Wound, it was as if someone knocked the breath out of me. I remember wondering, "Is my type obvious to everyone else but me? Like it's written across my own forehead for everyone to read but I can't see it?"

After coming to terms with my type's so-called Childhood

Wound, I realized that it wasn't a true wound but a painful misunderstanding that I internalized and then lived out of.

I recently witnessed a little friend experience her so-called Childhood Wound or Kidlife Crisis in real time. Phileena and I were babysitting for some friends who had to take an unexpected trip out of town. They left their five-year-old daughter, Ameena, with us for a couple of nights.

After breakfast one morning, before taking Ameena to kindergarten, Phileena asked if she wanted to help us wake our dog, Basil. Now Basil loves to sleep in and really doesn't get up until we sing him this goofy song that Phileena's mom used to sing to her in the mornings when she was little. As soon as Phileena or I start the little melody, Basil promptly rolls over on his back, buries his head in the blankets, and opens up his heart. It's actually pretty sweet.

As we sang to him, Ameena started giggling, but after a few seconds she suddenly became visibly pained. Phileena immediately stopped the song and asked, "What's wrong, honey, are you okay?" And without pause Ameena wistfully replied, "My mom and dad never sing me a morning song to make me happy."

Now Ameena's parents are dear friends of ours and the truth is they are some of the best parents we know. Ameena's tender heart couldn't be in better hands than those of her loving mom and dad.

Her reaction to watching Basil's response to our morning song triggered something within Ameena that exposed her own innocent desire to be loved. It wasn't a wound, and she's not been wounded by her parents; it was an experience of Kidlife Crisis revealing to her the reality that there are other ways of being loved. It was a simple recognition that there's more room in her heart than two humans, even the best parents on the planet, can entirely fill.

THE KIDLIFE CRISIS

These Kidlife Crises that we all experience are the purest cries of our hearts to be filled with love. They are the realizations that even in the most loving relationships we couldn't possibly receive all the love we're given. Our Kidlife Crisis is the confirmation bias that we're imperfect and imperfectly loved.

I've never been comfortable with the language of the Enneagram's notion of Childhood Wounds because it implies that someone or something hurt the tenderest part of our self, even if that emotional injury was unintentional (and of course, even unintentional wounds experienced as wounds create real pain and real consequences). That sure puts a lot of pressure on parents and caregivers. It also legitimizes any undeserved sense of blame we may levy at those entrusted to care for and protect our early childhood environments.

I perceive these so-called Childhood Wounds as confirmation biases, proving to our fragile, young egos that something has gone missing and is lost—namely the best of our authentic selves.

As already noted, the Enneagram's so-called Childhood Wounds are not always *real* wounds that were (intentionally or unintentionally for that matter) inflicted upon us; they're more accurately pain-filled misunderstandings. The pain is real, but *the wounds are often confused memories.* And memories are simply the metaphors of impressions that we need to assign meaning to in the development of our experiences.

This is why we must recognize the limits of memory. Take, for example, the suspicion leveled at eyewitness testimony in a court of law; though admissible and often heavily trusted, it is still largely considered unreliable. We can't trust the accuracy of our memories because we need our memories to serve as symbols—the symbols that help make our own stories have substance and meaning.

This is not to diminish the real pain and trauma that so many have experienced in their childhood. It's to help bring into focus that these so-called Childhood Wounds aren't the source or cause of type. We actually use type to contend with the real wounds and trauma experienced in our imperfect early holding environments (and yes, every single one of us grew up imperfectly).

There's something I need to clear up here. In the past, I've often said "we're born our type," yet this statement is a lazy one, because it's not the complete picture. What I really believe is we are born *purposed*. I'm convinced we are born to bring a gift into the world that will help heal the world when we're in sync with our destined reason for *being*. But when we experience our Kidlife Crisis we are jarred out of this purposed destiny, and type inevitably shows up in nine different, precisely patterned ways. This is why we need deconditioning from the power that type holds over us. That's not to say we can truly get rid of type, but there is a kind of living *beyond* type that keeps it accountable.

I should also make it clear that I fundamentally believe type is nature not nurture, because I also fundamentally believe our lives aren't accidental—they exist for a purpose. I don't believe in a random birth lottery that indiscriminately casts souls across the earth as though they are seed being scattered in a field. *Our lives are purposed*; each and every one of us was born for a reason. This purposed reason for being points back to our Essence.

The problem is, as little kids we don't feel as if we have permission to let this Essence shine, so we box it up or tuck it away in our shadow. We experience a shock to our sense of being, much akin to a midlife crisis, but this one happens when we're still children—a Kidlife Crisis.

When I was growing up, popular films portrayed the midlife crisis, as an identity crisis usually incepted by cultural constructs related to failure, loss, or simply the inner child not wanting to grow up. It's the realization of our mortality which frequently leads to a desperate need to get back to youth.

The cliché descriptions put a middle-aged man in a sporty red car or seducing a much younger lover; women got an even worse version of the cliché when depicted as overindulgent white-wine drinkers, menopausal, and emotionally unstable due to their changing hormones. Popular renderings of midlife crises were full of dismissive shame. There was, and still is, a lack of compassion for those wading through these murky waters of one of life's major identity transitions.

How times have changed. When I was younger, we were told of a looming midlife crisis around our fiftieth birthday and warned it would last as long as ten years. Today it appears that people in at least some Western societies are having two (or three) midlife crises. The first usually hits in our early-to-mid thirties, the second in our late forties to early fifties.

As real as these identity transitions may feel, they don't change anything about our Essence. These crises serve to realign us with lost Essence, a much-too-late invitation to face the little boxes into which we've tucked our authentic selves.

The Enneagram's so-called Childhood Wounds can be compared to a pre-midlife crisis—an early jarring out of our preconscious self, the undistorted unconscious self that is nearly impossible to remember or bring into awareness.

Our Kidlife Crisis is generally the accident of not being loved perfectly while simultaneously not being able to receive love perfectly. These Kidlife Crises aren't solely the confirmation bias of what we've lost touch with, as evidenced through our Passion, but are the inner conflicts we misunderstand and then live out of.

Let's consider how these inner conflicts play out for each type.

Type One	Compliance Check	Flexible Standards vs. Inflexible Fears
Type Two	Care Collision	Nurturing vs. Protective Love
Type Three	Closeness (Con)Fusion	Veneration vs. Adoration (Respect vs. Love)
Type Four	Credibility Complex	Authenticity vs. Accuracy
Type Five	Controlled Constraint	Inside vs. Outside Containment
Type Six	Concern Collusion	Inner vs. Outer Authority Angst
Type Seven	Crush Collection	Empty Heart vs. Full Imagination
Type Eight	Conflicted Conversion	Arrested vs. Accelerated Childhood
Type Nine	Compassion Compromise	Expressed vs. Repressed Love

Type One's Compliance Check: Flexible Standards vs. Inflexible Fears

For those dominant[1] in type One, this Kidlife Crisis was an inner Compliance Check. Born to be a source of goodness, their Basic Fear of being innately corrupt caused Ones to become obsessively submissive to their inner critic. This resulted in Ones being some of the most principled people. All the little Ones wanted was to be loved (just like all of us in nine different ways), and they intuited they would have to earn this love through compliance to the expectations set by their caregivers. The crisis occurred when those expectations were unclear or inconsistent.

---

1. I picked up this "dominant in type . . ." language from my dear friend and professional colleague, Dr. Avon Manney. It's one of the ways our phraseology of type can affirm that though we have a dominant type we still possess the energies and raw materials of *all* nine types within us.

Maybe their family moved around changing homes or cities, or maybe other siblings were introduced into the household, creating changing, arbitrary, and otherwise flexible standards. Whatever the case, the flexibility of their holding environments created unpredictable expectations that the One's inflexible fear of being intrinsically flawed couldn't deal with. There was a collision of flexible external standards and inflexible fears of innate corruption. As a result, Ones learned to turn inward, accessing their own resources for devising the criteria for how to live and causing them to double down on their inner compliance for what it means to be principled. If they could now just live into their own (albeit unrealistic) standards and expectations for perfection, then maybe they'd finally be less debased than their fear suggests.

Type Two's Care Collision: Nurturing vs. Protective Love

Poor little Twos suffered their Kidlife Crisis as a Care Collision, the impact of love's rival expressions: protection and nurturing. Can you imagine young Twos putting their childlike hearts into the world while generously giving themselves away? What benevolence! The power of their innocence and the force of their 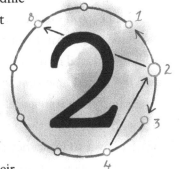 presence opened up the hearts of all those in their emotional orbit. They made the rest of us feel as if it was okay to get in touch with the tender parts of our emotional selves. But there was a caregiver who watched all of this with concern (conscious or unconscious). They were afraid that someone would take advantage of the Twos' open-heartedness, afraid that someone would break their precious young heart. Stepping in to shelter and guard the heart of a young

Two was the most loving way this adult could care for them. The problem was, the little Two's fluency in gifting nurturing love was regularly mirrored by others with a similar quality of love. So, when a caregiver responded with *protective* love the young Two felt rejected, failing to comprehend protection as another way to express love. Subsequently, Twos doubled down on a nurturing stance in presenting love and determined this is how they'd eventually win back the love they gave away to the protective caregiver.

Type Three's Closeness (Con)Fusion: Veneration vs. Adoration

When it comes to Threes, I really get gooey inside, feeling the pain they must never have given themselves permission to experience. The Threes' ache is rooted in their Basic Fear and centers around questions like, "Am I really loved or just respected?" "Am I valuable enough to be loved or must I prove my worth?" These questions hollowed out their heart at a young age. Having fused the emptiness of their hearts with the closest nurturing heart they could find, they gave themselves over to what they perceive as valuable journeys of warranting self-acceptance through accomplishments in order to secure the love they desired. You see, Threes aren't really preoccupied with winning or losing. They're not really consumed with achievements. Nor are they narcissistically image conscious. They just want the emptiness of their hearts to be filled with love—a love that sees and affirms their intrinsic value. But as little kids they quickly realized when they performed well or were recognized for behaviors that were positively reinforced, something entered that hollowed-out heart center. Veneration became the low-hanging fruit they could substitute for real love. Their confusion around respect as an alternate for love led to an addictive drive to be seen, recognized, and accepted through their accomplishments. Because Threes fear they don't have inherent worth, their Kidlife Crisis was a convoluted relationship to closeness—confusing veneration for pure adoring love.

Type Four's Credibility Complex: Authenticity vs. Accuracy

The aching heart of the Four also wants to be known and loved but suffers their Kidlife Crisis as an experience of complex emotions that feel authentic; however, the circumstances assumed responsible for those feelings allow for multiple perspectives or alternative narratives. That's not to diminish the depth of feeling associated with those memories. But it does require an accurate interrogation of how those memories are portrayed. Attuned to every detail of all things beautiful outside themselves, Fours can draw forward each splendid and magnificent facet in everything they encounter—everything and everyone *but* themselves. Unable to recognize their own beauty unearths a deep sense of frustration that is aimed at both the nurturing and protective caregiving energies in their imperfect holding environments. They perceive love to have been withheld, and frame this as the reason they can't discover their own authentic selves. As a result, they inaccurately blame factors and forces outside themselves, causing those influences to suffer alongside them. The inaccuracy of how they remember their early holding environments can't be challenged because their inner sense of being entirely authentic keeps them tethered to the illusions of what caused their loss of identity. This suffering, and the ways they pass it around, becomes a fatalistic cycle of staying distant from the truth that the source of their identity is love and it has actually never been withheld. The love that they want has always been with them; they've just felt disconnected from it. The very love they desire and the very love they're born to share has always been there.

Type Five's Controlled Constraint: Inside vs. Outside Containment

Much like Fours, those dominant in type Five are also heartbreakingly misunderstood. The misunderstanding of the Four is rooted in the depth and range of their emotional eloquence, while the misunderstanding of Fives is grounded in their brilliant cerebral skill. This one also breaks my heart because the Kidlife Crisis of the Five might be one of the most catastrophic misunderstandings of mismanaged attempts to offer and receive love. Generally, little Fives were fairly self-contained. They didn't appear to require a lot of attention. Even as young children they possessed a savvy level of controlled constraint. To their caregiver, it appeared that their range of emotions were on a very tight and simple spectrum, even though their emotional world may have in fact run very, very deep. The competent inner control of the Five's emotional life presented as a child with few needs and few demands. A relieved parent or thankful caregiver presumed their little Five required less shielding oversight and smothering care than perhaps another sibling needed or demanded. But in the mind of the young Five, the parental support of their perceived independence was a painful predicament which caused them to wonder what was wrong with them. Why didn't they get to go out for ice cream after school like their peers or ride in the front seat with dad like their other siblings often did? Why were they left unattended more frequently than their sisters or brothers? What deficiency in them was the source of the distance they felt from their parent or caregivers? Seeking to understand all this, Fives brought these concerns inward (inner containment), examining and attempting to understand them, eventually concluding that they were actually just fine. Conversely, it *had* to be their caregiver or parents that were their problem, leading to the Five's skillful outer containment. The missteps in feeling rejected and then rejecting is the accident of love acutely suffered as the Kidlife Crisis of Fives, a painful revolving door of unintended rejection.

Type Six's Concern Collusion: Inner vs. Outer Authority Angst

Sixes value security and experience love when they feel safe. From an early age they looked to their caregiver to provide that sense of safety. They came to believe that if they colluded with their concerns and found a way to subvert any looming danger or potential threat, then they would experience love. Sixes experienced their Kidlife Crisis in relationship to their insecurities and who would ultimately keep them safe. They wanted to be taken care of by a protective presence who would allay all that fueled their apprehensions. The problem was that no one could dispel their fears for them. Disappointed and feeling let down by their outer authority, they turned to an anxious inner authority. Attempting to overcome their fears, instead they colluded with them. Concern collusion then led to a never-ending cycle of authority angst: "Who will protect me?

The world isn't safe. And if you won't protect me and I can't protect myself, then I'll do everything I can to protect you." They learned to do this through risk management as a means of getting the love they desired. The importance they place on security informed their ideas about how to care for their loved ones. This is why threat forecasting, contingency planning, and worst-case-scenario thinking are love languages for Sixes. The painful irony of their Kidlife Crisis is experienced in them by internalizing unreasonably severe outcomes for how bad things might get and doing this on behalf of everyone else, hoping we won't have to suffer the consequences of their most outlandish worries.

Type Seven's Crush Collection: Empty Heart vs. Full Imagination

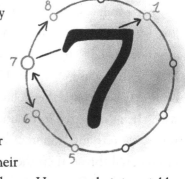

Despite their difficulty in connecting with their heart, Sevens deeply want to love and be loved. As little kids this idealization for love was projected outside of them. They thought love would be found "out there." So, they reached to the heart of a nurturing parent or caregiver (their first "crush") to assist in their attempts to connect with their own heart. However, their insatiable curiosity caused them to easily grow bored of what held their attention in the present. Boredom led to frustration, and rather than take ownership of this, it was projected onto the source of their attention. Subsequently, Sevens moved from one crush to the next, consuming as much as their imagination enabled them to before tedious monotony set them in search of another heart to devour. Now, let me be clear, these "hearts" and "crushes" take the shape of anything that holds potential meaning—a person, an experience, an idea, a hobby, etc. Young Sevens didn't set out to move from one infatuation to the next, nor do they desire this as adults. What's happening behind the scenes here is their subconscious effort to avoid entering their own heart, which seems empty to them. Turning toward what appears to be an empty heart creates a fear that the pain of emptiness will be too much for them to bear. This Kidlife Crisis is one of running away from their inner agony while collecting premature painful departures from commitments that potentially could bring them back to their heart, where they might discover, after all, a fullness of love.

Type Eight's Conflicted Conversion: Arrested vs. Accelerated Childhood

The Eight's Kidlife Crisis has to do with their lost childhood. They grew up too quickly and yet a part of their growth was stunted, resulting in an unmistakable inner child. Young Eights perceived their vulnerability as weakness and therefore rejected the nurturing love of their caregiver. They are (metaphorically or actually) the child who didn't want to be held. Presenting older or stronger than they actually were created a conflicted conversion. They converted to an older, stronger version of themselves before they were ready. This led to an arrested innocence—an inner child whose growth was stunted—and an accelerated childhood—they grew up too fast. This didn't toughen them up, though Eights present as pretty tough. It merely fossilized an arrested development of the part of them that never fully matured. Those tender parts never got to come out and play because they felt like they needed to be stronger than they were ready to be. This is why you come across so many full-grown adult Eights innocently rocking their My Little Pony T-shirts, Star Wars action figure collections, or Hello Kitty lunchboxes—these accessories and toys are hooks to that arrested part of their childhood that had to prematurely solidify and is now trying to be reclaimed. The Eight's Kidlife Crisis was a conflicted conversion, not in a religious sense, but more like a metamorphosis that skipped a step in the process of a child transforming into adulthood. It's like the child who walked before they crawled. It might appear incredible, but the child must learn to crawl in order to meet critical aspects of childhood development. Likewise, as an adult, the Eight has to recover their vulnerability and learn how to meet those tender places with nurturing love to realize the wholeness that has been missing. As grownups, the residue of this Kidlife Crisis shows up in their struggle to be vulnerable. This is sometimes observed when they try to protect that tender place by presenting as lewd or combative, degenerate, or contrarian. Nearly all Eights demonstrate this through their need to be against something. Their difficulty with accepting their innocence is the painful reminder that they've misunderstood it as weakness, when all along it's the source of their formidable strength.

Type Nine's Compassion Compromise: Expressed vs. Repressed Love

Finally, we turn to the sensitivity of Nines who are born to be a source of love. They hold an incredible capacity of concern for others. That compassion is easily directed outward but leaves the Nine minimizing their own needs and desires. As children, their intuitive attunement to love needed an outward focus because turning that compassion inward seemed selfish—the opposite of the Nine's gift for loving self-sacrifice. Their delicate sensitivities to those in their early holding environments became the focus of their attention, allowing young Nines to prioritize the needs of those around them, at the expense of their own. Their Kidlife Crisis was a trade-off entrenched in compassion—compassion for others but not for self. Learning to express love for everyone else only led to repressing love for themselves. Self-minimizing habitualized into self-forgetting, leading to an unconscious resentment or anger. The Nine's anger is dormant because to acknowledge it would seem unloving to the Nine. How could expressing irritation be loving? Yet the denial of their own needs is the very source of their hidden resentments and masked anger.

BELONGING STARTS WITH COMPASSION FOR SELF

Reframing these so-called Childhood Wounds to Kidlife Crises makes room for compassionate self-embrace. It's important to affirm that even these Kidlife Crises belong to our whole selves. Learning to accept them is key in learning to accept the whole of our stories. As Brené Brown writes, "True belonging only happens when we present our authentic, imperfect selves to the world; our sense of belonging can never be greater than our level of self-acceptance."[2]

If I'm honest, this is a struggle for me.

Holding Our Weeping Inner Child with Compassion

My folks were amazing; they went above and beyond what could have been expected of them. But realizing that my parents did their

---

2. Brené Brown, *Daring Greatly: How the Courage to Be Vulnerable Transforms the Way We Live, Love, Parent, and Lead* (New York, NY: Penguin Books, 2012), 145.

best to provide and care for me still doesn't take away the impression of what may or may not have been missing. Affirming they loved me as best they knew how still doesn't make my early holding environment less flawed. They did their best, and all I can do to honor that, as well as my imperfect humanity, is to live my best. And that sometimes means grieving the parts of myself that still need to be integrated into my whole, authentic self.

When this comes up with my psychotherapist (and yes, if you're a parent you too will someday be the focus of at least a few therapy sessions . . .), he asks me to hold the fragment of myself that wants to belong, that wants more love, as if it were a crying baby who needs to be cared for. Demonstrating what he wants me to do, he'll interlock his fingers palms upward and place his hands in front of his heart as if he's holding an infant.

For a long time, this little gesture pissed me off.

No way was I going to put my hands together and cradle an imaginary baby, even my own projected inner child. Reluctantly, I'd try to hide an eye roll, quiet my frustrated exhale, and play along.

Of course, it never worked for me because I wouldn't let myself go there. My resistance to my own vulnerability made it impossible for me to make peace with what still hurt my inner child's heart.

Reminds me of when one of my nieces visited my office and saw a wood-carved statue of a balled-up Buddha hunched over, sitting on a table. Probably four or five years old back then, Claire inquired, "What's that?"

"It's the Weeping Buddha," I replied.

"Why is he weeping?" her sweet little smoky voice asked.

I explained, "He's crying because of the pain in the world."

Disgusted and without hesitation she blurted out, "Well he doesn't have to do that if he doesn't want to!"

And she was correct; no one can make us face pain. No one can do the hard work of allowing our aches to belong—even my therapist, as gifted as he might be.

Like my niece, I was disgusted with my pain, but I wasn't going to go there. That is, until I remembered a little girl who I used to take care of when I lived in India.

Immediately after completing university I moved to Chennai and helped start South Asia's first pediatric AIDS care home for children orphaned because of the disease or born HIV+. At a time in my life when I should have been visiting the delivery rooms of my friends' first children, I more frequently found myself at the gravesite of a small girl or boy we had buried way too early.

Because I was the only single person working at the home, I usually got called on to handle overnight shifts when we were understaffed. Rare as they were, when we needed help late at night it was usually because there was a sick child who needed extra attention. One such night we had just admitted an eight-month-old baby girl named Bimala.

She was adorable. She was also very sick. Her tiny undernourished body was covered in rashes, her back full of bedsores and blisters. Like many small HIV+ children, her mouth was full of open wounds.

I arrived at the home around 8 that night and would leave the next morning by 7. In Bimala's room, one of my coworkers, Victoria, set out milk powder and a thermos filled with hot water. She also left a couple of diapers just in case . . .

It wasn't long before Bimala woke up the first time, sobbing in pain from all the ways she hurt. I picked her up trying to comfort her, and suddenly I felt a warm wetness on my chest that dripped down my stomach—urine everywhere. That was just the beginning. She was so sick with dysentery that I changed her diapers several times throughout the night.

Between short periods of rest, she kept waking up crying and crying. I'd try to keep her warm by holding her close to my body. Though I couldn't take her pain away, I did everything I could think of to comfort her. I was shaken. It was awful. This poor child enduring unimaginable suffering, not able to make sense of it, and there was nothing I could do to alleviate it.

I just had to let her cry. I just had to be present to her. I just had to show her as much love as I could from my own broken heart.

Holding Bimala with compassion, embracing her with love, was an excruciating practice for learning to offer myself that same acceptance and care.

The next time my therapist asked me to cradle this fragmented part of myself, I thought of Bimala—honoring this small child so deserving of all love and care—and tried to practice presence genuinely.

Let's attempt to bring this same compassion into how we cultivate an honest relationship with our type by briefly exploring nine compassionate blueprints for the different ways we express ourselves through personality.

4

Practicing Compassion
toward Our Type

A Fresh Take on the Origins of Personality

Enneagram types are the nine unique combinations of the three-card hand we're dealt from the shuffled deck of our scrambled Intelligence Centers: our body intelligence, cognitive intelligence, and emotional intelligence. These jumbled combinations lead with a bias for one of the Centers—intuiting, feeling, or thinking—that is simultaneously sustained and supported by a secondary Center, with a held-back Center that is denied or stifled from participating in this trichotomy of perception. Triangulating how our three Centers are arranged facilitates a *stacked* flow of attention with supported focus.

The stacked preference of the dominant Center, supported by one's secondary Center, provides our earliest clues to our Enneagram type's Basic Fear. In other words, this particular loss of contact with Essence will become our permanent state of inner fragmentation. How we perceive our Kidlife Crisis, and the Basic Fear that develops from this as a result, creates the life script that will shape so many of our experiences. This perceived reality, though generally far from the objective reality of our early holding environment, gives shape to the story we begin telling ourselves about who we are, thus allowing the figurative soft cartilage of pre-type to calcify into the skeletal structure of personality.

And while this may help outline how the psyche begins to dress itself up with idiosyncrasies, it's important to remember that we are more than our type.

TYPE ONE

Holy Idea	Holy Perfection
Virtue	Serenity
Basic Desire	To be good, to have integrity
Basic Fear	Being bad, imbalanced, defective, corrupt
Fixation	Resentment
Passion	Anger

Honorable, responsible, honest, consistent, hard-working, reliable, and full of integrity, Ones strive for principled excellence as moral duty. This comes from their Basic Fear of somehow being irredeemable or morally corrupt. That's ironic because Ones are among the most ethical people out there.

Incredibly disciplined, you can count on a One to follow through with their commitments. The downside to this shows up when we fail to be true to the promises that *we've* made to Ones—including missing deadlines or not carrying our fair share of responsibility when something on our team or in our relationship goes wrong.

Among the initiating types of the Enneagram, Ones are extremely decisive. This points to their clarity of vision and their determination of purpose. Because they are in the Instinctive Center, their clear decisiveness can be trusted and usually proves itself to be on point.

As Ones learn to grow in fluency with their Instinctive Center, their ability to practice accurate and astute discernment also grows.

Just remember to be gentle and kind to the Ones in your life. Their inner critic may be the most severe of all Enneagram types, and so they already know what they've messed up, gotten wrong, or failed at, which means any criticism of the One sears their soul. So be accommodating and forgiving if or when you need to point something out to them.

TYPE TWO

Holy Idea	Holy Will, Holy Freedom
Virtue	Humility
Basic Desire	To feel love
Basic Fear	Being unloved
Fixation	Flattery
Passion	Pride

Loving, nurturing, devoted, empathetic, generous, supportive, other-focused, and helpful, Twos strive for lavish love through self-sacrifice. Rooted in love—the source of the Enneagram's nurturing ground—those dominant in type Two spend a considerable amount of their energy caring for others better than they care for themselves.

Their presence is disarming. In a sense, it seems like everything in their being is inviting others into a warm embrace where Essence can be seen, known, held, and affirmed.

Though highly in tune with their emotional fluencies, Twos can be overly sentimental as a way of affirming the gifts in each of their relationships and how no two connections in their lives could be mistaken for the other.

Without becoming too smothering or manipulative, the real strength of Twos can be experienced in their engaging care and concern for others. They really do know how to love, and they sincerely find joy in self-sacrificing for those they cherish.

But don't let a Two overdo it in your relationship with them. Don't simply take without finding caring ways to give back to them. And make sure to learn exactly how the Twos in your life want and need to be loved. If you don't, they will gratefully receive the limited love you offer, but eventually they will find it hollow or come to resent you for not being as attentive to your care for them as they are for you.

Because Twos have explored the inner landscape of their own hearts, they carry the potential to be a midwife to our emotional truth. So, listen carefully when they offer to help navigate the complexities of your feelings.

TYPE THREE

Determined, ambitious, calculated, driven, competitive, practical, confident, and efficient, Threes strive for appreciative recognition through curated successes.

Holy Idea	Holy Harmony, Holy Law, Holy Hope
Virtue	Truthfulness, Authenticity
Basic Desire	To feel valuable
Basic Fear	Being worthless
Fixation	Vanity
Passion	Deceit

The adaptability of those dominant in type Three is remarkable. They're able to pivot and adjust to their climate, culture, or community expectations with instant, effortless smoothness. This, however, exposes their deep need to reconnect with the emptiness in their heart by earning connections through recognition, affirmation, or affiliation.

Further, Threes are among the most composed of all Enneagram types. Their ability to stay levelheaded under great stress is what allows them to earn the trust of others. And though there's a lot of competitive drive going on under the surface, they may never show this side of their selves (even competition with themselves as part of their grand self-perfection project).

Ultimately, at their best, Threes are self-controlled and demonstrate a kind of reservedness that ultimately leads to a deep sadness in their relationships. They imagine that perhaps they're not allowed to bring their self forward because it might be too spectacular for others. For Threes to come home to the gift of their truest selves requires that they learn to live their *own* lives—remembering there is absolutely nothing they have to do based on anyone else's expectations.

In your relationships with Threes, give room for them to shine while also giving them room to fail. Don't forget they need affirmation, especially for the behind-the-scenes contributions they make. And find creative ways to affirm their sense of being, not simply their contributions or accomplishments.

TYPE FOUR

Holy Idea	Holy Origin
Virtue	Equanimity, Emotional Balance
Basic Desire	To be themselves
Basic Fear	Having no identity or significance
Fixation	Melancholy
Passion	Envy

Sensitive, expressive, compassionate, introspective, sympathetic, idealistic, pensive, and emotionally attuned, Fours strive for the discovery of identity through faithful authenticity.

It's unfortunate that Fours are so misunderstood in most Enneagram materials, but this truly illuminates how remarkably different they are from all the other types (including how different they are from all other Fours). Their creativity is far more than a trait reserved for Fours. Deep within, there is a desire to experience what is beautiful and fabulous in the world as an attempt to mirror back to themselves what might be beautiful and fabulous within them.

Also mistaken as generally introverted, Fours do tend to turn inward with the hope to know themselves better so they can locate the source of their being.

One of the withdrawn types, Fours sometimes step back in relationships, not because they are smug or elitist but as a subconscious attempt to test their self-abandonment narrative. Subconsciously, many Fours feel as if they've been abandoned, so when they withdraw in relationships it's just one more way to prove to themselves that if we don't step forward, or toward them, then we've also abandoned them.

So, in your relationships with Fours, honor their boundaries, but prove your commitments through acceptance, patience, and validation of what is honestly exceptional about them—and don't exaggerate; they'll sniff that out. Use honest language from the heart.

TYPE FIVE

Holy Idea	Holy Omniscience, Holy Transparency
Virtue	Detachment
Basic Desire	To be capable and competent
Basic Fear	Being helpless, incompetent, and incapable
Fixation	Stinginess
Passion	Avarice

Objective, insightful, steady, thoughtful, systematic, detached, eccentric, and fiercely independent, Fives strive for decisive clarity through thoughtful conclusions.

There is not a more focused type than those dominant in Five. Their ability to narrow their attention to any issue, topic, or concern is phenomenal. With determined concentration, Fives can give themselves over to thorough evaluation and analysis of anything thrown their way. But this can lead to fascination that borders on obsession.

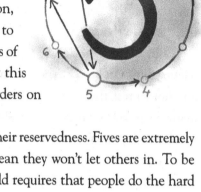

It's also important to honor their reservedness. Fives are extremely private people, which doesn't mean they won't let others in. To be let into the Fives' relational world requires that people do the hard work of listening well and asking open-ended questions that get to the heart of the issue. When a Five opens up to you, offer patience for their thorough processing—whether it be internal musing or external verbalization.

Perhaps the most boundaried of the types, Fives need to know in advance what is expected and required of them. This is why I usually encourage people not to assume Fives will pick up a random call but might need a text putting them on alert that you have a question and will call in a day or two. This gives the Five time to budget in their mind what energy and attention they're actually able to offer.

Once you earn the trust of a Five, you may never know a more generous and faithful companion who is eager to help at a moment's notice. Just make sure to find creative and thoughtful ways to love the Fives in your life. And allow your care for them to be the invitation for them to learn to take better care of themselves.

For Fives to wake up to their own potential and live into the beauty of all their gifts, they may find Father Richard Rohr's classic advice helpful: ". . . we don't think ourselves into new ways of living, we live ourselves into new ways of thinking."[1]

TYPE SIX

Holy Idea	Holy Strength, Holy Faith
Virtue	Courage
Basic Desire	To have support and guidance
Basic Fear	Being without support and guidance
Fixation	Cowardice
Passion	Fear

Faithful, collaborative, dependable, re-assuring, loyal, conscientious, trust-worthy, and community-minded, Sixes strive for steady constancy through confident loyalty.

The steadfastness of Sixes is unmatched by the other Enneagram types. Once a Six makes a commitment to a team, community, or partner, it's unthinkable to them to break that commitment. Their loyalty is a test of their own inner observer who treads in the waters of doubt and uncertainty, fueling the constant mental tug-o-wars Sixes chronically suffer. If they can prove their allegiances, then perhaps they can earn back a reciprocal devotion. But be careful. If a Six perceives you as no

---

1. Father Richard Rohr, "Journey to the Center," December 28, 2015. https://cac.org /journey-to-the-center-2015-12-28/.

longer worthy of loyalty, they may do everything they can to expose you as what they perceive you to be—dangerous.

Sixes are also the preeminent contingency planners, always thinking through worst-case scenarios as a way of threat-forecasting their concerns. This is often incredibly taxing on their mental well-being and can drum up a lot of panic or anxiety. But underneath it all is their subconscious desire to ensure stability and safety for those they love.

Once aligned with their truth and sense of their own inner strength, Sixes are the most courageous of the types and we'll follow them wherever they'll lead us.

Remember to listen to the subtext of their concerns and heed their warnings, because Sixes are usually right regarding the things about which they express trepidation. Also remember to remind them of how strong they are: it's not that they don't believe it deep down inside; it's just they sometimes need external validation to remember the gift of their courage.

TYPE SEVEN

Holy Idea	Holy Wisdom, Holy Work, Holy Plan
Virtue	Sobriety
Basic Desire	To be satisfied
Basic Fear	Being trapped in pain and deprivation
Fixation	Planning
Passion	Gluttony

Curious, energetic, charming, playful, imaginative, optimistic, spontaneous, upbeat, adventurous, and fast-thinking problem solvers, Sevens strive for imaginative freedom through inspired independence.

Clearly the most jovial of all Enneagram types, Sevens are among the
most likable and relatable of people.
They find natural ways to identify
connections with those around
them, partly because they want to
take us along for the ride of their
enthusiasm but also because they're
frequently looking outside themselves to
find the markers of what seems missing inside themselves.

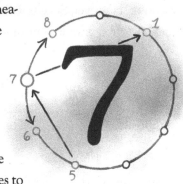

Not necessarily extroverted, Sevens are generally outgoing.
Sevens present their energy up from their hearts and out into the
vigorous ways they live into their reality. This upward drive is just
one of the ways they attempt to maintain distance from the pain in
their hearts that keeps them on the move and overly positive while
also out of their hearts and into their minds.

They really are the fastest thinkers and incredible problem
solvers; in a sense they're seers of the beyond and can predict what's
around the next corner or trends. Because they have such a quick
mind, they can be misunderstood as bored in conversations which
they find mundane and are often blown off as too playful or sarcastic.

So, remember to consciously take Sevens seriously. Don't dismiss
them. Don't relegate them to brainstorming sessions, but involve
them in strategic discussions as well, because they likely hold the
solutions to your largest questions or most treacherous quagmires.
Learn to encourage Sevens to find a way back to their own hearts,
the very source of their abundant potential but the place they most
naturally avoid.

And finally, because Sevens are on the run from the pain hidden
in their hearts, it's very difficult for them to be present—in fact, I
joke around that Sevens go on vacation so they can plan their next

vacation. However, Sevens will only find what they want when they are honest about what is missing—even if that is a painful confession.

TYPE EIGHT

Holy Idea	Holy Truth
Virtue	Innocence
Basic Desire	To protect themselves
Basic Fear	Being harmed, controlled, and violated
Fixation	Vengeance
Passion	Lust

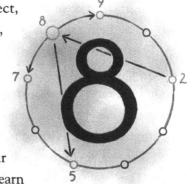

Powerful, active, impulsive, direct, assertive, strong, truthful, protective, and justice-oriented, Eights strive for impassioned intensity for unfettered autonomy.

Eights are truly magnanimous, larger-than-life kinds of people who fill a room with their presence and energy. When they learn to love and accept themselves, the love they offer others is so intense it almost knocks them down. But this is a slippery slope because many Eights project concern and care into their environments as a way of extending outward what they won't extend inward—compassion for their own vulnerabilities and their own inner child.

Experienced as unabashed, Eights are usually pretty uninhibited in the excessiveness of their impulsiveness. They act from the gut and can learn to parlay the energy of their Instinctive Center through their clear intuition.

Perhaps the most determined (though not always as stubborn as Nines) of the types, Eights will force their way, opinion, or energy on a lesser aware partner or those they perceive as lacking confidence. This is part of how they test folks, pressing and pushing to sort out who will stand up to them and fight back. If you don't back down, you'll earn their respect and have a protector who will take amazing care of you.

In relationships with Eights, remember they are as tenacious as they come across but not as tough as they present. They are looking for permission to explore their own inner tenderness and allow their inner child to feel safe in relationships. Make sure you extend that kind of care if or when an Eight ever opens up. And never use their vulnerability against them—it steals the safety they need to learn in expressing the parts of themselves they often mistake as weak.

TYPE NINE

Holy Idea	Holy Love
Virtue	Action
Basic Desire	Peace of mind and wholeness
Basic Fear	Loss, separation, and fragmentation
Fixation	Indolence
Passion	Sloth

Conciliatory, peace-filled, stable, easy going, understanding, self-effacing, balanced, affable, receptive, accepting, and patient, Nines strive for harmonious peacefulness and congruent repose.

Though accommodating, those dominant in type Nine are more stubbornly
set on not being disruptive or both-
ersome in their environments. So,
when they present as obliging, the
sad truth is that something they
care about is being subconsciously
relegated to the back of their minds
or hearts.

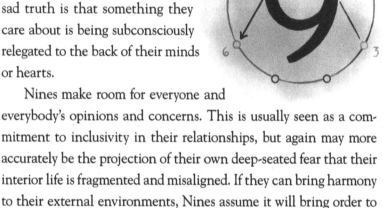

Nines make room for everyone and
everybody's opinions and concerns. This is usually seen as a commitment to inclusivity in their relationships, but again may more
accurately be the projection of their own deep-seated fear that their
interior life is fragmented and misaligned. If they can bring harmony
to their external environments, Nines assume it will bring order to
their internal clutter. Externalizing harmony serves to keep them
asleep to the very things they need to be awakened to.

Maybe the most stubborn of all the Enneagram types, Nines
won't aggressively resist but rather find subtle means of opposing
by what seems like obstinate compliance. Sure, they might act
agreeable on the outside, but if pushed too hard or expected to do
something faster than they perceive is possible, they'll slow way down
to recalibrate and reflect on what they presume is being taken from
them. This is considered by Nines a violation, and so be warned that
they work on a different clock and are motivated very differently
from others.

In relationships with Nines, give them space. They do have a
natural tendency to fuse with those they care about. Honor their
need for autonomy. This is crucial in their relationships. Otherwise,
everyone loses because Nines no longer own the gift of the parts of
themselves they choose to offer another.

TYPE AS AN INVITATION TO
RADICAL COMPASSION

Historically, much of the modern Enneagram literature generally lacks compassion for type. It's as if discovering your type had to come by way of shame or humiliation—the greater the degree of discomfort the type description created, the greater chance that it was yours. On the contrary, we can realize type through compassion. If we can actually come to understand and accept the gifts of our type, including the challenges hidden within, then compassion for self becomes the pathway to compassion for others.

5

The Dynamic Movement
of the Enneagram

Wing Theories and the Meaning
of the Crisscrossing Lines

Something that sets the Enneagram apart from other character structure systems is its dynamism. There are lots of moving parts at play inside and around the circle.

Some of the earliest teachers of the Enneagram of Personality believe the tension between our wings and the interplay of the types' connected relationships (shown inside the Enneagram's circle with the crisscrossing lines) are actually the most important aspects of type structure.

The first of which is the theories about the wings.

Simply put, each type has access to two wings, the adjacent numbers clockwise and counterclockwise to your dominant type. For example, type One could have a Nine or a Two wing (sometimes noted as 1w9 or 1w2) or both, just like type Seven might have a Six or an Eight wing (noted as 7w6 or 7w8) or both.

Essentially the wings serve to balance your type, which seems simple enough, but not in the Enneagram community where there are counterpoints for everything. I often joke around that the Enneagram is worse than religion because the parochial and competitive pettiness of some Enneagram theorists is almost too much to handle.

But before diving into this shallow-but-wide pool of wing theories I need to admit something: I'm an *EnneaUniversalist*—I more or less can find some validity in nearly every one of the prominent Enneagram theories out there. If there's something you've learned about your type and it works for you, then by all means I encourage you to go with your *EnneaPragmatism* until the concept no longer serves your inner work and personal growth. This applies to the various ideas about the wings.

PROMINENT WING THEORIES

Let's review just a handful of them.

1. **Wings Are Fundamental to Type Structure.** Many of the Enneagram of Personality's original teachers affirm that the wings are more important than our dominant type. This comes from the notion that the interaction of type with its wings is the alchemic process that creates the basis for type. Another way to understand this might be that type is the distortion of our two wings in conflict, creating between them the resolution which becomes our type. If our type is fundamentally the distillation of the interplay of our wings, then it's inaccurate to suggest someone is merely a One with a Two wing or a One with a Nine wing, rather a One may have a more pronounced wing but essentially is a One with *both* wings.

2. **Wings Are Inconsequential.** Some distinguished authors and teachers don't think the wings really impact type all that much and are more or less ambivalent about them. It's not to suggest they don't exist, so not an outright dismissal, but more a kind of sidelining of their possible influence on reshaping dominant type.

3. **Emergence of Wings as Evidence of Maturity.** My first Enneagram teacher, mentor, and friend Father Richard Rohr has taught that our wings become more prominent and our dominant type less noticeable the more mature we become.

4. **Wings Half Life.** There are authorities out there who think accessing our wings has to do with phases of life. One of these models proposes that we have easier access to one wing during the first half of life, but that ease of contact shifts to the other wing during our second half of life.

5. **Wings Imprinted on Fingerprints.** One of the most intriguing models was developed by Rafael de J. Henriquez Theran (the founder and director of the Ariel Foundation for Research and Integral Development of the Human Being in Bogotá, Colombia). His research attempts to prove that type is physiologically derived and encoded with a governing wing on our fingerprints![1] I disregarded this theory until I read his research and noticed my fingerprint pattern aligned with his theory of what my type and pronounced wing should be. Busted!

6. **Wings as Ally and Shadow Points.** One of my Enneagram teachers, Jewish mythologist and author Michael Goldberg, has this gorgeous idea that our clockwise wing is our *Ally Point*, "something of an antidote to one's Enneagram style, a practical source of leverage,"[2] while the *Shadow Point* is the counterclockwise wing, "the rejected part of the self [that] types cast a particular shadow behind."[3] Here we have two invitations, one to access the underdeveloped best of ourselves, the second to excavate the beautiful yet neglected parts of self.

1. Rafael de J. Henriquez Theran, "Enneatypes and Fingerprints," *Enneagram Monthly* 19, no. 3 (March/April 2013, issue 196): 1, 15–22.
2. Michael J. Goldberg, *The Nine Ways of Working: How to Use the Enneagram to Discovery Your Natural Strengths and Work More Effectively* (Cambridge, MA: Da Capo Press, 1996), 15.
3. Ibid., 14.

7. **Wing Fluidity.** Finally, *and* in addition to all these brilliant ideas, I more or less believe we can consciously vacillate between our wings with fluidity. There will be times when one wing will be more important to our mental, emotional, social, or spiritual growth while at other times we may need to find accountability in the supplementary wing. Leaning into either or both simply enhances our becoming and belonging as we continue to say "yes" to ourselves.

Again, I find some value in all these notions of how the wings work to balance or enhance type. If you're interested in delving deeper into a detailed description of the eighteen types with their pronounced wings, check out the material the Enneagram Institute has developed on this aspect.

Type + Wing	Enneagram Institute Name
One wing Nine	The Idealist
One wing Two	The Advocate
Two wing One	The Servant
Two wing Three	The Host or Hostess
Three wing Two	The Charmer or Star
Three wing Four	The Professional
Four wing Three	The Aristocrat
Four wing Five	The Bohemian
Five wing Four	The Iconoclast
Five wing Six	The Problem-Solver
Six wing Five	The Defender
Six wing Seven	The Buddy

(cont.)

Type + Wing	Enneagram Institute Name
Seven wing Six	The Entertainer
Seven wing Eight	The Realist
Eight wing Seven	The Independent or Maverick
Eight wing Nine	The Bear
Nine wing Eight	The Referee
Nine wing One	The Philosopher or Dreamer

CONFLUENCE AROUND THE
OUTSIDE EDGE OF THE CIRCLE

The confluence theory was proposed by Naranjo as a way to understand that type doesn't emerge independently of its wings. Type may actually be the *aggregation* of its clockwise wing falling into its counterclockwise wing—a leapfrog game that produces life in the empty spaces it jumps over. This is most clearly depicted in the way that confluence creates the Enneagram's Passion.

For example:

- Nine ↻ Seven | What is *lust* for type Eight if it's not mere lazy (Nine) gluttony (Seven), a substitution of thoughtless desire for true love?
- Eight ↻ Six | And *gluttony* for Seven is simply lust (Eight) falling into fear (Six), the voracious concern that there won't be enough, giving rise to the intense drive to consume it all.
- Seven ↻ Five | At Six *fear* then becomes gluttonous (Seven) greed (Five), a selfish loss of courage fortified by insatiable concern for more than one already has.

- Six ↺ Four | For Fives *avarice* is concocted when fear (Six) falls into envy (Four), an anxious jealousy that greedily grabs for more.
- Five ↺ Three | Four's *envy* is nothing short of greed (Five) tumbling into vanity (Naranjo swapped type Three's Passion and Fixation), illustrating that conceited, acquisitive, selfishness produces jealousy, as if one deserves what they want.
- Four ↺ Two | The *vanity* of Three is clearly the product of envious (Four) pride (Two); it's an inflated view of self, derived from jealous arrogance.
- Three ↺ One | Two's *pride* then is conflated when vanity (Three) falls into anger (One), a kind of contemptuousness that only conceited resentment allows for.
- Two ↺ Nine | One's *anger* can be understood in the mixing of pride (Two) and laziness (Nine), or viewing resentment as indolent arrogance.
- One ↺ Eight | Finally, the Nine's *sloth* is formed when anger (One) falls into lust (Eight) because annoyed intensity is just lazy passion.

INTEGRATION, DISINTEGRATION, AND THE INNER FLOW

Another dynamic element of the Enneagram is the crisscrossing lines inside the circle. The connections these lines make tell a rich story of the fluid nature of type. The lines have been explained in a variety of ways that I believe harmonize. Again, as an *EnneaUniversalist*, I think the range of interpretations here makes this aspect of the Enneagram one of its most powerful qualities.

INTEGRATION

DISINTEGRATION

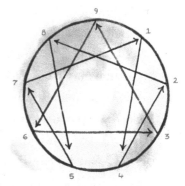

Theory of the Crisscrossing Lines 1: Integration and Disintegration

Nearly everyone who knows the basics of the Enneagram is familiar with the theory of Integration and Disintegration. It's not uncommon to hear someone say, "As a Six, when I'm healthy I *integrate* to a Nine," or, "Look at that stressed-out Four *disintegrating* to a Two." The theory basically suggests that when in healthy and unhealthy inner states we find movement along the lines that connect our dominant type to either our Heart Point or Security Type (in health) or our Stress Point or Stress Type (in unhealth). Pretty straightforward, and most of us can attest to at least some version of this through personal experience.

However, there are quite a few misunderstandings even in this simplest analysis of the meaning of these lines.

Misconception #1: We Become *Our Heart or Stress Point*

The first mistake that people make is assuming they *become* their Heart Point or Stress Point. Personality experts agree that the fundamental make-up of our personalities doesn't change very significantly, even over time. And this is true in the Enneagram. As an Eight. I don't *become* a Two when I'm centered, nor do I *become* a

Five when stressed out. When I'm not doing well, I'm still an Eight, just struggling with my Eight-hole-ness. And when I'm at the top of my game, I'm still an Eight. The movement isn't *from* our dominant type but is more like a reach *toward* one of these other two points on the circle.

Misconception #2: The Disintegration Path Is Always Harmful

The second nuance that is important to understand here is the different relationships we have with our so-called Heart and Stress Points. Generally speaking, it's fair to say we *borrow* some of the positive traits of our Heart Point to augment the affirmative features of our dominant type. It's like adding sugar or milk to a cup of coffee; it doesn't fundamentally change the nature of coffee, but it might enhance the flavors that already existed in the coffee itself. However, the reach toward our Stress Point has less to do with accessing the negative characteristic elements of that type; in one theory, it's specifically the unhealthy *manipulation tactics* of our Stress Point that are drawn into our dominant type. When we experience ourselves starting to manipulate like another type, it's likely we are falling down a psycho-spiritual hole of inner despair. When this happens, it is clearly time to snap out of whatever destructive patterns are allowing this behavior. Though this evidences the reality that we are losing our way, this reach can be understood as a corrective, subconscious, self-preserving tactic to prevent us from getting worse or staying stuck in a place we desperately need freedom from.

Misconception #3: Healthy and Unhealthy Types All Present the Same

The third gaffe that frequently arises in discussions pertaining to the theory of Integration and Disintegration has to do with the terms "healthy" and "unhealthy" versions of type. This is where my

EnneaUniversalism is cruelly tested because when I hear someone arbitrarily say, "*Healthy* Sevens look like . . ." or "*Unhealthy* Nines demonstrate . . ." my brain cringes and I try to bite my tongue. It's problematic because the person suggesting "health" or "unhealth" generally is appealing to a subjective bias of how they experience their own inner states. And then they indiscriminately apply that to others. Who's to say what health for me or you is expressed as? We all have different ways of expressing this.

Thankfully we have an expert we can appeal to in the brilliant work of the late Don Riso, who developed the Enneagram's *Levels of Development*. Essentially, Don taught we are all moving up and down a nine-rung ladder of psycho-spiritual health based on the power we give to our type's Basic Fear. (Yep, there are *nine* renderings of each type's Basic Fear and they've all been described in lucid detail.) The more we believe the lie of our fear, the further down this ladder, or these levels, we move. The less power we ascribe to the distorted truth with which our fear tries to delude us, the higher up this ladder we can progress.[4] In the *Levels of Development* there's nothing arbitrary about the descriptions of healthy and unhealthy types. They're clearly defined and eloquently detailed.

Misconception #4: Integration and Disintegration Are Foundational Concepts

Moreover, and this is the real bummer for folks who only understand the intersecting lines crossing through the center of the Enneagram as Integration and Disintegration, the author of this theory actually abandoned the idea. Claudio Naranjo was taking part in a Q&A session with a group of students when allegedly, freestyling

---

4. For a brief description of the Levels of Development, check out the Enneagram Institute's website: https://www.enneagraminstitute.com/levels-of-development.

his answers, he responded off the top of his head that the arrows illustrated Integration and Disintegration. Years later he refuted the theory. While not a full-out rejection of the idea, he considerably backs away from it:

> Another element I contributed in those days has to do with the movement of the arrows in the enneagram. Now this has become a matter of dogma, almost—that retrogression in the movement of the arrows represents a shift toward integration, and that progression with the arrows spells disintegration. That is an idea that I tentatively put forward. Indeed, I remarked that this was not part of the tradition, because I didn't want it to become a misunderstanding "in the name of higher authority," so to say. And I will parenthetically remark that I continue to be tentative; or rather, now I see that it has a relative validity, but both movements are part of transformation; both movements involve difficulties yet are processes that can result in an integration.[5]

Misconception #5: Stress Must Be Avoided at All Costs

Fifth, I don't necessarily think that stress (sometimes postulated as the cause of disintegration to our Stress Point or Stress Type) is always bad. Some of us perform best under stress. Consider also that when you use or strengthen a muscle, you're actually *stressing* it. To imply that stress is always a bad thing loses sight of the necessity of stress for growth. Stress can indeed hold for us a powerful invitation to growth.

---

5. Naranjo, Claudio, "A Report to the 'First International Enneagram Conference' at Stanford University, 1994 [Transcript of the Video-taped Presentation]." *Enneagram Monthly* 2, no. 2 (February 1996): 16.

Theory of the Crisscrossing Lines 2: High Side, Low Side

Another prevalent teaching of these lines is regularly expressed as the idea that every type can access the *high side* and the *low side* of each of the two numbers they are connected to. For example, type Six can reach to both Nine and Three to access the high side, or some of the best aspects of those numbers, as well as the low side or the more negative aspects of those types' structures. It's a generous form of Integration and Disintegration in that it affirms the good and the bad in both reaches and in both directions.

Like moving from one bar to the next on the old monkey bars of your childhood playground, when we reach for both numbers, we are progressing, moving forward in a dynamic flow of high and low momentum.

Theory of the Crisscrossing Lines 3: Soul Child

Infrequently introduced in this conversation is the theory of the *Soul Child* as an alternative for the Heart Point or direction of Integration.

I first came across this in the teachings of Father Richard Rohr, who suggests that our *Soul Child* is the type we were born, but the so-called Childhood Wound thrust us across the Enneagram along our path of Disintegration to our Stress Point. In his understanding of the theory, our Heart Point is actually our true Enneatype and we spend our lives trying to get home to our *Soul Child*. I like this idea because it speaks to our original innocence, something that most of us have experienced in relationship to the reach toward our Heart Point. But the truth is, this was never the original design of this tradition.

Hameed Ali (the founder of the Ridhwan School of the Diamond Approach, who uses the pen name A. H. Almaas) originally proposed the *Soul Child* as the neglected aspects of our self that we left behind in our childhood, while the rest of our character structure continued to develop. Sandra Maitri explains it like this:

> Our soul child is a part of our consciousness that was arrested in its development when we were very young, and so it did not mature with the rest of us and therefore feels experientially like a part of us that is a child. It is not simply a younger version of ourselves as we are now; it is the part of us that was not helped, fully allowed, and supported as children. Its qualities—which as we shall see are those of our heart point—were not acceptable for one reason or another within our childhood environment, and so we learned to suppress these aspects of our ourselves. Our personality developed around this sealed-off part of us, largely in reaction to it. Since these characteristics were not accepted, we developed other ones that were—those of the following point moving along the inner flow of the enneagram—our ennea-type. These parts of ourselves that were acceptable to our parents and supported by the environment matured, while the soul child remained behind, gradually becoming hidden away in our unconscious.[6]

What Hameed Ali and Maitri are getting at is the childlike quality of our type hidden away in our sub- and unconsciousness that needs to be metabolized into our dominant type. We generally experience our *Soul Child* in its more negative expressions, which isn't always a bad thing. Sometimes letting these messy bits of ourselves belong can be a compassionate coming to terms with them. To clarify this, Enneagram author and teacher Ginger

6. Sandra Maitri, *The Spiritual Dimensions of the Enneagram: Nine Faces of the Soul* (New York, NY: Jeremy P. Tarcher/Putnam, 2000), 249.

Lapid-Bogda describes the *Soul Child* as our "disowned childlike self"[7]—it has to be compassionately welcomed for us to become whole. To absorb the separated facets of this *Soul Child* requires that we engage every aspect of it; we have to let it "act out" in a sense so that it can mature and become wholly part of us. For a Five that means letting your type Eight Soul Child be a bully and express its aggression as well as its tender vulnerability. For a One it will require letting that type Seven Soul Child loose to consume all that it desires (even in detrimental ways) and run from its pain as well as find the joy of letting it live into its curiosity and playfulness.

Theory of the Crisscrossing Lines 4: Stuck or Located?

Finally, I've heard Michael Goldberg (the Jewish mythologist who discovered the Enneagram tucked away in Homer's classic work *The Odyssey*) suggest in passing that perhaps we're not stuck at a point on the outside circumference of the Enneagram's circle; rather we're located somewhere along these paths in between points in the middle of the circle. He suggests, "the lines are the basic building blocks of the Enneagram, not the points. An enneagram line is an archetype, a collection of themes. . . . These themes are meant to be engaged, participated in, and wrestled with. At one end of the archetype/line is a point, the most extreme position in the argument. This is an enneagram number. But the enneagram number does not stand by itself. It remains part of a line, part of an ongoing story with its opposite, at the other end of the line."[8]

---

7. Ginger Lapid-Bogda, "Enneagram Theory: Soul Child; Maybe Not; Disowned Childlike Self; Perhaps," *The Enneagram in Business* online, December 12, 2010: https://theenneagramin business.com/theory/enneagram-theory-soul-child-maybe-not-disowned-childlike-self-perhaps/.

8. Michael Goldberg, "The Lines Are the Basic Building Blocks of the Enneagram, Not the Points," *IEA Ninepoints* online, October 1, 2014, https://ieaninepoints.com/2014/10/01

Here is the basis for how we come to understand the idea that we possess within us the energies or aspects of *all* nine types. It's through the movement of this Inner Flow that the evidence of every other type can be accessed by our dominant type through dynamic movement.

Theory of the Crisscrossing Lines 5: Inner Flow

Mapping the lines toward the Stress Points or Stress Types in Disintegration has traditionally been called the *Inner Flow* of the Enneagram as it is the natural, unhindered direction of the arrows. This is why, in the older books, Enneagrams are always drawn with the arrows pointing to the so-called path of Disintegration or toward the Stress Point.[9] That used to make me a

INNER FLOW

wee bit sad because the optimist in me thought surely drawing the Enneagram's arrows aiming to the Heart Point *has* to be the goal or at least our hoped-for intent. When I eventually asked one of the old-school teachers why it was traditionally portrayed in stress, she explained that the Inner Flow is the effortless move from one type to the next in a movement for restoration and reconciliation. This pathway allows for what is incompletely developed to be celebrated and completed through the perpetual movement toward what it

---

/the-lines -are-the-basic-building-blocks-of-the-enneagram-not-the-points-by-michael -goldberg/.

9. The original Enneagrams drawn in the earliest book shows the arrows moving *forward toward* so-called Disintegration or Stress Points, which explains the commonly used phrase "moving against the arrows" when referencing the movement along the lines toward the so-called Heart Point or Security Point.

needs most. Maitri explains it this way, "[I]t is a further elaboration, result, and reaction to"[10] its dominant type. And rather than using "disintegration" or "stress" to describe these movements, the language Maitri uses is the *Defended Point*, which she suggests is used to bolster the defense needed to keep our egos asleep or to further fortify the grasp type holds over us.

For twenty years my wife and I were involved with an international humanitarian organization with projects in fifteen nations. During that time, we lived, worked, and traveled in over seventy countries. There were plenty of spots we never visited, but all my wife Phileena wanted was to travel to the Grand Canyon in Arizona. Whenever we sat down to plan out our holidays, she'd bring it up again, "What about the Grand Canyon?" And I'd dismissively respond, "What? We haven't been to the Khyber Pass yet; why would we want to visit the Grand Canyon?"

We never did make it to the Khyber Pass before we adopted our sweet dog Basil. Falling head over heels for him motivated me to consider vacations we could enjoy with our pet. As it turns out, we're probably not allowed to take Basil with us to Pakistan and Afghanistan. The Grand Canyon seemed to me like the next best thing. So, on a recent holiday, Phileena, Basil, and I did end up driving the 3,000-mile round trip to this natural world wonder. It turns out, the Grand Canyon is pretty grand.

I had this ridiculous idea—just like in the cartoons from my childhood—that once we finally got there I'd walk up to the edge of the canyon and holler at the top of my lungs, "Burrito!" hoping to hear it echo off the deep valley walls. Gave it a try. Must have done it wrong. No echo.

---

10. Sandra Maitri, *The Spiritual Dimensions of the Enneagram: Nine Faces of the Soul* (New York, NY: Jeremy P Tarcher/Putnam, 2000), 245.

The Inner Flow, however, *is* the echo of our souls moving from one point to the next, following the arrows through the Enneagram. Much like an echo, the reverb of subsequent types may be less and less perceptible as it goes, but eventually they will find a route all the way to our Enneatype, allowing us to incorporate qualities of each of them into our dominant type.

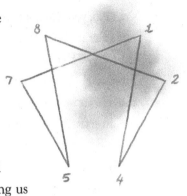

Let's examine how the natural and original direction of the lines work, starting with point One:

One → Four For Ones who've exhausted themselves through compliance to every imaginable standard, there's an inevitable fatigue that will eventually lead to more resentment unless a One drops down into the gifts of type Four that affirm for them they truly *are* exceptional and their alignment with excellence is what makes them beautifully unique.

Four → Two At point Four, however, if that exceptionalism is overdone it can produce entitlement, which ultimately leads to further isolation for a type that already feels pretty separate from the others. So, Four has to move toward Two, embracing themselves, feeling the embrace of others, and finally embracing those outside their secluded heart to make loving connection with the world.

Two → Eight Twos, however, tend to overreach with their embrace of the mythical other, generously pouring themselves out in their significant relationships. This can be draining, and when Twos feel emotionally depleted or used up, the reach to point Eight is a necessary taking back of their power as if to

say, "No, you will *not* take advantage of me anymore" or "I will
not tolerate being taken for granted another damn day!"

Eight → Five But at point Eight the inclination to intensely
protect their own vulnerabilities by overpresenting their
tough exterior not only wears themselves down, but it's also
grueling for those around them. So, Eights have to drop down
to Five to reflect on the toomuchness of their experience
of themselves and how that's projected outward. At point
Five there is safety to accurately evaluate how to be more
approachable in the world.

Five → Seven This is all well and good for Fives who prefer
living a cerebral life in their mind-palaces, reflecting on the
minutiae of human behavior. Yet just like their neighbor
the Four, interiorizing their gift will further detach them
from their world by pushing them into mental isolation.
Reaching out to Seven, however, activates their conclusions
and requires they live into all the fabulous ideas they've
dreamt up by embodying the concepts they've figured out.

Seven → One The energetic living into every conceivable and
trivial idea at point Seven can engender excessiveness. Sure,
it's a blast to be along for the ride with a Seven who's out to
experience it all, but that too has its limits. Seven's unhealthy
relationship with constraint must be held in check, which is
why their reach to point One is so critical for their thriving.
At point One, the Seven is reminded that boundaries and
rules are necessary for human flourishing and something not
to be resisted but rather celebrated.

While this movement echoes through the Enneagram's irregular
hexagon, the inner flow is simultaneously processing through the
equilateral triangle in the middle of the circle starting at point Nine.

Nine → Six Nines are notorious for taking
on the energy, opinions, desires, or concerns of
everyone else but themselves. Giving away their
own aspirations is akin to living someone else's
life, which Nines quietly go along with.
Dropping down to point Six wakes the
Nine up from their internal slumber by
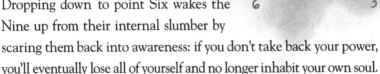
scaring them back into awareness: if you don't take back your power,
you'll eventually lose all of yourself and no longer inhabit your own soul.

Six → Three At point Six (along with the Three, one of the
Enneagram's Shock Points[11]) the jarring back to self through whatever
threats can be constructive; it's just the overuse of giving in to their
concerns that drums up an inner anxiety. This burden is too much
for anyone to carry, especially the Six, whose addiction to distress is
overly agitating to everyone around them. The more they think about
what upsets them, the more fixated they become on their mental
unease. And so their reach to point Three is always for freedom from
these worries through initiating the solutions they require.

Three → Nine The driving energy of point Three will get things
sorted out and won't allow their fears to get the best of them. Efficient
problem solving is one of many ways Threes add value to their lives
and stability to their relationships, but at what cost? If Threes continue to live out of the emptiness of their hearts, chasing value outside
themselves as if it's a trade-off for bringing it back inside themselves,

---

11. If all Enneagram types are simply a diminished or faded version of type Nine which
is centered at the top of the circle, then Types Three and Six are sometimes called the Shock
Points. Beginning at the top of the circle and flowing downward from Nine, the most intense
or brightest energies of Eight and One start a momentum that eventually slows as it drops to the
most reserved or boundaried energies at the bottom of the circle with Five and Four. The Shock
Points keep the flow moving, shocking the downward movement and maintaining the flow of
this momentum. The jolt is also noted because it seems the space below these Shock Points is
unexpected. Consider the flow from the Passion of Three (deceit) to the emotional purity of Four
or the sometimes anxiety-driven mental uncertainty of Six flowing into the cerebral confidence
of Five. These reaches seem much further below the Shock Points than they do above them.

they'll need to reach to Nine. At point Nine, Threes slow down and stubbornly arrest their momentum to earn what has always been ascribed to them. Here they find true peace.

UNIQUE LUMINARY ROLES FOR ALL TYPES

To wrap up these assorted renderings of understanding type, I want to highlight that every type plays a unique role in showing the other types how *becoming* is fundamentally a movement of belonging. I call these specially designed functions that each type plays "luminary roles" because if each of the nine types can reconcile what's unreconciled within it, we all benefit from the example to continue on our inward journeys of integration. Once one learns to make room for all parts of the dynamic personality system, one can then manifest more wholeness and ultimately more Essence in the world. This reminds me of when Phileena says, "To the extent we are transformed, the world can be transformed."

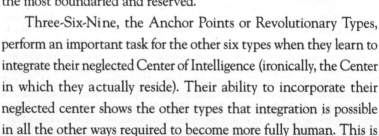

Starting at the top of the circle, we'll follow the types as they fall off both sides of the Nine. The naturally diminishing intensity of types from Eight and One are the most extremely expressed, all the way down to types Four and Five who are the most boundaried and reserved.

Three-Six-Nine, the Anchor Points or Revolutionary Types, perform an important task for the other six types when they learn to integrate their neglected Center of Intelligence (ironically, the Center in which they actually reside). Their ability to incorporate their neglected center shows the other types that integration is possible in all the other ways required to become more fully human. This is a path of belonging, remembering that the very thing which seems furthest from us was always waiting for us right there inside our own hearts, minds, and bodies.

One and Eight sit at the top of the circle flanking type Nine with all the lost intensity that point Nine seems to have forgotten. In most cases it's undeniable that One and Eight are the most forceful and insistent of the types; there's a kind of charging at life these two types express: Eights attacking outward while Ones indicting inward. This demanding drive contained within the structure of these two types is what makes Ones and Eights the initiating types of the Enneagram instigating for the good and the bad forceful energy that is very difficult to stop, even pretty tough to slow down.

Twos and Sevens are the anomalies of the Enneagram, because they are the only two types that don't have natural connections to all the Centers of Intelligence. When you look at a drawing of the Enneagram, you'll notice that type Two's wings

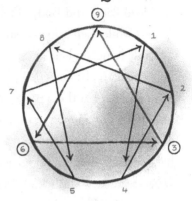

**TYPES 3-6-9
LUMINARY ROLE**

**INTEGRATING
REPRESSED CENTERS**

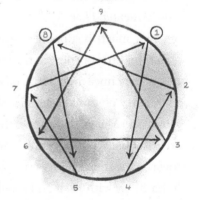

**TYPES 1-8
LUMINARY ROLE**

**EXTERNAL-INTERNAL
BALANCE**

are in the Body (One) and Heart (Three) Centers and their paths also stay in the Body (Eight) and Heart (Four)—there's no contact with the Head Center. Similarly, type Seven's wings are located in the Head (Six) and Body (Eight) Centers while their arrows point to the Body (One) and Head (Five)—there's no natural connection to the Heart Center. For these two types, finding a way to incorporate their missing Center shows the rest of us that a chrysalis-esque transformation always creates new life in dead places.

Fours and Fives who sit on the edge of the Enneagram's *Existential Hole*, the gap at the bottom of the circle, serve to illuminate two important luminary roles for the other types. But first a word about this *Existential Hole*.

Not much has been written about this little opening at the bottom of the Enneagram's circle other than a few obscure articles in old *Enneagram Monthly* back issues that are essentially out of print. Some theorize the true Enneagram is one in harmony with itself and should be drawn with three equilateral triangles (seen in what are sometimes called the Harmony Triads or the Dominant Affect Groups) that connect type Two to Five and Four to Seven. This would explain why Two and Seven appear to be awkward anomalies; originally, they were

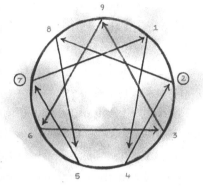

**TYPES 2-7
LUMINARY ROLE**

**INCORPORATING
THE LOST CENTER**

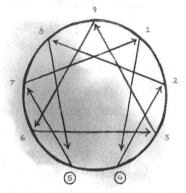

**TYPES 4-5
LUMINARY ROLE**

**CONNECTING
HEAD *AND* HEART**

connected to all three Centers. In this theory, the circle was broken open through the introduction of original sin, pushing the invisible line from Five to Two up, now Five to Seven, while simultaneously pushing the invisible line from Four to Seven up, now Four to One.

I can accept that to a point if we examine the first two stories of human sin found in the pages of the Hebrew Scriptures.

In the first instance (Genesis 2:4–3:24) we find Eve desiring divine understanding, reminiscent of type Five's *need to understand*. Prior to eating the fruit, she did not yet possess the knowledge of good from evil. Her desire to understand, and so be like God, was what led her to eat of the fruit, even though she was instructed not to. While the consequences of her action are understood to be demeritorious, can we not find some empathy toward Eve? So often we think of "sin" as malevolently intended. But Eve was simply desiring to understand. And remember she didn't yet know right from wrong. Surely we can summon compassion for her and for all of us who unintentionally mess up from time to time.

The second story of human sin (Genesis 4:1–26) is written for us in the tale of Cain killing his brother Abel as a painful expression of feeling left out or unloved by God. Cain's jealously (reminiscent of the *envy* of type Four) was a malformed expression of his desire for God to accept his gifts like Abel's offerings were received. While we are not obligated to condone Cain's murder of his brother, we can recognize his "hate" was really a disguised longing for acceptance. The tragedy is that this got the best of him. But we can honestly understand the hurt behind the hate, and again find some compassion for such deeply harbored pain.

So, if the sins of Eve and Cain represent the break in the bottom of the circle, then part of the work of Fours and Fives is to close that break.

But wait just a second here, because maybe that opening isn't where original sin entered the human story. Another way to understand this gap at the bottom of the circle might be that the *Existential Hole* is the birth canal of all that's good and true and beautiful about humanity—falling from love (at the top of the circle, type Nine's Holy Idea) and flowing through the entire Enneagram out past these two gatekeepers, Four and Five.

That sounds like an integration of all the Centers: Nine's Body Center, Four's Heart Center, and Five's Head Center. But this is where things get tough, because as the saying goes, "The longest journey you will make in your lifetime is from your head to your heart."

This is the work of *becoming*, not closing that gap but *connecting* the circle of life by bringing together two aspects of our selves that seem diametrically opposed to one another. Not upgrading to some better, faster, stronger version of ourselves, but becoming our true selves by remembering who we have always been. We can never be perfect. But life itself is the process of becoming. So, we are invited to bring everything, even the most disparate parts of ourselves, into belonging. That's some pretty tough work, but Fours and Fives get to carry that for us.

The other role Fours and Fives play for the rest of the Enneagram is the ability to shoulder the weight of this human community we're part of. The Fours at the bottom of the circle seem to carry the emotional weight of the whole Enneagram, while the Fives seem to shoulder the mental well-being of all nine types. That's a lot to endure, a lot to hold in tension for the rest of us. But they do it with grace and honor. And we thank them for allowing us to rest on their responsibility to anchor the best of our mental and emotional states in the flow of a circle that won't be broken open.

Understanding our type on the surface level doesn't help us recognize what's behind it. There's so much more to be discovered in the shadows. But it's difficult to enter the unknown, and very few of us have the courage to enter that cave and explore what has to be brought into awareness. So, let's make that brave step together.

PART II

BRINGING OUR THINKING CENTER BACK *to* BELONGING

6

The First Truth We Tell Ourselves

Exploring the Holy Ideas

There's almost always a cave scene woven into every great story. The cave (also symbolized through settings such as a desert, swamp, valley, the wilderness—just about anywhere one can go to find a critical truth for their sense of meaning) is meant to be a symbol of our shadow. It's an inevitable stop in the pilgrimage of nurturing our spirituality. The problem is, we generally won't go there willingly. It usually takes crisis to get us there.

STAR WARS

I grew up watching *Star Wars* movies. The nine (yep, there it is again . . .) films span three generations of an intergalactic power struggle of the Skywalker family's collective psyches to make peace with their own shadow. Throughout the character development of the Skywalker dynasty, the viewer is knocked back and forth with the s/hero and villain in each of them. In episode five, *The Empire Strikes Back* (1980), Luke Skywalker finds his own cave on Dagobah, an abandoned world covered in misty swamps and steaming bayous.

While training with his new guru Yoda, a green-skinned 900-hundred-year-old mystic (a sort of tiny little dragon himself), Luke grows impatient and wants to accelerate the process. He's trying to figure out the difference between recognizing the light from the shadow when he encounters his cold, dark cave. Peering into it he asks his master, "What's in there?" and Yoda replies, "Only what you take with you."

As Luke enters, Yoda instructs him to leave his weapons behind, yet Luke ignores the counsel. Once inside, his nemesis Darth Vader emerges from the shadow with his lightsaber drawn. Luke reaches for his own energy sword and in the ensuing duel beheads Vader. As the mask of his slain adversary rolls to the ground it opens to reveal Luke's face.

Pretty powerful stuff for a kitschy science fiction film.

I doubt my nieces and nephew are going to get all nerdy about *Star Wars* like I did, but in the past few years Disney has released several other films they do love, and in each of them a hollow, cavernous den of discovery shows up.

INSIDE OUT

Inside Out (2015) follows the story of Riley, a girl from Minnesota who has to say goodbye to her childhood home when her family relocates to

San Francisco. The move is especially difficult on Riley. Her feelings, personified as the main characters (Joy—the ringleader of these five primary emotions—Sadness, Fear, Disgust, and Anger), struggle to help Riley live in the present while retaining her nostalgic core memories from the past. But Sadness keeps touching Riley's happy memories, turning them into desolations. A struggle ensues between Joy and Sadness, who both want to shape Riley's sense of self as it's rooted in her memory. While journeying through the part of Riley's psyche that contains her long-term memories, Joy and Sadness encounter her childhood imaginary friend Bing Bong—a happy-go-lucky fluffy pink creature (mostly elephant mixed up with a little cat, dolphin, and cotton-candy fur) with a multicolored flower pinned to his lapel who cries candy tears.

Effervescent Bing Bong is up to the challenge to help Riley because all he ever wanted is for her to be happy. But this culminates in a heart-wrenching scene that takes place in the "Memory Dump," the recollection memorial aspect of Riley's mind where memories gradually fade away and go to die—another such cave. It's in this valley that Bing Bong sacrifices himself for Joy. A tear-jerking symbol of the ego needing to let go of childish hang-ups, the resistance to growing up that eventually acts out in our midlife crises.

MOANA

Or let's take *Moana* (2016), the story of a young Polynesian chieftess-in-waiting who's destined to save her community but first needs to find the heart of Te Fiti, a magical greenstone that created the islands and all life on them. Her grandmother brings Moana to a secret cave (a symbol of her repressed past that stifles the possibility of her future) full of abandoned ships that have been docked for generations. Not to be stuck on the island, Moana takes one of the boats and ineptly sets sail, only to be overcome by a typhoon and shipwrecked on a faraway island. It's here that she meets a shapeshifting demigod Maui who had stolen (and then lost) the heart of Te Fiti. He imprisons Moana in a cave, representative of what was holding her back from realizing her strength, and attempts to steal her boat. She escapes, and the two reluctantly join forces on a quest to retrieve the enchanted stone and save humanity. But Maui's also lost his magical fishhook that must be retrieved for him to be successful. It's in yet *another* cave, a symbol of Moana's hidden inner resources, where she and Maui recover the fishhook from a giant jewel-encrusted, gold-covered coconut crab, a sort of sea dragon guarding hidden treasure.

The caves in *Moana* seem to represent her past, her present, and her future, which stay in a cycle that eventuates into her aligning desire with Essence, uncovering her identity, and allowing her to protect her community as she liberates herself.

COCO

Finally, in *Coco* (2017) we encounter the story of gifted twelve-year-old guitar player Miguel and his search through the realm of the dead to reveal the hidden identity of his great-great-grandfather, hoping that this revelation will eradicate his family's ban on music. Miguel teams up with a fading soul and fellow guitarist Héctor to help discover his family's patriarch. On the verge of exposing the long-held secret, the two are captured and thrown into an underground cavern where (spoiler alert!) it's revealed that Héctor's true identity is in fact Miguel's long lost great-great-grandfather. The cave here symbolizes belonging.

FACING THE SHADOW TO
DISCOVER OUR HOLY IDEA

These stories are loaded with signs pointing to the complexity of what can be lost and what can be found in all our shadows. Take for instance the companions highlighted in these tales. In each of these cases, it appears they are the projection of what is lost or missing in the protagonist's psyche: Yoda for Luke is a projected image of desired wisdom; Bing Bong for Riley is an image of forgotten innocence; Maui for Moana is a projected sense of unrealized strength; and Héctor for Miguel is a symbol of familial belonging.

All these discoveries happen in caves. All these insights come through struggle. All these realizations also require a companion—an inner witness or an inner child.

The universal wisdom is clear. In the journey of remembering our soul's created purpose and releasing from our false sense of self, there's a cave each of us must enter. It's a cave that requires courage of us, yet within, a buried treasure awaits. This treasure is a lost part of our self that all of us have hidden in our shadow. Our inner child is eager to accompany us into these cavernous, shadowy places so that the truth of our identity can be recovered and remembered.

The Enneagram calls this lost treasure the evidence of our type's Holy Idea and Virtue working together.

HOLY IDEAS

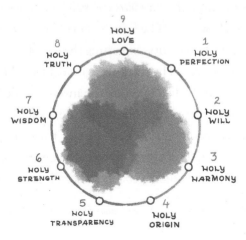

You may remember, the Holy Ideas were one of the first four Enneagons that Óscar Ichazo taught, and of those four, perhaps the most misunderstood.

Ichazo explained them as the unconditioned self's higher mental states. He presented them as the nine essential qualities of humanity's divine nature. Some have even suggested they are the nine faces of God. Regardless, along with the Virtues (the unconditioned self's higher emotional states), the Holy Ideas are a key ingredient in the foundational components that make up our Essence.

These nine divine thoughts are usually skipped over in most Enneagram teachings or grossly mistaught because they don't necessarily mean what they say. Ironically, the terms applied to them are vague at best, which leads to quite a bit of confusion. Further, there are very few resources out there to help us understand what is meant by the Holy Ideas.

Hameed Ali, one of the first students in Claudio Naranjo's original SAT program, centralized the Holy Ideas in the framework for his Diamond Approach to Self-Realization. His groundbreaking book, *Facets of Unity: The Enneagram of Holy Ideas*, is an unprecedented text on this obscure aspect of human character structure. Ali views the Holy Ideas as the nine *objective views of reality* or *unobscured perceptions of what is*. He writes, "The Enneagram of Fixations reflects the deluded or egoic view of reality, expressing the loss of the enlightened view, which is represented by the Enneagram of Holy Ideas."[1] It can then be argued that the Fixations are the inverse of the Holy Ideas.

If these unobstructed views of reality are, as Ichazo suggested, the *psycho-catalyzers* on our journey of inner transformation, then they might be the principal aspect of the entire Enneagram tradition.

Aligning with the truest version of ourselves and the gift we

---

1. A.H. Almaas, *Facets of Unity: The Enneagram of Holy Ideas* (Boston, MA: Shambhala 2002), 6.

were born to bring forward into the world requires a compassionate clarity of our own inner landscape. It demands we tell ourselves the truth, which is why the Holy Ideas are at their core *the first truths we need to tell ourselves.*

Acceptance and belonging of these Holy Ideas makes way for the path of inner clarity and spiritual openness by showing us what has been forgotten. This focused work will unearth everything. This is the painful yet ultimately rewarding process of excavating our lost Essence. It all begins with telling ourselves the truth.

Several years ago, I attempted to press into the Holy Idea for my Enneagram type, Holy Truth. At its core Holy Truth is a rejection of the lies of dualism, affirming that nonduality is the compassionate belonging of all. Eights however want to reduce this divine thought to a sort of "speaking the truth in love," which generally lacks tenderness and doesn't usually come across as very loving. The Holy Idea of Truth invites every Eight to practice nonduality by gently accepting every aspect of self. For Eights, that includes the vulnerable aspects we think are weak as well as the hardened aspects that frequently become weaponized in our relationships.

I had no idea how devastating this acceptance of this Holy Idea was going to be. Everything was turned inside out and upside down in my life. Years later I'm barely reassembling the pieces of the tumultuous reframing of everything I thought I knew was true.

I entered my own egoic cave to face my shadow, where this treasure of a Holy Idea had been hidden. But I was not prepared for the changes that ensued, however positive they might be.

Each of us at some point in our life will have to make a decision: will we follow the innocence of our inner child into the cave of our soul, face our shadow, and be transformed by the Holy Idea? Or will we stay stuck in the patterns that keep us in the shadow?

Sounds great, right?

The thing is, we all want to experience belonging, but few of us are willing to do the messy work necessary to achieve it. To unearth buried treasure or excavate our Essence means our hands are bound to get dirty. We're lucky if we start this journey in our twenties. Figuratively, it's as if we're tasked with the labor of digging through that first layer of egoic soil covering up our Essence, that loose dirt mixed in with stinky manure. Wait until our thirties to get started, and once we've gotten through the compost of our psyches, we've then got to dig up the mucky clay that's entombed our gifts. By our forties we're taking this work in shifts as the stony gravel and rocky soil is much heavier to extract. In our fifties getting started requires a spiritual jackhammer to break through the fossilized lies we've built a life around. And if we wait until our sixties (or beyond) to start excavating our Essence, it's likely we'll need some heavy machinery and a team of professionals to crack the core of our ego. It's not impossible, but like I said, it's dirty work.

SO HOW DO WE GO ABOUT
RECOVERING OUR HOLY IDEAS?

I believe the Holy Ideas are the *first truth* we must tell ourselves to wake up from the slumber of our forgetfulness and live into the gift of our belovedness. And these first truths help us return to our divine mind aligned with love, or the mind as it was always purposed to be.

Not to be cliché, but I've worked out a framework for implementing these divine thoughts in our personal lives. I call them "the ABCs of the Holy Ideas":

A as an *Affirmation*, the assertation of our inner truth with which our soul longs to reconnect

B a *Belief,* the celebrated acceptance of our truth that leads
to freedom

C a *Confession,* the acknowledgment of these divine thoughts
as necessary for transformation

Type One

Traditional Holy Idea	Holy Perfection
Affirmation	I am complete when I celebrate my imperfections.
Belief	I believe there is a divinely compassionate intrinsic perfection of love within.
Confession	I accept what is, as it is, starting with my perfectly flawed self.

The concept of perfection cannot lead to precise experiences of exactness or correctness. This affirmation of divine perfection is an inner state of discovering perfect love within. Ones are perfect *just* as they are; nothing more or less is required of them than to merely *be.* Celebrating their perfection means accepting the gifts and limits of their humanity. This requires compassion for what is intrinsically true of all humans: we are not as bad as our worst failures; we are better than our best successes. This also requires a reorientation in how we understand ourselves: God is not as hard on us as we are on ourselves. Ones who learn to find beauty in their flaws join the rest of humanity, holding hands with love, and making room for all of us as they've made room for all of themselves.

Type Two

Traditional Holy Idea	Holy Will, Holy Freedom
Affirmation	I am a cocreator with love.
Belief	I believe there is unconditional freedom to be loved and to love.
Confession	I willingly release all obligations to my sense of indispensability.

The strength of type Two is found aligning with inner or divine will, realizing they are a participator in love rather than the driver or source of it. Holy Will creates freedom to not give oneself away but to become instead a liberated participant in the flow of love exchanged in relationship—love that 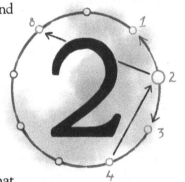 gives *and* receives. The will of the Two allows one to not be in charge of all their human connections. They can flow from the source and cocreate with their relationships rather than be the god of them. Holy Will is the strength of the Two that allows for true freedom.

Humility is not a means to an end; it is the passageway through which a soul journeys toward its truest source of strength, its will. As a virtue, humility is the principle that flows from love. Humility allows for one to affirm that they need something and someone outside their self, which is simultaneously a recognition of their need for belonging and an admission they are not the source of belonging. Twos who embrace their divine humility are able to will their cocreative fecundity in relationships, never apart from the other, allowing themselves to need without being needy. Moving from humiliation to honor is the move from self-importance to self-love.

Type Three

Traditional Holy Idea	Holy Hope, Holy Law, Holy Harmony
Affirmation	I am changed by love.
Belief	I believe there is an inherent value in all souls.
Confession	I embrace the permanence of my value that cannot be earned.

The divine mind, that is centered in its Holy Idea, creates through loving and compassionate order, and this creation is not dependent on us. Affirming the divine plan for creation changes in us the desire to control our efforts in altering reality to somehow attain value. Instead of attempting to change 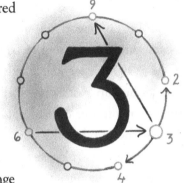 their world to attain value, Threes are changed by the world; discovering there is nothing they can do to earn love. Threes align with this interior change when they are able to be taken into their ground of being and find the seed of transformation and source of love. Awareness of the harmonious perfection in the laws of nature is the source of hope—hope for lasting change. When Threes live into their Holy Idea, conversion is realized as transformation, changing illusions of worth from merit-based pursuits to alliance with inherent worth. Here they discover they cannot change themselves to be loved, for they are inherently and unconditionally loved as they are.

Type Four

If we affirm that all people are significant because of their holy origin, then we likewise affirm no one is without a basis for belonging.

Traditional Holy Idea	Holy Origin
Affirmation	I am connected to love.
Belief	I believe there is a divine source in all life.
Confession	I am conscious of compassionate belonging.

Furthermore, we can then assume aligning with that basis is what assigns
meaning. The emotional ache to
locate source in the soul of Fours
is the evidence that source exists,
just as human restlessness with
time points to our eternal nature.
The divine mind of the Four owns
this for themselves. Connecting with the

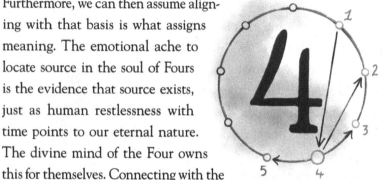

source of love requires connecting with self, accepting oneself, and
allowing oneself to be loved unconditionally. Here, connection is
simply the echo of love reverberating from one soul to the next—
being without doing.

Type Five

Traditional Holy Idea	Holy Transparency, Holy Omniscience
Affirmation	Love is the coherence that holds everything together.
Belief	I believe there is divine truth in silence, there is love in the unknown.
Confession	I am rooted in mystery.

Many spiritual teachers have suggested the first language of the
divine was silence. In the silence, love is no longer anonymous though
it's known without name. Fives who allow themselves to surrender to

the mystery of this unnamed yet know-able love stand in the long line of all mystics before and beyond them, affirming that not needing to know everything is the only thing one needs to know. With transparency, they realize, "Love is what I've always held because love has always held me." Here they discover the coher-

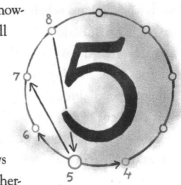

ence that they've longed for; it's love that holds everything together.

Everything resonates to the universal frequency of love. There are actually no answers the Five has to find because love is the answer to every need, the solution to every problem, the completion to what is missing. If they can be compassionate with themselves in silence, they will be able to perceive love.

Type Six

Traditional Holy Idea	Holy Faith, Holy Strength
Affirmation	I am courageous because of love.
Belief	I believe there is divine love grounded in compassion that liberates fear.
Confession	I make an option for the absurd to believe beyond belief.

Doubt isn't the opposite of faith; certainty is. Faith requires making an option for the absurd, hoping for something better than could be imagined. One doesn't need to believe the things they put their faith in, because faith and belief are falsely correlated aspects of a larger commitment to trust. Faith is rooted in love and grounded in truth. Faith is hope-filled. Faith is courageous doubt. Now courage doesn't imply a lack of fear—just as faith needs doubt, courage needs fear. Courage is being honest with fear, facing the illusions and truths it conceals. In a quasi-spiritual trust fall, the divine mind of Sixes finds authentic peace through liberating their concerns by putting on their courage—seemingly the most absurd option they can make.

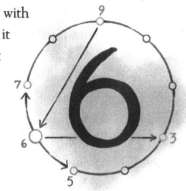

Type Seven

Traditional Holy Idea	Holy Wisdom, Holy Work, Holy Plan
Affirmation	In the present I am loved.
Belief	I believe constancy through constraint leads to contentment.
Confession	I affirm the enoughness of each moment.

The wisdom of love is experienced in the present. One cannot participate in the present while fixated on anticipating the future, just as a preoccupied mind can't occupy the moment that holds it. The painful struggle for Sevens demands they slow down the fast-paced brilliance of their minds long enough to remember

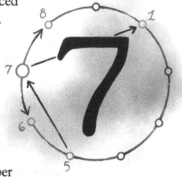

that the present moment is always enough, for in it every moment of our past is held and every potential moment of our future is incubated. This moment, *now*, is the only moment that matters. This present moment holds every answer and every question. The enoughness of now is the compassionate embrace of love's patience which has consistently and constantly waited to be held. This divine thought of Sevens celebrates constancy through constraint, as evidence of their spiritual flourishing.

Type Eight

Traditional Holy Idea	Holy Truth
Affirmation	I am held in compassionate love.
Belief	I believe all truth comes from the source of love.
Confession	I willingly surrender to love.

Truth is the severe mercy of love showing its tender aspects. It is an invitation to love. The strength of the Eight is surrendering to love and discovering they are held with compassion. In this embrace, the Eight can be vulnerable. But in such an exchange, rejection is possible.

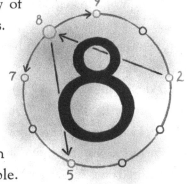

Opening to this possibility is true strength. Being sensitive to the potential pain incurred by rejection is true courage. To close oneself off from either the joy or sorrow balanced on the knife's edge of rejection is controlling. And any effort to exert control is an overcompensation of weakness.

Learning to let go of control is the way Eights make peace with their power—a power that is realized in the mastery of self rather than attempting to control others. As Lao Tsu suggests, "Mastering others is strength. Mastering yourself is true power." The divine mind of the Eight opens their vulnerable heart, inviting them to bear their most woundable and tender selves as the validation of their power.

Type Nine

Traditional Holy Idea	Holy Love
Affirmation	I cooperate with love.
Belief	I believe love anchors my being in compassionate self-awareness.
Confession	I am a source of love because I first love myself.

To be love is divine. To be divine is to cooperate with love. Located at the top of the Enneagram's circle rests the Nine like a full moon or the risen sun, permeating the world with rays of love beaming from the clarity of their divine mind. Nines know to love is to be loved. To be love is to start by loving oneself without condition, commentary, or constraint. The experience of love has to be an internalized one. And when the divine mind cooperates with love, it sparks action and activates love in the world.

THE HOLY IDEAS AND THE ESSENCE OF LOVE

As the poet and mystic Mawlana Jalal-al-Din Rumi mused, "I searched for God and found only myself. I searched for myself and found only God." The Holy Ideas are not emotional states or experiences but unobstructed views of reality that embody the essence of love. Because fundamentally, love doesn't objectify what it holds with attention; rather love makes the object its subject. And it takes a divine mind to realize this—both a conception realization, but more than that, an embodied reality lived in the world.

7

Making Peace *with* Our Fixations

The Counterforce of the Holy Ideas

Y ou know those microfiber cloths that are used to clean the lenses of eyeglasses? They're really helpful for clarifying our perception and helping us see better through the lenses. Once you're used to nice clean eyeglasses, the scratches, dust, and the little flaws that can't be polished away become more apparent.

The Holy Ideas are like those microfiber cloths we use to clean the lenses of our consciousness. Just as the Holy Ideas bring clarity, the Enneagram's Fixations are the spots and flecks of dust that threaten to obstruct the lenses. Before long, our Fixations calcify and become truly fixed. Suddenly, it becomes seemingly easier to learn to see *around* these specks in our vision, rather than doing the work of removing them with our Holy Idea. In this way, our Fixations keep us stuck. They prevent us from observing the wholeness of our own beauty and the beauty of the world around us. When we learn to pay attention to these hang-ups and engage them head-on, rather than trying to ignore and accommodate them like dust on our eyeglasses, we expand our ability to perceive the inherent good in ourselves.

This allows for the gifts of our Holy Idea to come forward.

Conversations about the Holy Ideas naturally bring us to the Fixations. The Holy Ideas and Fixations are the two sides of the mental coin our Head Center flips over and over and over again. If the Holy Ideas can be understood as the *first truths* we have to tell ourselves, then the Fixations are the *original lies* that keep us trapped in the fiction of our illusions.

Fixations are like mental stowaways; though part of type structure, they're kinds of psychological fugitives that sneak into our shadow, hiding from our Holy Idea, but ultimately needing to be exposed for the lies they tell us.

Prominent theories on how type is formed suggest that, while still in our infancy, a Fixation crystalized in one of our three Instincts, thus producing the container for what our personality was to become. This suggests that the soul work for each of us requires a loosening of this fossilized Fixation—wiping away the dust or polishing out the scratches of our lenses. The move *from fixated to free* is our ultimate liberation. But the solidification process of these Fixations—distorting our sense of self—is a lifelong project. Generally, we unconsciously allow the Fixation to become the driver in our minds, pushing our Holy Ideas to the background. That's how they become so convincing, so believable. Just as our Holy Ideas bring us back to the truth about our Essence, our Fixations are constantly making mental justification for the mindsets that keep us disconnected from our Essence.

The journey into belonging invites us into awareness of our Fixations, so that we might walk the path of freedom.

FIXATIONS AND FRANKENSTEIN

I liken the Fixations to the monster created by Dr. Victor Frankenstein in Mary Shelley's classic novel.

Remarkably, the author was just eighteen years old when she wrote the book, and when it was published shortly after her twentieth birthday there were originally only 500 copies printed. Though it took nearly ten years for the success of the book to be realized, Mary Shelley's life had been and would continue to be marked by intense suffering.

Shelley's mother, Mary Wollstonecraft, a radical first-wave feminist (even considered the foremother of the British feminist movement), died just eleven days after giving birth to Mary. Shelley herself would lose three of her four children. The premature deaths of her partner and other family members, some by suicide, forged an early adulthood marked by unimaginable pain and suffering.

I can't help but think all that anguish Shelley suffered throughout her lifetime was projected on the monster she wrote about. Shelley's monster has become an embedded icon in the horror fiction genre, inspiring countless derivative stories and characters. And hundreds of authors, literary critics, filmmakers, and storytellers have retold her classic tale, taking wide liberties to adapt and reinterpret the story to fit their agenda.

Ironically, the monster is never named in Shelley's work, though he is often misidentified in popular culture as Frankenstein, when in fact this is the name of the creature's creator and not the creature himself. And this creature's adopted erroneous name has become woven into pejorative colloquialisms, used to describe things that seem unnatural or monster-esque. Take for example "frankenfoods," a term to describe genetically modified animal or plant-based foods.

If you've never read the novel or need a quick refresher, *Frankenstein* begins curiously at the end of the story, describing an Arctic expedition undertaken by fictitious explorer Robert Walton. Walton is writing letters to his sister detailing his adventures when he peers out the window of his ship at an eight-foot tall, yellow-skinned creature cruising along the snow on a dogsled. Not long after, another dogsled is seen chasing this monster, this one led by Dr. Victor Frankenstein, the monster's creator or parent figure.

Victor, who isn't well, boards Walton's ship and begins to account an unorthodox creation myth where he plays the role of creator, in a sense assuming godlike powers.

As a young man, Victor finds dazzling success as a scientist and becomes obsessed with reanimating the dead. His experiments start with animal parts, but soon he's collecting bits of corpses plundered from graveyards and brings an experiment to life with electricity— literally creating a monster. To his surprise, Victor is sickened by his creation and rejects it. Ironically, he's repulsed when his experiment *does* succeed—so horrified by it, he runs away. Tragically he becomes a kind of father to a child he can't or won't love.

So rejected, the nameless creature goes into hiding. By observing various characters throughout the story, he learns to speak, read, and write, and soon longs for companionship. When the creature is reunited with his creator, he asks for a partner, but when that doesn't work out the creature begins wreaking havoc on Victor's life through a series of revenge killings (including Victor's younger brother, newlywed wife, and others).

Victor pledges to kill the monster he's created. An epic chase ensues that leads them both to the Arctic, where Victor dies on Walton's ship, and the creature, who earlier in the work refers to himself as a fallen angel, looks back on his life with regret and sorrow. In the end the monster blames his abandonment for all the human life he took. He's so grief-filled because of it all that he vows to take his own life.

For our purposes here, let's consider *Frankenstein* to be a story about a doctor being punished (experienced by the loss of his family, friends, and in the end his own life) for creating the *wrong kind* of life out of death.

Victor's attempt to renew life is less about the redemptive possibility of life defying death and more about an attempt at power and playing God.

It's a distorted creation story. If we view Victor Frankenstein as a manipulator of life, one whose attempts at resurrection are about his own display of power rather than bringing new life for another, then we can't help but experience some sympathy for the so-called monster (yet another symbol of a dragon).

The creature didn't ask to be brought to life. The creature suffered the rejection of its creator. When the creature experienced and expressed his loneliness, he was denied the relationships he longed for. Ultimately abandoned, the rest of the creature's story plays out through retaliation and regret. Even at the end of the story, the monster laments that he didn't mean to cause harm.

FRANKENSTEIN FIXATIONS

At the moment our Kidlife Crisis sets in and the light of our Holy Idea (our unobstructed view of all that's good in us and the world) goes out, something necessarily has to fill the void created by this existential darkness. Rather than returning to our Holy Idea through affirmations, reoriented beliefs, and confessions, we reanimate the experience of what we *thought* it was by bringing to life a mental

Fixation, much like Frankenstein's monster. Yet this reanimation is always an alternative to the Holy Ideas, a far lesser alternative to the natural vibrancy of life.

Unlike our Holy Ideas, these Fixations are conditioned with the biases of a victim mentality. And just as you might imagine, this victim mentality changes the narrative we tell ourselves about our life.

Much like Dr. Frankenstein, who was hoping to resurrect life from death, we give our Fixations a free pass because we are using them as an alternative to the true Essence that was lost. And just as the monster Dr. Frankenstein created, our Fixation is dressed up to make it *seem* human so that we can justify its existence. But that doesn't mean it *is* real. The sense of aliveness we feel in resuscitating what was lost is likewise an illusion.

And yes, at a certain point we begin to realize that we no longer can control it but rather it controls us—creating pain and loss in our lives, relationships, and communities.

As we observe the harmful and addictive thought patterns created by them, the Fixations become a kind of monster we vow must be destroyed. But they're always one step ahead of us, turning everything upside down and inside out. They become more powerful and disruptive than we could have envisioned. Consequently, like Dr. Frankenstein, we spend most of our lives chasing after the wreckage of our Fixation's unintended consequences.

Sure, we may be repulsed by these unbecoming bits of our personalities, but the truth is we created them out of mental and emotional scraps—what we could salvage of the malformed memory of our Essence once we lost contact with it. Our Fixations only exist because we continue to reanimate them with false hope. Even when we find minor victories, it's as if we can never fully destroy the monster it's become.

But the good news is, even our Fixation belongs. Rather than resist it, which only makes it stronger, the path of liberation is found when we welcome it with compassion, making room for it at the table—not the head of the table but still a welcomed guest. In learning to accommodate space for our Fixation we are actively reminded of the lie that has caused so much havoc in our lives and thus keep our vulnerabilities in active awareness.

We must learn to allow for our Fixation to find its proper place on the landscape of our interior lives, as an honest part of our full self. And when we make peace with it, the Fixation is no longer an enemy that derails us every chance it gets but is now an integrated aspect of our ego structure that reminds us when we lose contact with our Holy Idea. Almost like a power gauge, awareness of our Fixation offers us alerted consciousness when we're slipping back into old patterns and addictive behaviors. Bringing our Fixation into view helps us realize that it does not define us and is not perhaps as powerful as we've previously believed. If not kept regularly in sight, however, it holds the power to destroy others and ourselves. Just as Frankenstein's monster didn't need to be brought to life, our returning to our Fixation only resuscitates it, causing us and those we love harm.

Type One	Resentment
Type Two	Flattery
Type Three	Vanity
Type Four	Melancholy
Type Five	Stinginess
Type Six	Cowardice
Type Seven	Planning
Type Eight	Vengeance
Type Nine	Indolence

FIXATIONS

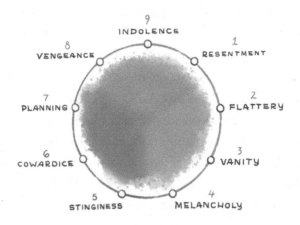

A REVIEW OF THE FIXATIONS

Since the Fixations were one of the first four Enneagons shared by Ichazo, they're among the most commonly referenced type components, yet there has been very little substantive work to develop how they are experienced by the nine types. It's a bit surprising and frankly disappointing, especially because our Fixation has so much power over our sense of self and how we present that self in the world. You see, if our Enneatype is fundamentally rooted in the ordering of our Centers of Intelligence, then the pre-conscious preferences of our dominant type can't help but expose what our psyche will fixate on once our Kidlife Crisis happens. Once we're fixated, we've built the perfect trap—a self-made prison to keep our Holy Idea contained, sidelined so it's out of the way. Then the Fixation takes over in three basic operation modes.

Fixations as Preoccupations

First the Fixations operate as *preoccupations*. These are mental blocks that distort our Holy Ideas, or our trusted and true view of the world. As a preoccupation, the Fixation proves itself determined to react in one of nine ways to combat the internal and external pressures we experience but don't want to follow back to our truest self. Even the term *preoccupation* assumes that conceptually we will be mentally occupied or fixated with an addictive, intellectually biased response even before that response may be required to face challenges. Being occupied *before* needing to be occupied takes up a lot of energy that causes our minds to stay numb and distracted from the truth at hand.

Fixations as Obsessions

Second, the Fixations show up as nine mental *obsessions* that possess the addictive power to completely overrun any clear-minded clearheadedness. The psychology of addiction, as understood on a biological level, reveals how deeply rooted the Fixations truly are. The obsessive nature of having to cope with life through these mental habits actually alters our brain chemistry—creating neuro-grooves of automatic thought and behavior that aren't easily subverted. This is what we mean by our conditioned personalities. Thankfully, science has made the revolutionary discovery that our brains can change. This is referred to as neuroplasticity. New neuropathways can be created, freeing us from the obsessive nature of our Fixation. Contemplative practice, like meditation, is one such method that helps facilitate a relaxing of our mental Fixation's neuro-constructs. But calming these obsessions is painfully devastating work because most of us don't know who we are without them.

Fixations as Complexes

Finally, the Fixations more than anything are a *complex*, a collection of networked delusions that are tethered to our Instincts (which we'll talk more about later in this book), Centers of Intelligence, and Kidlife Crisis, and are defended by our Passions. This *complex* of fixedness is why it's so hard to stop allowing the Fixation to think for us. It's as if our Fixation is a cerebral autopilot on a collision course. The *complex* nature of our Fixations is why we continue to circle back to destructive habits that seem to cause us to make the same mistakes over and over, time after time. If it were only as simple as practicing presence to overcome the *preoccupation*, or loosening addictive patterns to liberate us from it as an *obsession*, then many more of us would find the freedom in our life that could drive us back to the clarity provided by our Holy Ideas. But deconstructing the scaffolding of our Fixation is the work of a lifetime. And as soon as we think we've made significant strides, we're confronted with the difficult reality that there may actually be more layers to the Fixations than any other aspect of our character structure.

Type One: Resentment

For those dominant in type One there is a constant preoccupation with structure, order, and process, all of which are rooted in an obsession with perfection. This all has its basis and bias in the Basic Fear of Ones, which is that they are somehow inherently corrupt and beyond redemp-tion. Because of their preoccupation with how the world (and themselves) *should be*, their obsession with what is wrong or flawed within them leads to a form of internalized *resentment*. They resent themselves for knowing how they ought to live when they fail to comply with their unrealistic standards. The complex in this case is located in the dualism of their notions of right versus wrong, good versus bad, and perfect versus imperfect. To loosen the vise grip that resentment holds, the One's mental state of mind requires a movement to nonduality. The nondual mind realizes there is nuance between the binaries of right and wrong, good and bad, or perfection and imperfection. This of course requires *all* these concepts to breathe in unison while holding each other in tension.

Type Two: Flattery

As we have come to love those dominant in type Two for being so sacrificial and caring, we're often surprised by the ugly underside of the "love" they share in their significant relationships. Twos are primarily concerned with being a source of nurturing care in their world, which leads to their preoccupa- 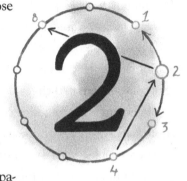 tion with heart-to-heart connections. How could there be anything wrong with that, one might wonder? But when their drive to include and be included in the lives of their loved ones becomes an obsession, their blameless motivations get derailed. When their relationships don't pan out in the way they hoped, they turn inward to determine if they are to be blamed, and this is where their *flattery* shows up. They unconsciously flatter themselves. How could *they* be the source of what is unsatisfying in their relationships? *They* are the partner or friend who cares more, gives more, sacrifices more, and loves more. The flattery here is how they cope with what they perceive is still missing in their relationship with others, yet are somehow still capable of meeting those missing needs. The complex nature of their Fixation requires that they learn to love themselves first, as practice for learning to love others second. But how could the Two drop their deep-seated needs related to connections and their natural focus on inclusion if they've yet to relate to every part of their inner lives—especially the parts of them that are yet to fully be included?

Type Three: Vanity

Claudio Naranjo famously swapped the Three's Passion (deceit) and Fixation (vanity). However, to honor the traditional framing of the Fixations, we will appeal to the language of *vanity*. Vanity for Threes shows up as a preoccupation with curating a desirable self-image, meaningful contributions in their relationships,

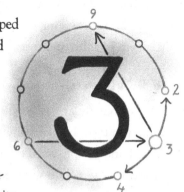

and alignment with causes or concerns that help make the world a better place. Again, it sure doesn't seem like there's much off base here, but when coupled with an obsession to prove their worth (vanity), those dominant in type Three end up stuck on a hamster wheel of trying to earn the value they're fundamentally afraid they've lost touch with. The Fixation complex for the Three ties together their carefully curated, projected image with their desire to prove their worth—all the while stagnating in their Basic Fear that they do not have intrinsic value other than what is validated outside them. Dualism in this case requires winners and losers, and for the Three, winning isn't the point, it's just one of the easiest ways to earn the validation that assuages their fear. And when they assume they've successfully achieved the state of validation they think will afford them the love they want, their *vanity* kicks in. They convince themselves they've actually done it—they've actually accomplished "being loved." Vanity for the Three is the delusion of believing their own lies, perpetually keeping them disconnected from something they could never earn in the first place.

Type Four: Melancholy

If Fours are chronically preoccupied with authenticity as a means of exploring the truth of their own story, then how could they not be obsessed with the genuine substance behind everything? This is why Fours are sometimes caricatured as being overly particular or sometimes a bit snobbish about their preferences. What's not understood when such judgments are made is the pain Fours quietly suffer. Their pain is that of having conceptualized the ideal

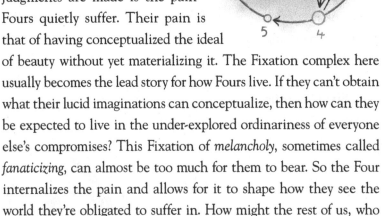

of beauty without yet materializing it. The Fixation complex here usually becomes the lead story for how Fours live. If they can't obtain what their lucid imaginations can conceptualize, then how can they be expected to live in the under-explored ordinariness of everyone else's compromises? This Fixation of *melancholy*, sometimes called *fanaticizing*, can almost be too much for them to bear. So the Four internalizes the pain and allows for it to shape how they see the world they're obligated to suffer in. How might the rest of us, who are less emotionally astute, possess the capacity to shoulder some of their pain with or for them?

Type Five: Stinginess

Fives are further misunderstood when the term *stinginess* is applied to their Fixation. It's not that Fives are un-generous misers; quite the opposite is true. It's just evidence that their preoccupation is holding onto un-certainty as a way of showing their love in relationships. Their obses-sion with finding solutions, analyzing threats, reframing questions, or getting to the bottom of the world's multifarious quandries is how they attempt to display love. Sadly, it's not always seen or experienced as loving because it's based more in cerebral energy than heart-forwardness. Nonetheless, when Fives can be left to their own resources to uncover all that is hidden, it comes across in social settings or relationships as a form of *stinginess*, also sometimes called *retention*. The Fixation complex for the Five is the lair that their mental meanderings think needs to be guarded from outside distractions. Ironically, it's their own musings that more frequently distract them from their mental pursuits.

Type Six: Cowardice

It's almost as if the traditional terms applied to the Fixations just get worse and worse as we go around the circle, especially when those dominant in type Six have to contend with *cowardice* as their Type's Fixation. This comes from their preoccupation with threat forecasting as a way of caring for those in their social circles and relationships. If a Six can do contingency planning for every worst-case scenario, then they'll have already sorted out what will be required to avert any potential or possible harm that may be looming around every unpredictable corner. Their obsession is with threats and how to deal with said threats. This obsession for Sixes vacillates between avoiding possible threats or taking them head-on, but even the path they choose is racked with self-doubt, further bracing the Fixation complex that keeps them second guessing their innate courage and uncompromising faith.

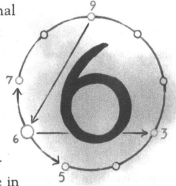

Type Seven: Planning

The energy of those dominant in type Seven is absolutely astonishing compared to those of other types. The up-and-out flow of the Seven keeps them on the move, which is not only entertaining to observe and participate in but a true curiosity to personality experts. The preoccupation of the

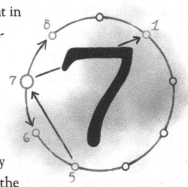

Seven is simply that: preoccupation. Sevens are smart enough to know that their pleasurable pursuits will always come to an end, so why wait and see what's waiting for them on the backside of an experience when they can imagine what will come next after their current experience is complete? This preoccupation with preoccupation is entirely unsatisfying and leads to obsessiveness with what they can consume—be it experiences, relationships, or knowledge. It's actually their Basic Fear of being trapped in the unexplored pain of their hearts that keeps them so curious. They constantly look outside themselves as a way of maintaining their perpetually distracted state of being. The Seven's Fixation complex of *planning*—sometimes called *anticipation*—is the obvious source of their suffering. Their inability or unwillingness to stop planning and be present to their own pain will always be the original source of the pain they're trying to avoid.

Type Eight: Vengeance

Though Eights seemingly have no qualms expressing their anger, it's generally an expression of their difficulty with experiencing their own sadness. Rather than being honest with their feelings, Eights catalyze them into an externalized projection of control, which is the persistent preoccupation of Eights. They want to maintain a

heightened sense of autonomy, independence, and self-sufficiency. This
preoccupation with control leads
to their obsession with power as
the antidote to anything they
perceive as weakness. Thus, a
Fixation complex forms around
Eight's notions of what it means
to avoid being taken advantage of,
betrayed, or harmed through preemp-

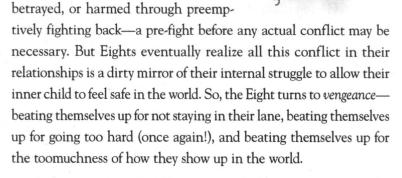

tively fighting back—a pre-fight before any actual conflict may be
necessary. But Eights eventually realize all this conflict in their
relationships is a dirty mirror of their internal struggle to allow their
inner child to feel safe in the world. So, the Eight turns to *vengeance*—
beating themselves up for not staying in their lane, beating themselves
up for going too hard (once again!), and beating themselves up for
the toomuchness of how they show up in the world.

Type Nine: Indolence

Indolence is a lazy word for how Nines
present as inactive in their world.
That's why the Fixation of the Nine
is sometimes alternatively called
rumination. Because Nines desire
uninterrupted interior harmony,
they will do nearly anything to avoid
that being disrupted. However, the
easiest way for them to maintain their

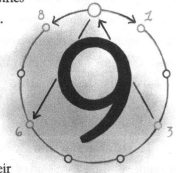

peace of mind is to cause as little friction in the world as possible. Their
sluggish preoccupation with avoidance goes unexamined and leads to a
kind of listless obsession with remaining unbothered by not bothering

their environment. The Fixation complex is a complicated network of internal drivers that puts the brakes on all the external drivers in their lives. Ironically, the Nines spend so much energy trying not to be energetic, they are perceived to be lazy when in fact they're internally exhausted from all their efforts to avoid disruption and friction.

A FIXATION INTERNALIZED IS A FIXATION EXTERNALIZED

Now if the implicit isn't yet explicit, then let me try to make this as clear as possible. We internalize our Fixation to perfect its efficiency so that when it's externalized, we express it with striking fluency. Essentially, we project outside of ourselves what we've perfected inside ourselves. This is equally true for both the good and the bad.

For example, as someone dominant in type Eight, my Fixation is traditionally considered *vengeance*. I often joke around (even though it's not really funny) that if you mess with any of my friends, I'll identity-theft you. Well, that's pretty brutal and it's also pretty spot-on for the intensity of an Eight's vengeance. Additionally, my wife Phileena brought it to my attention early on that I'm notorious for getting someone back ten times worse for an offense (a harmless one or a more serious one). I'm able to conjure up such dramatic reactions to the world around me because I've avenged so much inside myself (unnecessarily of course and often disproportionately more severe than needed) that bringing it outside myself feels like I'm on vacation from my Fixation. The problem is, when it's externalized, no one else can be on *their* vacation.

Or let's explore the Fixation of the One, the type that first taught me compassion for all types. Their *resentment* toward themselves for being unable to live into their unrealistic idealizations of perfection is a losing scenario for everyone. Of course, they'll inevitably have to resent themselves if they imagine they are the only people who have the clarity to imagine and embody excellence in all things. So, give them a break if they sometimes come across a little critical or fussy with your imperfections, because when they finally let that internal resentment leak into their external relationships it's like they're finally giving themselves a break from the torment of their own inner critic. Yes, sometimes they come across as a little salty and grumpy, but thank goodness for that! It's an indicator they feel safe enough to share one of the most challenging parts of themselves.

All of this is even more reason to get honest with our whole selves. Because whatever qualities are growing inside of us, for better or for worse, will become outwardly apparent in our lives.

DON'T THINK ABOUT THE POLAR BEAR

Once we understand the nature of our Fixation and come to terms with the harm it's caused ourselves and others, what do we do with it? How can we make peace with it? How do we relax its preoccupied and obsessive nature?

For many of us, bringing anything—including the cognizance of our Fixation—into conscious awareness only seems to give a thought or concept more power over us. Recognizing the need to be observant of my Fixation almost seems to make me more preoccupied and obsessed with it. How is that helpful? I mean, if now I'm constantly thinking about vengeance, then what's the point?

In 1987, a Harvard University social psychologist, the late Daniel Wegner (considered the founding father of thought suppression research), launched a research project inspired by a line from Fyodor Dostoevsky's *Winter Notes on Summer Impressions*, his account of traveling through Western Europe. In a chapter called, "An Essay Concerning the Bourgeois," Dostoevsky writes, "Try to pose for yourself this task: not to think of a polar bear, and you will see that cursed thing come to mind every minute."

Wegner proposed that when we attempt to suppress a thought, it actually gives that thought more prominence in our mind and subsequently brings it to the forefront of our thinking patterns and processes. This theory was published in the *Journal of Personality and Social Psychology* in 1987[1] and became known as *Ironic Process Theory, Ironic Rebound,* or the *White Bear Problem.*

Wegner's research involved two test groups. The first group was given five minutes to articulate their conscious thoughts but were instructed specifically not to think of a polar bear. If members of this first group did bring to mind a polar bear, they were required to ring a bell. Members of this first group rang that bell on average more than once per minute. The group was then instructed to narrate their thoughts for an additional five minutes. This time they were allowed (even encouraged) to think of a polar bear but still needed to ring the bell when they did.

The second group was given the opposite instructions: to think

1. Daniel M. Wegner, David J. Schneider, Samuel R. Carter, and Teri L. White, "Paradoxical Effects of Thought Suppression," *Journal of Personality and Social Psychology* 53, no 1 (1987): 5–13.

of the bear for the first five minutes and then attempt to not think of the polar bear for the second five minutes.

As you can imagine, the first group experienced a significant rebound effect, which caused them to think of the polar bear at an even higher rate during the latter part of the experiment—substantially higher than the second group's reporting of the bear coming into awareness.

What Wegner was highlighting is the phenomenon that when tasked to avoid a thought there's still part of our mind that will "check in" on that thought periodically to ensure it's not a distraction, creating the irony of thinking about what we're not supposed to think about.

The Fixations work similarly to this Ironic Process Theory. On one hand, when we attempt to mute the Fixation's voice, somehow it only amplifies it. On the other hand, the urgent work of turning the volume down on its voice requires a commitment to redirect the influence of these thoughts.

Wegner's research offered strategies for dealing with this problem, such as finding an alternative distraction to mitigate the frequency of an unwanted thought. He'd sometimes direct his test groups to think of a red car whenever the polar bear came to mind, thus allowing for a substitute distraction. In other cases, Wegner instructed people to schedule or postpone when they would allow themselves to be preoccupied by unwanted thoughts, as if scheduling your worries for Monday afternoons gave those thoughts the ability to "be," but now on your terms not theirs. He also worked with people to welcome those thoughts, confronting them head-on, and taking command of the sway they held over one's attention.

Wegner also concurred that mindfulness practices over time could aid in suppressing unwanted thoughts. That's when I got really interested in his research because I've personally found the Loving Kindness mediation to be one of the most effective ways of working with my Fixation.

A LOVING KINDNESS MEDITATION
FOR OUR FIXATION

As I've mentioned, I can be pretty hard on myself. I've often said that you can't punish an Enneagram type Eight harder than they'll punish themselves (I even get *myself* back ten times worse!). Thanks, mental Fixation *vengeance*!

When I slip up or mess up, when I hurt someone, when I allow my frustration to get the best of me, or when I'm just *too much* (again . . .) I really let myself have it. The mental tapes start playing, "You're such an idiot, man!" or, "Stop being such a jerk all the time!" or, "Why are you *still* so stupid?"

I'll never forget sitting in my psychotherapist's office years ago, replaying some of my most difficult moments while offering him commentary of how foolishly I was acting. He quickly observed that when I could no longer recruit someone to punish me, I'd enlist my inner critic to pick up the slack. It was that day he taught me a little mantra, a three-line mindfulness practice that changed my life.

I started repeating these three short lines silently in my mind for several minutes each morning, and then I took it on the road and aligned these lines with my breath while I was out walking Basil or sitting on an airplane while traveling.

The Loving Kindness meditation is an unconditional, inclusive meditation practice that aids in the development of radical compassion for yourself and others. Called *metta bhavana* in the Buddhist tradition, this practice may be adapted or used as a tool for coming into greater awareness of our own belovedness. When practicing a Loving Kindness meditation, we're instructed to dial down the voice of our inner critic, muting her self-criticism and internal commentary.

At the beginning of moving this practice to a discipline, we focus on ourselves first. Then, once we've developed compassionate loving kindness (even for the hardest parts of ourselves to accept), we expand the meditation to include the people in our lives.

Let me offer an example of one of the Loving Kindness meditations I frequently practice:

> *May I be filled with faith.*
> *May I be a source of hope.*
> *May I be aligned with love.*

After falling into a natural cadence with these lines and really owning them as intentions for myself, I'm able to include others in successive stages of acceptance through this practice. The subsequent stages of this practice include: (1) those who love me, (2) those I love, (3) those who are difficult for me, and (4) those in my larger community. The meditation evolves into phrases like this:

> *May you/we be filled with faith.*
> *May you/we be a source of hope.*
> *May you/we be aligned with love.*

To develop your own practice is simple:

1. Choose a few affirming statements or phrases that attend to a tender part of your heart.
2. Determine those you intend to include in this practice, those who you hope will also benefit from your mindful loving kindness.
3. Assume a posture that is relaxed while remaining attentive and alert. If you're able, sit upright in a comfortable chair or with your legs crossed on the ground. Close your eyes or allow your gaze to gently drift to the floor two to three feet in front

of you. Draw attention to your breathing and allow it to return you to the present moment every time you get distracted.

4. Begin your practice by repeating your own affirming phrases for three or four minutes. (You may even want to give yourself more time at the outset of habitualizing this meditation.) After a few minutes, begin to affirm these statements for others, offering each successive movement an additional three or four minutes. Ideally you would spend fifteen to twenty minutes with this practice but, depending on your time constraints, you may be able to accomplish these stages in a briefer amount of time.

Similar to all contemplative practices, the fruit of this practice won't be found in the meditation itself but demonstrated in your active life. The practice transforms our inner critic to a compassionate inner witness or a non-judging inner observer. By activating the "observer" or "witness" function of this aspect of mind, we discover compassionate acceptance of the whole of who we are.

When we can learn radical self-acceptance through this practice, it inevitably leads to more compassionate living with others. This is why the meditation naturally incorporates additional people in the practice.

Once my loving kindness meditation seems to take effect, I sense my heart opening to first make room for myself and then for those in my life who are included in my practice. It usually goes something like this:

1. I practice for myself, including my inner child and my inner critic.
2. I practice for a person who has taught me about self-acceptance and compassion, usually a mentor or teacher (past or present).
3. I practice for a person whom I love and care for deeply (I imagine them sitting with me).

4. When I feel rooted in the loving kindness being generated, I try to practice for a person who is difficult for me, someone who has hurt or betrayed me.

5. I practice for my local community, for my extended community, and for those near and far who are suffering.

When aligning this with our Enneagram type, the practice helps suppress the unwanted voices and thoughts our inner critic and Fixation inflict upon our tenderness and goodness. Let me suggest a type-specific mantra that can be incorporated as a Loving Kindness meditation for each of the nine types.

Type One

> *May I be at ease.*
> *May I breathe peacefully.*
> *May I find freedom in rest.*

Type Two

> *May I offer love.*
> *May I receive love.*
> *May I love myself.*

Type Three

> *May I own my worth.*
> *May I own my value.*
> *May I be embraced by love.*

Type Four

> *May I see myself.*
> *May I know myself.*
> *May I love myself.*

Type Five

> *May I be here now.*
> *May I say yes to silence.*
> *May I let go.*

Type Six

> *May I embrace my fears.*
> *May I embrace my faith.*
> *May I embrace my courage.*

Type Seven

> *May I be free.*
> *May I be content.*
> *May I rest in this moment.*

Type Eight

> *May I be openhearted.*
> *May I be loving.*
> *May I be vulnerable.*

Type Nine

> *May I be present.*
> *May I own my power.*
> *May I have inner peace.*

LEARNING TO LAUGH AT OURSELVES

Once we've learned self-acceptance and compassion, we're now able to find a sense of humor and laugh at ourselves. My spiritual director, Father Larry Gillick, helped me understand this through a little word play.

During one of our sessions he explained that *humus* is the equivalent in Latin for our English words "dirt," "soil," or "ground." And *humus* is the same etymological root for our words for "humanity" and "humility."

Of course, the connection of dirt or soil with "humanity" makes sense. We learn in the Hebrew Scriptures, in the third chapter of Genesis, that we came from dust and so we shall return. This is one of the reasons our Muslim sisters and brothers touch their head to the ground five times a day in prayer. It's a reminder of their connectedness with the earth. It's also a posture of humility.

The connection of "humility" with the ground also makes sense, at least on an intuitive level. As a university student I spent almost a year in Jerusalem. Since Bethlehem is only six miles south of Jerusalem, I visited the city several times during my stay. There's a church in Bethlehem that was built to commemorate the birthplace of the Christ. Legend says this ornate place of worship was built over the space where Jesus was born. It's believed that the actual place of the Christ's birth, the very spot where he was laid in a feeding trough, is in the basement of the church. This sacred point is covered in marble with a golden star in the center of the floor marking the exact place of the manger. To visit, you must enter through a tiny door. Now, I'm not exactly what you might call a tall fella. In fact, I'm the shortest of my brothers, what I think of as "fun size." But even though I'm "fun size," that door is pretty small, even for me. It was intentionally designed so that to pass through it, you must bow down. Visitors are forced to approach the birthplace of the Christ in a posture of humility, with the head submitted below their heart, and their face pressed as close to the ground, or the soil, as possible. Humility is not a means to an end. Rather, humility is the door through which we must enter to be welcomed into the presence of divine love.

Connecting our humanity and humility is one of the marks of

the spiritual journey, to recognize that we are not God, that our efforts do not save us, nor do our notions of the accuracy of our beliefs or doctrines or religious traditions. We put our hope in something beyond, better than us, more beautiful than we can imagine. And then we cling to the humility that we are worthy of this divine love, that we deserve it (not that we have to earn it) because we were created for it.

But what Father Gillick shared with me that completely caught me off guard was the connection that "humor" had to *humus*. This connection of humor to *humus* and subsequently to humanity and humility is more elusive. Father Gillick tried to explain it to me like this. Imagine a four-year-old child dressing up in their mother's heels and evening gown. The humor is in that image, in the humility of the child's humanity. The humility of a little one, a child wanting to be a big person, is humorous. We get it wrong because the humor of the humility of our humanity is that we think we don't deserve to be bigger than we think we are. And so, we mistakenly try to make ourselves smaller (false humility). But playing small serves no one. That's not funny; it's tragic.

A little girl or boy hoping and knowing that they may grow into a fabulous adult with power and realized potential is what is at play here. Each of us is invited to embrace the humor of the humility of our humanity, that we too are more beautiful than we could imagine. We carry within us more promise and potential than we could desire. And we are loved more than we want to be loved.

The other connection is something Father Richard Rohr reminded me of in a recent conversation. He said that until we've done our shadow work, we probably don't have a sense of humor about ourselves. And this is one of the things the Enneagram teaches us—that we are vulnerable to a common crack in our souls that we will continue to return to until we become aware of it, make peace with it, and integrate it.

Now simple awareness of our flawedness won't remove it from us. And this is key. Remember, it's about belonging. So, when we find ourselves falling back into old patterns, addictions, or harmful behaviors, we have to be able to laugh at ourselves as one of the ways of disarming those tendencies. When we find the humor in these predictable patterns in our lives, we've unlocked one more way to practice the humility of the gift of our humanity.

This is the path of excavating our Essence. This is what is required to make peace with our Fixations and allow them to belong. This is the journey to finding compassion and loving kindness for ourselves and everyone else.

To excavate Essence, we have to dig through a lot of mud. To unearth buried treasure, we have to get our hands dirty and dig deep into our soul. There's no other way to get there.

PART III

BRINGING OUR FEELING CENTER BACK *to* BELONGING

8

Gifts *of the* Heart

Exploring the Virtues

Some of history's earliest performance activism is recorded in the Hebrew Scriptures. One of my favorite accounts is that of Yonah son of Amittai (יונה), or Jonah—yep, the man who ended up chilling in the stomach of a sea monster for three days.

My old Sunday school teachers used to love rolling out the old Jonah story, getting wild on their flannelgraphs, warning us that if we were unfaithful to the divine calling on our lives, we'd suffer a similar fate—a spiritual time out. Yeah, we probably wouldn't be slopping around in the slimy guts of a whale, but there would be a contextual equivalent and we would eventually consent to our divine destinies.

Today, many Bible scholars think the story to be satirical fiction, but its lasting value and cultural impact attest to its universal significance.

Jonah, one of the twelve Minor Prophets in the Hebrew Scriptures, was from the northern kingdom of Israel. His story takes place around the eighth century BCE but was probably written a few hundred years later. The little book is just over 1,000 words long, but it's unforgettably dense with imagery and allegory.

The tale begins with conflict. God puts the 120,000 residents of Nineveh (located in modern-day Iraq) on alert: they face the threat of destruction if they don't repent. To be fair, God enlists a ringer to give them a chance and commands Jonah to travel to Nineveh and warn the people of their looming annihilation. But Jonah, less than interested, replied, "Nah, I'm not really a fan of the Ninevites and was thinking of making holiday in Tarshish that week anyway. Sorry God, I guess you'll just have to obliterate them all. Darn." Promptly, Jonah rushes off to buy his ticket to Tarshish, jumps onboard a ship, and begins his journey.

As can be imagined, God's not super-duper down with Jonah bouncing like that, so God sends a violent tempest to flush Jonah out. The crew of the ship are absolutely terrified by the storm and make quick work of Jonah, swiftly throwing him overboard into the sea.

While treading water in an effort to save himself from drowning, a large fish swallows Jonah whole. And this is where the reluctant prophet will stay for three days, in the belly of this aquatic beast before he's vomited onto shore. After washing off the fish stink, Jonah finally concedes and makes his way to Nineveh to reluctantly deliver the message: "Y'all have forty days to get right with God or you're goners."

To his surprise, the Ninevites listen and respond. He convinces an entire city to turn to God in mass conversion and avert their own destruction. Even Jonah's surprised at his success. Turns out he's a better preacher than he thought.

But Jonah is still a little salty from the sea and still a little bitter about having to be used by God to save folks he doesn't particularly care for. So, he sulks outside the city under the shade of a plant, hoping God will destroy the town nonetheless.

Worn out from Jonah's attitude, God sends a worm to eat the stem of the shade-bearing plant, which pushes Jonah over the edge. That's the last straw!

Embittered, Jonah lashes out at God, who then confronts Jonah's shadow and reveals the prophet's projection. You see, Jonah resented God's compassion toward the Ninevites, whom Jonah did not believe were worthy of being saved. But on a deeper level, Jonah's outsized anger reveals that something much more personal was going on here: all along it was the unresolved aspects of Jonah's *own* psyche that he wouldn't allow to be redeemed. You see, whatever is internalized will inevitably be externalized. Whatever we despise in ourselves we can be sure to despise in others. And one of the saddest parts is, like Jonah, we often fail to observe our own projection.

It begs the question for us all: who don't we want to receive salvation? Who won't we allow to be welcomed into beloved community? Who don't we want to belong?

The answer to these questions is likely found in our own hearts. We must dare to face the parts of ourselves that we don't want to be brought into the light. We must dare to bring forward the parts of ourselves that we would rather leave unredeemed in the shadows. And when we do, like Jonah, we are bound to find more compassion available to us than we would ever have allowed for ourselves.

Somehow, many of us think there are parts of us that can't be salvaged, that are un-savable. It's our lack of imagination and our malformed notions of love that keep us stuck. But we know this: love by its nature needs to be expressed. Just as God wants us to thrive in our purpose (even more than we want to thrive), God also loves us even more than we want to be loved. Love starts with embracing the courage to enter the cave of our own shadow, slay the dragon who guards the unexcavated treasures of our Essence, and compassionately make peace with every aspect of who we are—the good *and* the bad.

Just as Jonah got stuck in the belly of the fish, we too get stuck in our own shadows when we try to run away from dealing with them. When we refuse to own our shadow, often it ends up owning us.

I'm afraid the surprising realization many of us need to come to is simply this: it's the best (not worst) parts of ourselves that are easier to reject than the more challenging aspects of our personalities. Jonah couldn't accept his chosenness by God; he couldn't accept the success of his message; and he surely couldn't accept the possibility that his spiritual community was about to get much bigger, making more space for him to belong. Like Jonah, we actually coddle our Passions (the inverse of our Virtue) and Fixations (the inverse of our Holy Idea) by allowing them to have the final say. We assume a victim mentality at the expense of our soul's created purpose.

It's Our Holy Ideas and our Virtues that are the most powerful means we have to bring us back to our true Essence. Ironically, it's our Holy Ideas and Virtues that we just can't seem to make room for.

WHAT PARTS OF OUR IDENTITY DO WE HAVE THE MOST TROUBLE ACCEPTING?

Moving from the hard work of self-observation to the compassionate work of self-remembering leads us to the thrilling work of living into the gift of our freedom. But this is harder than we realize because many of us suffer from a spiritual fear of heights. It's as if we only allow ourselves so much growth before we start doubting or before we roll out our inner critic's mental tapes calling out our subconscious imposter syndrome.

It's like this. Our physical bodies have a set point or a weight range that's biologically programmed for optimal functioning. The set point isn't always the ideal weight for our height and age, but it's where our bodies have learned to manage. These set points are stubborn, that's why some of us struggle to lose weight and keep it off. I've attempted to drop fifteen to twenty pounds from time to time, but when I'm successful it's not long before that lost weight somehow, slowly but surely, creeps back.

What we learn from our body's set point is that if we want to lose weight and keep it off, then we need to maintain a *new* set point for an extended period of time so our body's intelligence can reorient and recalibrate.

I believe the same is true for our psycho-spiritual health. We all seem to get stuck at a comfortable psycho-spiritual set point that keeps us from growing. And it's daunting to shake up this set point because it requires much of us.

This is why meditation is so hard for most of us. But it's also why meditation is so important for all of us. I love the old Blaise Pascal assertion: "All human evil comes from this: our inability to sit still in a chair for half an hour."

Once we find a contemplative practice that seems to work, there's some early excitement about the impact it has on us and the immediate changes we experience. But it doesn't take long for the difficulty to show up once our practice sets in and the demands of life become distracting strains on our commitments to mindfulness. It's also frustrating for those of us who experience positive changes at the beginning of adopting a new practice, only to have those transformations drastically slow down if not stall entirely.

One of the founding board members of our nonprofit organization and one of our dearest mentors, the late Father Thomas Keating, used to instruct folks incorporating a Centering Prayer practice to commit to two twenty-minute meditation sits twice a day for six months before giving up on the practice. It really does take that long for most of us to experience a change in our psycho-spiritual set points.

Sadly, most of us won't give it six months. We'd rather stay comfortable where we've learned to function. This kind of stretching feels too hard to commit to, even though the bigger picture shows the real and rewarding benefits that we'd like to have . . . if only we could have them without all the work. Others of us do embark on a commitment to our inner work, only to second-guess the fruits of the transformation we experience.

I've suffered this self-limiting commitment to my own stalled set points over the years. At certain points in my life, especially when I found myself on the verge of much-needed spiritual breakthrough, I'd somehow convince myself I didn't deserve the growth I had worked so hard for, or that I wasn't worthy of it. Just as I was about to live into some of the gifts of my contemplative practices, a part of me tucked in the darkness of my shadow would self-sabotage and subvert my growth. There was a fragment of my identity that wanted to keep the whole of myself stuck in the past where things seemed familiar and comfortable, even if unhealthy.

This is where friends showed up and community became so important.

I can't image a better illustration than what may be the most visually enthralling ten minutes of modern cinematic storytelling. Set in 1740 near where Argentina, Brazil, and Paraguay share borders, the 1986 film *The Mission* tells the story of two men, Father Gabriel, a Spanish Jesuit missionary priest played by Jeremy Irons, and Rodrigo Mendoza, a mercenary slave trader played by Robert De Niro (who coincidentally happened to play Frankenstein's monster in a 1994 film).

The priest and the soldier fight for the souls and the bodies of the same Guaraní tribe. One attempts to convert them to colonial Christianity; the other traffics them as slaves to plantations owned by colonial Christians.

After returning from an expedition to enslave captured members of the tribe, Rodrigo Mendoza discovers that his younger brother and fiancée are having an affair. Out of rage he kills his brother. Then out of sorrow he requests the most severe penance from Father Gabriel. Consequently, he undertakes an agonizing journey of reconciliation.

Rodrigo Mendoza is invited to join the Jesuit mission in the mountains, but part of his atonement journey is to bundle up his armor and sword, the symbols of his past transgressions, and drag them with a rope as he climbs a treacherous mountain to the Jesuit's mission. The climb is arduous, to say the least, as Mendoza navigates jagged rocks while the bundled net of his former military tactical gear constantly gets trapped in the crevices.

Upon arriving at the mission, completely exhausted and on his knees, unable to take another step, members of the Guaraní tribe recognize Mendoza. One of them grabs a long knife and rushes up to him, pressing the blade against his throat. The Jesuits back off, realizing that because of the injustices Mendoza has inflicted upon this community, the tribe must deal with this on their own terms. After a few tense moments, the young man uses the knife to cut Mendoza's burden loose, freeing him from his past and welcoming him into this new future.

I've watched and re-watched this film more times than I can count, but that scene gets me every single time. I'm an awful, slobbering mess with each viewing.

What a powerful story of belonging. What a powerful snapshot of forgiveness.

You see, the burdens we drag through life and try to reconcile are inevitably too heavy for us to carry. In some cases, we unnecessarily tether ourselves to our pasts, waiting for the offended persons of our previous lives to free us through their forgiveness. We need both the experience of belonging to others and the experience of belonging to ourselves. When we either accept the whole of ourselves, or experience others' acceptance of the whole of us, it makes belonging more possible on both accounts.

Like the Guaraní tribe members, the Holy Ideas and Virtues stand to greet us with all our baggage and set us free.

Why do we tie ourselves to the burdens of our Passions and Fixations? Why won't we allow ourselves to let go and embrace the truest parts, the most beautiful parts of ourselves, that for whatever reasons we've forgotten? Perhaps in part because our baggage is familiar to us, even comfortable. But there's no denying it weighs us down.

If the Enneagram only offers nine mirrors for us to see ourselves without also offering nine road maps for what we do with self-knowledge, then we can't help but spin the wheels of fueling our narcissism and harming the tenderest parts of ourselves.

As we read in the story of Jonah, self-observation is essential for course-correcting on the path of transformation. We cannot help but externalize what's going on in our interior lives. If we disparage, reject, or dishonor any part of ourselves, we will disparage, reject, or dishonor the same in those around us. But what if we turned the tables and found that the inverse is equally true?

I believe the Enneagram's most essential invitation is toward self-compassion. If we can practice radical self-acceptance for ourselves, we cannot help but extend that very same undiscriminating acceptance toward others. And that compassion leads to gentleness with self and a renewed love for the world. If our interior life is centered in the reality of our belovedness, we will in turn project such a force of love into the world. In Enneagram language, the Virtues are the gifts of the heart that is centered in the reality of so radical a love.

WHAT ARE THE VIRTUES?

VIRTUES

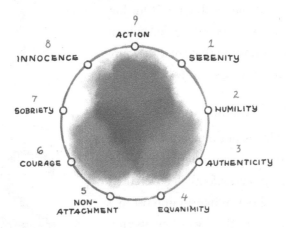

The English word *virtue* is generally defined as ethical and principled morality, an almost unattainable notion of integrity. But the Latin roots for the word *virtue* are located in the word *vir*, which simply means "human."

That sounds like good news. To be virtuous simply means to be human.

In *EnneaLanguage* the Virtues are the sincerest and most authentic part of our hearts that were forgotten as a result of our Kidlife Crisis. While the Holy Ideas are the gifts of the mind as it was made to be, the Virtues are the gifts of the heart as it was purposed to be. Together, they are the evidence of the mind and heart that is grounded in its belovedness. Along with the Holy Ideas, the Virtues are the purest part of our truest self.

Fundamentally, the Enneagram's Virtues are the realized gifts of a heart centered and at peace with itself. The Virtues can't be forced, nor do they need to be proven. They simply exist as the fragrance of our souls bearing witness to our goodness in the world.

Type One: Serenity

The Virtue of type One is the peace-fulness of living in harmony with one's flaws. The *serenity* is that type One has made peace with their wounded human condition, knowing that their flaws are what makes them perfectly beautiful.

Type Two: Humility

Humility is not a means to an end but the proof of one's internal strength. My old high school football coach used to say humility was like an iron fist in a velvet glove. For the Two, remembering their Essence is a return to the mighty potency of their unpretentious ownership of all that is fabulous about themselves.

Type Three: Authenticity

Type Threes who pursue love through external validation know deep down in-side the counterfeit currency of love's sub-stitutes. This is why for Threes to return to themselves they must accept that they were always loved. This is the most truth-ful or *authentic* way of being themselves.

Type Four: Equanimity

Equanimity is a kind of level-headed level-heartedness that allows for those dom-inant in type Four to live in centered spaces

rather than in the overindulgence of their emotional highs and lows. For the Four to return to their equanimity is their gift to stay grounded and present even while their interior lives are tossed to the extremes.

Type Five: Nonattachment

Traditionally, Ichazo labeled type Five's Virtue as *detachment*, but I prefer *nonattachment* as an interior posture of openhandedness. Those dominant in type Five are constantly craving answers and ideas. Yet if we can't give something away, then we do not possess it but are possessed *by* it. Nonattachment isn't what we hold, but *how* we hold it. Type Five's virtue is making available to all what they have uncovered in their mental pursuits, rather than hoarding it for themselves.

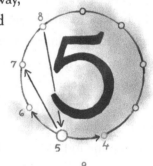

Type Six Courage

Though it may appear that Sixes don't believe in themselves, deep down inside at their core they know they have *courage*. Courage doesn't mean we won't be or aren't afraid. Courage is facing our fear and pressing into it anyway. Courage is disempowering the lies of fears by confronting them with the truth that we will not be overcome by them.

Type Seven: Sobriety

For the Seven, *sobriety* doesn't necessarily mean abstinence as much as it means learning how to hold the

object of their craving without being held by it. It's more about moderation than starvation. For the Seven to find the *enoughness* of every moment, they must return to what feels empty or unsatisfied in their hearts, and instead of looking to consume something outside of themselves, find the nourishment they're craving within.

Type Eight: Innocence

As much as those dominant in type Eight want to push against others, often appealing to inappropriate or vulgar comments and jokes or otherwise aggressive behavior as a subtle test to see who will stay with them, their *innocence* is the very thing they're attempting to hide. They hide their innocence first from themselves, then in their relationships. Eights who return to innocence realize this is where the depth of their power lies. Innocence is the strongest aspect of their character they can live into.

Type Nine: Action

Love in *action* is the illustrative characteristic of Nines. Waking up and living into their reality while actively engaging it reminds Nines of what was lost when they hid their deepest desires or whimsical wishes. Embracing life to the fullest, even if it still looks a little understated to the rest of us, brings the Nine home to their forgotten selves.

HOW DO WE LEARN TO
REMEMBER THE VIRTUES?

The Virtues are like a lullaby we haven't heard in years, yet it still quietly sings in the back of our minds and fills our hearts from time to time. When we come across that lullaby at a nursery or in a collection of children's cradlesongs, we can immediately recall the melody and all the lyrics. The Virtues are like that. They were never truly lost. They were just hidden away under the masks of our type and set in the back seat by our Enneagram Passion.

So how do we remember and reengage the gifts of these Virtues?

The bummer is, we can't afford to hold out for the next great Enneagram book that will be able to give us the language and understanding to realign with our Virtue. I'm guilty of this myself; visit me at my office and you'll notice behind my desk a few hundred Enneagram books, but none specifically on the Virtues. After all these years of trying to chase down every resource I could find on the Virtues, I've come up short. That's because there's nothing better than the mere practice of remembering what's always been true about myself. This isn't something you can learn by reading someone else's ideas or going through a workshop. Returning to your Virtue requires an intentionality, going inward and learning to love yourself. Breathing into my own innocence releases and frees my Virtue to come out and play. Holding myself with compassion reminds me of the innocence of my inner child that doesn't want to be hurt, just loved and safe to be held.

Embodying the ideals of our Virtues by being present to the whole of us is a return to our humanity.

The nature of the emotional quality of being is something that has to be experienced in our hearts; it's a practical owning of our innate beauty that is made evident through the kind of soul-making that places our heart in the center of our experience.

WHY DO THE VIRTUES MATTER AND
HOW DO THEY RELATE TO BELONGING?

Each Virtue spotlights *our soul's indispensable purpose for being.* They're rooted in our original righteousness and the core of our Essence. Once aligned with our Virtue, the path to belonging becomes clear and the journey to becoming is given a much-needed restart.

The Virtues are the clearest snapshot of what's detectable in our Essence. Though they may be the most likeable aspects of type structure, they are also the easiest to dismiss, the first part of ourselves that we assume can be blown off or downplayed. But the Virtues remind us that making room for the whole of who we are allows for room to be made for the whole of who others are.

When we can allow our Virtue to take the lead in what guides our sense of being, we start to experience how the Enneagram supports our flourishing in relationships, in community, in friendships, and ultimately in how we live faithfully into our vocational commitments. We're animated by the Virtues when moving from self-observation to self-remembering, and then into the thrilling work of seeing ourselves and the world with new eyes so that we can live more freely and love more beautifully.

Still, some of us feel as if our Virtue is some distant memory lost in the mental fog of what can't be recalled. In a sense that's likely true. It's not something we can cerebrally bring forward but something we effortlessly live emotionally into. The Virtue is the fruit of a centered heart that knows we are loved, first by ourselves so that we can be loved by others.

This is why many of us love hearing stories about our childhood—especially the stories we've forgotten but adults still remember. I grew up loving to listen to my parents tell tale after tale of the tiny version of myself living out of my innocence. Such sweet recollections of the discovery of awareness or selfless sacrifice. There's something amazing about the tenderness of children. Sadly, much of that is forgotten as we grow older.

My first job after graduating university was in a children's home in South India. The kids we cared for had come from really, really difficult backgrounds. Many had lost a parent or two to the global AIDS pandemic. Many of the children's parents were leprosy survivors who'd been so marginalized in their communities they were unable to offer the care they wanted and desired for their children. And a number of those children were survivors of female infanticide. Despite the challenging environments the kids came from, there was still something remarkable about each and every one of them. The purest aspects of their Essence shone through in the ways they cared for each other, adopted each other into their larger surrogate family, and protected one another's vulnerabilities.

One summer I had some friends from Southern California visit. We were all at the children's home when a call came in from a desperate family who had found a two-month-old baby girl left at the beach. Severely undernourished and just moments from being washed out to sea where she'd face certain death, the child was rescued but had nowhere to go.

Of course, we took her in and cared for her as though she were our own. A couple I worked with named her Sheelu. She was given every comfort we could afford and the best medical care in the city. It wasn't long, however, until we found out Sheelu was deaf.

I'll never forget how the rest of the kids in the home looked out for her, taking such sweet care of their little sister. The kids even worked out their own shorthand sign language that was used at home with Sheelu, eager to learn the sign language Sheelu was picking up at school. The connections they made beyond words clearly came from their hearts and showed how beautiful each of them was.

Today those little kids are all grown up—many of them graduate students; others, professors or nurses; some of them have even become parents themselves. But when I'm able to visit them in India, they just want to hear stories about what they were like when they were little. And I love remembering back to those precious days when the kids were just two or three months or two or three years old.

There's something about our Virtues that shine brighter than we can imagine, that allow our inner child to find freedom to just be, but still seem to be hidden from us. They're easier for others to observe, and when someone reflects back to us the goodness that they see in us, we love it. Even if we can't fully own it, we somehow know it's true.

ACCESSING THE VIRTUES

What we come to learn about the Virtues is an age-old common truth: the very things we search for in our sacred texts, cherished mentors, or the newest books from our favorite authors can be supports for our process of remembering what we've always possessed within ourselves, *but* . . . what we are looking for has always been as close to us as our hearts.

No one else can help us locate or illuminate our Virtue. We get to find it for ourselves. We have to allow ourselves to be realigned with this Virtue. We must own it and allow it to own us.

Contemplative practice is one such way of accessing the gifts and fruits of our Virtues. In solitude, silence, and stillness, the qualities of our Virtue are remembered and fully received.

When looking for a guide, someone to show me how to open myself to all the ways my Virtue can come alive in the world, I often remember Mother Teresa and the little chapel she prayed in every day.

Had you visited Mother before she passed away back in 1997 or if you've made pilgrimage to her tomb since then, you likely stopped in the Missionaries of Charity's chapel on the second floor of their convent. It's a simple little spot—not much on the walls—and back when I used to spend more time there, not even chairs for guests to sit on. We'd just assume our spot on the floor during morning mass or afternoon adoration.

What always surprised me about Mother Teresa's chapel was the unbearable noise pollution that would pour in through the open windows. Each morning when the priest would stand behind a microphone to offer the daily homily, I would struggle to hear most of what he shared. The blaring of horns and the screeching traffic below drown out nearly every sacred word that was spoken in that place.

But you see, it wasn't the external space where Mother and her sisters went to pray; it was the internal gaze where they'd intentionally create interior solitude, silence, and stillness to find their center, to connect with divine love, and to unleash the fruits of their Virtues on the streets and in the slums of Calcutta.

Never have I seen a community with such open hearts.

Going inward allowed them to serve one another and their larger community. Discovering their belovedness gave them the ability to perceive the belovedness in others. And loving themselves made room for them to be a force of love in the world.

That force begins with the Virtues. All of this is accessible to each of us through the empowering nature of our Virtues. This is why accepting the gift of our Virtue is foundational to becoming the very best of ourselves. Learning to let the most radiant aspects of who we are come forth ultimately leads to compassionate living and loving in the world.

It reminds me of a story from the life of Sadhu Sundar Singh, the great India mystic who followed the teachings of Jesus while remaining contextually committed to the cultural religious practices and forms of his childhood faith, Sikhism. His fidelity to humanity was the evidence of his own virtue grounded in his contemplative practice. The Sadhu opened his heart to the world, and not only were those around him transformed but in turn he was saved from himself.

Born in Punjab in 1889, he was just thirty-nine years old when he set out on pilgrimage to Tibet, never to be heard from again. He regularly traveled through South Asia to teach and, over the course of his short life, even made several international trips to places like Australia, Britain, Burma, Ceylon, China, Japan, Malaya, and Tibet.

During one of his trips through Tibet, Sadhu Sundar Singh and a local guide were crossing a steep mountain pass still miles from their destination when the temperature suddenly dropped and a winter storm set in. As they hurriedly made their way in hopes of outracing the dangerously frigid weather, they stumbled upon the body of a fellow traveler they presumed was dead. But after checking on the man, the Sadhu realized he was barely alive and in desperate need of medical attention. As the Sadhu lifted the helpless man, wrapping himself and the weary pilgrim in his blanket, his guide protested, "If we try to save this man's life, we will all perish." And with that, the Tibetan guide rushed off ahead, leaving the other two behind. Soon it began snowing so heavily the Sadhu could hardly see his hand in front of his face. Every step forward was treacherous on the slippery path. As nightfall set in, the Sadhu could see his destination off in the distance, a small village just a few hundred yards away. Tragically he looked down and found the frozen body of his guide, literally within shouting distance of their destination.

Reflecting on the difficulty of the journey, the Sadhu concluded it was the struggle that saved him and the unfortunate traveler. The body heat generated from their laborious trek through the mountains kept them both alive.[1]

---

1. Kim Comer (ed.), *Wisdom of the Sadhu: Teachings of Sundar Singh* (Farmington, PA: Plough Publishing House, 2000), 135–136.

We know this to be true: the fruit of our love in the world not only saves others but ultimately saves us. This is why we need each other, and this is how the Virtues are guides to compassion. It's our Virtues that will heal the world, and this healing starts inside each of us, opening our hearts to our whole selves so that, when confronted with human need, injustice, and an opportunity to give of ourselves, we are capable not of "good works" or some projected benevolence project but of allowing ourselves to be saved. Opening our hearts to the world is the proof that our Virtues are alive and active, bearing witness to faith, hope, and love as they contagiously heal what's broken within and outside ourselves.

9

Making Peace *with the* Passions

The Counterforce of the Virtues

W ay back in 2006, Dwayne Carter Jr.—you may also know him
as Lil Wayne or Weezy or Tunechi or even Lil Tunechi—
started working on what would be his sixth studio album, *Tha Carter
III*. Now this was at a crucial time in modern music history: record
sales were down, online streaming did not yet exist, underground
mixtapes were still popping, and Lil Wayne was everywhere—MTV
even unofficially crowned him the "Hottest MC in the Game."

Like an adult version of the popular children's game *telephone*, I've
heard different versions of the origin story of *Tha Carter III*—the one
I wish was truest includes Lil Wayne pulling off one of crowdsourcing's
greatest heists.

By mid-2007, most of the album had (allegedly *unintentionally*)
leaked online. Fans and critics alike all weighed in on what they
loved and hated about the songs. Because of Lil Wayne's massive
popularity at the time, twenty of those songs were stitched together
by a DJ known as The Empire and released in the summer of 2007
as an unofficial mixtape called *The Drought is Over 2 (The Carter 3
Sessions)* or *The Carter III Mixtape*. In December of that same year,
Lil Wayne himself took a handful of those songs and released a
five-song EP called *The Leak*.

By the time the commercial studio album dropped in June 2008, the anticipation for his new project was at an all-time high. *Tha Carter III* ended up selling over one million copies in its first week alone and would become one of the top forty best-selling hip hop albums of all time.

Urban legend has it that Lil Wayne was behind it all. Leaking the songs helped him decide which ones to keep for the studio recording and which ones to float off for the informal mixtapes. Listening to all the critiques from listeners gave him crucial clues for how to re-record and perfect the most loved of the leaked songs. By the time the album dropped, Lil Wayne had crafted a nearly perfect project that was critically acclaimed and still considered one of hip hops greatest albums.

Now some of you are internally protesting: "But I don't like Lil Wayne, he has a dirty mouth" (sorry, so do I, but keep reading) or, "What does *Tha Carter III* have to do with the Enneagram?" (which we're getting to now . . .).

A couple of years ago I had an idea that maybe our Enneagram Passion isn't first and foremost a sin to begin with (even though the nine Passions are labeled with the terms for Christianity's nine capital sins). And even more nuanced, maybe we experience our Passion in three different ways—each held by our Intelligence Centers.

I hadn't heard anything like it at the time and didn't want to wade into the murky waters of *EnneaHeresy*. So, I decided to write down my ideas and float them to the *Enneagram Monthly* and then the International Enneagram Association's online forum, *IEA Nine Points*. In the spirit of Lil Wayne, I "leaked" the idea to let readers push back and help clarify or correct what I had gotten wrong. What follows may not get all the accolades that *Tha Carter III* did, but it does represent a carefully critiqued take on the Enneagram's Passions.

WHAT ARE THE PASSIONS?

Type One	Anger
Type Two	Pride
Type Three	Deceit
Type Four	Envy
Type Five	Avarice
Type Six	Fear
Type Seven	Gluttony
Type Eight	Lust
Type Nine	Sloth

PASSIONS

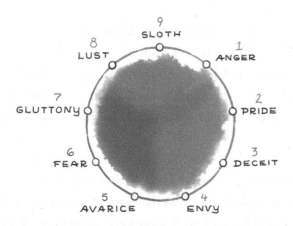

Before getting to that theory, however, it's important we're all on the same page when it comes to the Enneagram's Passions.

Many of us in the old days found it easiest to discern our own Enneagram type through reviewing the Passions. That's why it's frequently suggested that you'll know your type when you come across the one that makes you squirm or feel most humiliated. The Jesuits did their darnedest to rub some Bible on these Passions, explaining them as the *shape of our tragic flaw* or our *sin tendency*. This triggered shame or guilt in many of us. It also allowed us to really dig into our souls to find what our Enneagram type's emotional motivators were. That's why the Passions have become the lead story or the most popular of Ichazo's first four Enneagons and the Enneagram that enthusiasts are most familiar with. Because a lot of us don't know what to think about our feelings, the Passions seem to be the most honest character component of type structure.

So, what are the Passions?

When Óscar Ichazo first introduced the Enneagram to Claudio Naranjo, Óscar drew an Enneagram with the Passions assigned to each of the nine numbers and asked Claudio to locate himself on the circle. Typical in type Five fashion, it took Naranjo a couple of attempts before he accurately self-typed, but I can't help but think it was Naranjo's introduction to the Enneagram, through the Passions, that brought them to the center of modern teaching.

The Passions are our nine type-specific coping skills that suffer our disconnect from Essence; they are the evidence of our misery. They present themselves as the inverse or counterpoint of the Enneagram's Virtues. It could be said that the Passions are the shadow of the Virtues. Fundamentally, I believe our Passion is how our type, specifically in our heart, aches and longs to reconnect with the Virtue of our truest self. This ache is our soul's clarion call to return to home.

When our Basic Fear (that we are cut off from the possibility of realigning with our soul's created purpose for being) takes over and clouds the clarity of our perception, our Passion inevitably steps forward and becomes our first appeal to contending with this fear.

Essentially, it's an irrational emotional coping mechanism to try to quiet our Basic Fear.

It's as if our heart wants to coddle the rest of our being by saying, "It's okay, don't worry. Your emotions know how to take care of this loss." Our heart attempts to take care of the fear by enlisting the conditioned traditional expressions of how our Passion presents itself.

But when we are fear-driven, our Passion can very easily become a fatal flaw. One of the reasons our Passions seem to be so relatable is because they have this automatic and familiar nature about them. We don't have to think about turning over the keys of our soul to them; our Passions just step up and take over for us, without permission. And our subconscious finds a sort of comfort in this.

Once our Passions kick in, they also bring an indulgence toward addiction. This is aggravated by our Fixation's insistence that how our heart suffers our loss of contact with Essence "makes sense" to the Fixation. And as the mental Fixation convinces our emotional Passion that it's justified, a hamster wheel loop sets in and we find ourselves stuck in a constant cycle where our Passion and Fixation reinforce each other.

Over the years I've found it best to relate to my Passion with compassion rather than resistance. There's something childlike, not necessarily innocent but still naïve, about the attempts our Passion makes to have the final say. And just like a child who hasn't been afforded an adequate amount of control over their circumstances, caring affection through nurturing love, or reasonable security in their early holding environment, our own inner child acts out toward securing these "programs for happiness"[1] if they're not sufficiently

---

1. As a Yale University educated mental health professional turned monk, Father Thomas Keating extensively wrote about the idea that as children we all need adequate amounts of "power and control, affection and esteem, and security and survival" for healthy psychological development. However, as we mature, our human tendency to *overidentify* with

possessed. This acting-out is almost always expressed through the Passion. Because our ability to access the energy of our Passion starts early in life, it becomes habitualized and eventually normalized, an automatic response.

Though the traditional list of Passions seems fairly clear, they are much more mysterious than their labels suggest. Let's examine a few ways these Passions move within and without us, demonstrating their dynamic nature.

PASSION AND COUNTERPASSION

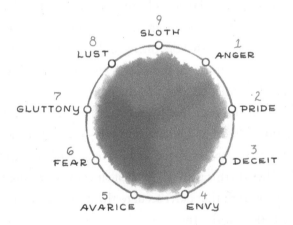

PASSIONS

In my last book, *The Sacred Enneagram*, I suggested the Anchor Points or the Revolutionary Types (types Three, Six, and Nine) carried

one of these programs for happiness keeps us developmentally and spiritually stuck. Father Keating suggests, "Without adequate fulfillment of these biological needs, we probably would not survive infancy. Since the experience of the presence of God is not there at the age we start to develop self-consciousness, these three instinctual needs are all we have with which to build a program for happiness. Without the help of reason to modify them, we build a universe with ourselves at the center, around which all human faculties revolve like planets around the sun." Thomas Keating, *The Human Condition: Contemplation and Transformation* (New York, NY: Paulist Press, 1999), 9–10.

within them a unique relationship to their Passion that showed itself through a kind of two-faced presentation.[2] Specifically, I intimated that if the *Counterphobic Six* was the only type that had two variants, then the existence of this deviation was actually an easy way to disprove the Enneagram, since after all, the Enneagram consistently proves itself as a fractal of triads. To demonstrate how the Anchor Points or the Revolutionary Types are consistently the exception of many of the Enneagram's *rules*, I wrote that in addition to a *Phobic* and *Counterphobic Six* there also is evidence of an *Active* and *Inactive Nine* as well as a *Genuine* and *Disingenuous Three*.

Since the publication of *The Sacred Enneagram*, I have come to realize when the *Counterphobic Six* was first identified there was very little conversation around the Subtypes or Instinctual Variants (let alone the Countertypes). But now we can assume the *Counterphobic Six* is actually the Countertype Six or Sexual Six (more on this in the next chapter).

Further, I do regret using the term *disingenuous* for type Three—of all six variants I mentioned, this was the most judging or discriminating language in a theory that was intended to be communicated in neutral terms. What I had intended to express was that there are two ways it appears: Threes either overshare or undershare their own inner truth. They do this through explicit sincerity or by implicitly hiding aspects of truth that don't seem to them to be consequential in their interactions with others.

Though I still believe types Three, Six, and Nine present their Passions through a pair of unlikely extremes, I've since come across Fabien and Patricia Chabreuil's theory that all nine types internalize or express the energy of a *counterpassion*.[3]

---

2. Christopher L. Heuertz, *The Sacred Enneagram: Finding Your Unique Path to Spiritual Growth* (Grand Rapids, MI: Zondervan, 2017), 100–101.

3. Fabien and Patricia Chabreuil, "Passion and Counterpassion," *Enneagram Monthly* (October 2002, issue 87): 1, 21–22.

Enneatype	Traditional Passion	Counterpassion*
One	Anger	Renouncement
Two	Pride	Self-Effacement
Three	Deceit	Self-Restraint
Four	Envy	Self-Sufficiency
Five	Avarice	Extravagance
Six	Fear	Temerity
Seven	Gluttony	Austerity
Eight	Lust	Wariness
Nine	Sloth	Hyperactivity

* This list is derived from the Chabreuil's article, "Passion and Counterpassion".

These counterpassions are not anomalies. Rather, they are the fraternal twins of our conditioned emotional responses hardwired to type structure. The problem is, when giving over to the drives of the counterpassions, we may presume we are operating closer to our Virtue than our Passion, which simply fortifies the power of our Passion over our emotional well-being. The subtlety here is of utmost importance to recognize. Otherwise, we experience a kind of self-delusion, assuming the counterpassion to be more virtuous than it truly is.

What the Chabreuils are helping us understand is the dynamic duality or the pedulumic dichotomy of our Passion by detailing the counterpassions as a "caricature of the virtue"[4]—a nuanced pivot that has profoundly painful consequences.

---

4. Ibid.

Type One

For example, they explain how type One, who is not conscious of their relationship to anger, tends to swing between *renouncement* and a kind of tolerant acquiescence. This allows for them to maintain a muted internal frustration that supports a self-deluded sense of moral superiority.

Type Two

The type Two who can't bear to face their pride, yet still suffers the compulsion of it, may express their counterpassion in the form of *self-effacement* or a kind of false humility that makes them feel as if they should be less important than they are. This self-diminishment isn't humility but an attack on the power of the strength their humility.

Type Three

When type Three is unaware of their tendencies to downplay all that is fabulous about them, they may reach toward a kind of *self-restraint* that's expressed through a reserved posture—still a subconscious tactic to manage others' perceptions of them.

Type Four

Fours suffer the pain of their envy until it's no longer bearable and then move into their counterpassion of *self-sufficiency*. This convinces them that they don't need anyone or anything to find centered contentment. However, the counterpassion in this case reinforces their inner abandonment narrative, *proving* to them the inability of others to see or love them adequately.

Type Five

The counterpassion hustle for type Five is a form of *extravagance* or indulging others with gifts, information, or even shared time that their beneficiary may not be able to comprehend or appreciate. The illusion of openhearted generosity in this case is still a controlled cupidity which allows the Five to maintain power over whatever resources they still quietly withhold.

Type Six

Of course, the most obvious of all counterpassions is that of type Six, whose attempt to overcompensate for their fear leads them to an audacious *temerity* or a boldness that appears as courage but is still veiled fear.

Type Seven

The ever-elusive Seven experiences their counterpassion through self-control and restraint. This is why the Chabreuils refer to it as *austerity*. When Sevens have overdone everything or are attempting to manage the external perceptions of their image, a dialing-in or dialing-back allows for a refocusing of their tendency toward excessiveness.

Type Eight

An Eight who extends their unhealthy relationship with control over their passion makes a counterpassion move toward *wariness* or caution, which may present as controlled simplicity or minimalism. There's still an intensity at play internally; the control however is demonstrated in the external appearance of excessively measured restraint.

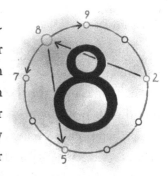

Type Nine

Finally, the unintended personal and social consequences of type Nine's sloth will sometimes cause them to move toward their counterpassion of *hyperactivity*. This is an obvious over-correction that is generally internally aimed at self-perfection projects. But when it is externally expressed, it tends to have an activist edge to it.

Of course, many of these counterpassions appear to have clear correlations to the Instincts and their Countertypes. However, the countermovement of the Passions seems to be accessible to all nine types as a self-deluding coping tactic to convince oneself of false inner growth. I'd venture to suggest that living out of our counterpassion is a form of spiritual bypass. This assumes that the repackaging of an experience of our Passion is somehow growth rather than the masquerading that it actually is.

THE INNER POLARITIES OF THE PASSIONS

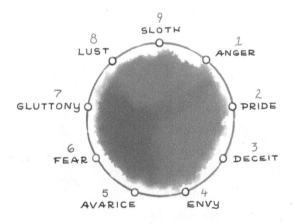

Another brilliant theory on the vibrant force of our Passions comes from Antonio Barbato and Jack Labanauskas (the cofounder and editor of *Enneagram Monthly*), who suggest the Passions are formed on a continuum of contractive and expansive energy. Labanauskas and Barbato call this gamut of expressions "Inner Polarities."[5]

---

5. Antonio Barbato and Jack Labanauskas, "Inner Polarities: The Structure of Passion," *Enneagram Monthly* (March 2000, issue 59): 1, 18–20; and Antonio Barbato and Jack Labanauskas, "Inner Polarities: The Structure of Passion (Part 2)," *Enneagram Monthly* (April 2000, issue 60): 8–9.

Enneatype	Traditional Passion	Inner Polarities*
One	Anger	Security ←→ Sensitivity
Two	Pride	Freedom ←→ Intimacy
Three	Deceit	Depersonalization ←→ Self-Interest
Four	Envy	Disorientation ←→ Vindication
Five	Avarice	Distrust ←→ Certitude
Six	Fear	Attack ←→ Surrender
Seven	Gluttony	Impermanence ←→ Sacrifice
Eight	Lust	Submission ←→ Supremacy
Nine	Sloth	Lethargy ←→ Hyperactivity

*This list is derived from Labanauskas and Barbato's articles, ""Inner Polarities: The Structure of Passion" (parts 1 and 2).

Type One

For those dominant in type One, their anger lives on a range between *security* and *sensitivity*, a display of their need for control as it relates to the deep sadness of living with their flaws. We know that anger is often disguised grief, and the sensitivity of the One to the pain of their imperfections must be

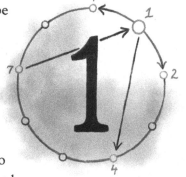

expressed. However, maintaining an image of control, even over their sadness and anger, is rooted in their sense of moral stability or an inner compass providing the security they need, knowing that in the end they are right. So, awareness of the sensitivities disguised in their anger allows for a homecoming to the pain in their hearts. This reminds them of the security of their inner strength as expressed through tender weakness.

Type Two

Type Twos find themselves vacillating between the poles of *freedom*
and *intimacy* as they relate to the
spectrum of their pride. If one of
the ways pride shows up for the
Two is restrained dominance in
relationships, then on one hand
their sense of superiority needs the
coddling of connection which can be

mistaken as intimacy. On the other hand, the shrewdness of their self-
importance needs some independence or freedom as a means of caring
for themselves in a way they fear no one else possibly could. Both of
these swing from a self-restrained sense of freedom (not needing others
though still desiring to be needed by others) to an expansive sense
of intimacy (the substitute for unconditional connection) emphasize
to the Two their inner authority, and they (often arrogantly) assume
themselves to be the governing authority in their connections.

Type Three

From *depersonalization* to *self-
interest*, type Three contends with
their deceit while rarely bringing
any amount of self-awareness to
what's at play within the polarities
of their Passion. For a Three to
have to own their feelings related
to their deprived sense of self-value
is almost too painful for them to bear.

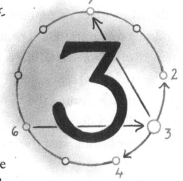

So rather than being honest with their aching heart, they further
distance themselves from their emotions by depersonalizing the

effects of their internalized fear. Within reach of the diminishment of their pain, however, is the remedy for it, a self-interested grab for attention, affirmation, recognition, or validation to tend to the hurt within. Of course, both reaches, in either extreme, keep Threes from being honest about the source of their emptiness as it relates to their notions of self-worth and self-love.

Type Four

Type Four suffers the polarities of their envy through *disorientation* and *vindication*. Both extremes are undergone as introjected deceptions of what seems to be lacking as a result of their perception of being unloved or inadequately cared for as children. The disorientation of not fundamentally knowing they are loved 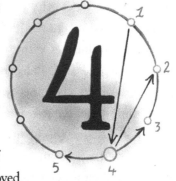 because of who they are comes from their sense of not knowing where they came from. This is sometimes aggravated further by their conflicted relationship with their own origin stories, an experience tethered to a lack of connection from parents or caregivers. The vindication corrects the disorientation by taking back the fierce inner strength of a Four, who further isolates themselves and punishes others for their emotional segregation. This vindication is a kind of emotional exoneration. It justifies the Four's extreme emotional swings as the source of their disorientation, rather than facing it as externalized envy of not having what they perceive others have come to possess.

Type Five

Type Five's Passion of avarice lives on a mental teeter-totter dithering between *distrust* and *certitude*. These are the two extremes of their acquisitiveness. Initially, they distrust their ability to protect the resources they've gathered. Subsequently, they learn to distrust their knack for knowing whether what they've attained will ever be sufficient. Nevertheless, a stabilizing mental overcorrection catapults them from concern to conviction, which

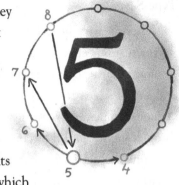

requires that they confidently double down on their assurances with an emotional certitude. Somewhere between the contractions of their distrust and amplifications of their certitude, Fives must learn to waiver in generous mystery in order to find their center.

Type Six

As always, Sixes are a study of contradictions. What may appear incongruous with fear, the Passion of type Six, is their fluctuating ambivalence. Sixes bounce between the polarity of *attack* and *surrender*. While some Sixes find reassurance in confrontational rebellion, there's still a tentative trepidation behind their strength—especially when it's

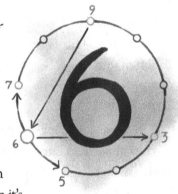

expressed as confrontation. Though attack is one way of combatting their inner fears, withdrawing through surrender isn't pure faintheartedness. Rather it's a kind of trusting in their apprehension—which is actually a counterpoint to their timid distress. Perhaps the most unpredictable of all polarities is the Six whose extensive capacity to attack is balanced by their restrained tendency to surrender. Both responses are volatile and erratic, while sensibly rooted in their deep need for permanency.

Type Seven

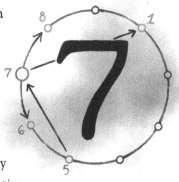

There is very little hesitance in the fluctuation between type Seven's Passion polarity of *impermanence* and *sacrifice*. To the Seven, the virtuous temperance or mitigating through sacrifice all that could be consumed is actually a calculated equation of the transience of the very impermanent focus of their attention. Sevens don't need to be warned of the impending end to that which brings them pleasure. They're well aware of the hollow gratification that distractions carry. So, to sacrifice those distractions appears as a move toward restraint or moderation, though it is still a gluttonous diversion to the emptiness they suffer. An unaware sway between impermanence and sacrifice hardens their addictive propensity for excessiveness. This is something they must compassionately allow to soften into true sober clearheadedness.

Type Eight

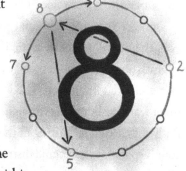

As those dominant in type Eight forcibly move from one extreme of their Passion (lust) to the other extreme, this relationship between *submission* and *supremacy* is revealed as an instinctual exploration of their power *and* their weakness. Just as all these inner polarities of the nine Passions are not dualistic skirmishes within the subconsciousness of type structure, the Eight (usually through great pain to themselves or others) learns that their absolute power is located in willing submission, while their most vulnerable weaknesses are humiliatingly exposed by their grasps for supremacy. Both reaches, however, are rooted in the lust of their impulsive desire for excessive power over themselves and their environments.

Let me offer a personal anecdote to embody this polarity. I used to be terrified of dogs. Until a day that changed all that for me. I'll never forget the interaction I had with a big scary-looking white dog that knew I was frightened by her. She walked right up to me. Sniffed me, as dogs do. Laid down on top of my feet and then rolled over, exposing her chest and belly. Not only was I horrified by this creature, but I was also a bit confused. Her human tried to calm me, "Look at that," he said. "She knows you're afraid of her and so she's vulnerably exposed her heart to you to reassure you that she's safe. Go ahead and scratch her chest so she knows you trust her." And just like that, I was completely challenged to reexamine my relationship with vulnerability, vacillating between submission as a means of communicating powerlessness, and supremacy over power through vulnerability.

Years ago, my spiritual director pointed out for me that the English word "vulnerable" comes from the Latin word for "wound." Therefore, to be vulnerable means to be capable of being wounded. I'd however prefer to be transparent. Ask me whatever you want, and for the most part I'll share anything with you, even my most shame-filled moments and spectacular failures. Not because I want us to be close, but because I use transparency as a hustle to avoid being vulnerable.

For me, being vulnerable is much more difficult than being transparent. It's painful exposing the parts of me that can be wounded. It's not impossible for me to share my feelings with someone, but it is incredibly difficult for me to trust people with my feelings. It's not easy for me to put my needs out there and give someone a chance to reject them. And so, what I usually do is work toward transparency as a distraction from my lack of vulnerability.

Type Nine

Finally, type Nine gracefully makes indirect moves between the polarities of sloth expressed through *lethargy* and *hyperactivity*. It bears repeating that the sloth of the Nine is not technically laziness but has more to do with prevention of suffering. So, what may appear to be lethargic is more rightly understood as the exhaustion 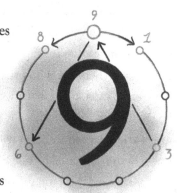 Nines feel from their efforts to maintain inner and outer peace. Their hyperactivity, nevertheless, is simultaneously a thoughtless determination to fill empty spaces with positive endeavors lest those moments of rest be consumed by painful memories, unmet needs, or unreconciled demands on their relationships or in their communities. This awkwardly shows up as the Nine attempts to overcompensate for the idle effects of their disconnect from the demands of their reality.

CONTOURS OF THE PASSIONS: An Enneagram Fractal of Hunger, Ache, and Restlessness

So, back to all this noise about Lil Wayne (finally). After having explored the counterpassions and inner polarities of the Passions, I'm still not convinced that the traditional labels of the Passions we just reviewed are all that helpful. Drum roll, please. Here comes my carefully critiqued theory.

Today, the Passions are a central element of nearly all serious Enneagram studies. Though they stand alone as some of the clearest archetypal components of human character structure, the language used to define the nine capital sins ascribed to the Enneagram's Passions is imprecise at best.

First, the inadequacy of the language is evident practically any time the Passions are presented. Enneagram authors and teachers typically reframe the traditional Passions to better describe them. For example, they will often suggest, "It's said that *lust* is the Passion of type Eight, but it's not simply sexual lust but the *lust for*

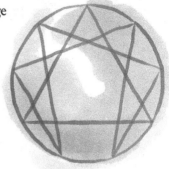

intensity," or, "The Passion of the Nine is *sloth*, less categorical laziness and perhaps more accurately described as *self-forgetting*, which may get closer to what is meant by the Nine's Passion."

Second, I don't believe the Passions are first and foremost "sins" nor the shape of one's tragic flaw, as often purported by those Enneagram students influenced through the Jesuit lineage. Claudio Naranjo's interpretation of the Passions as a "thirst for Being, ultimately based on a loss of contact with Being"[6]—connected to our original wound and our loss of innocence—seems as true to experience as any explanation. Certainly, when the Passions are overused as coping mechanisms, they quickly become addictions, and in addiction, sin can be present.

Third, I was at a workshop facilitated by Michael Goldberg where he shared the story of a conversation he had with Óscar Ichazo in the early 1990s. Considering he was working in his second language to portray such a profound teaching, Ichazo reflected to Goldberg that the English translation for some of the terms used with the Passions was insufficient, only an impression of what was meant by the substance of the Passions.

---

6. Claudio Naranjo, *The Enneagram of Society: Healing the Soul to Heal the World* (Nevada City, CA: Gateways Books and Tapes, 2004), 23.

PASSIONS

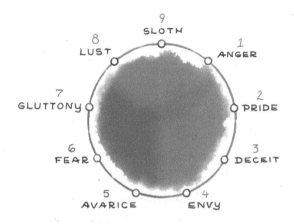

Now I'm absolutely convinced the triadic cosmology of the Enneagram is its strongest proof. Like a fractal that shows a naturally occurring infinite pattern replicated in a feedback loop, the hidden dimensions of the Enneagram come forward through its triads. It's much like the old pixelated "Magic Eye" images that disguise a 3D figure in a two-dimensional pattern. The harder you focus your attention to see the 3D picture emerge, the more difficult it is to see it. You have to *unfocus* or relax your gaze to allow the embedded image to be revealed.

Loosening the emotional grasp that our Passions hold over us is very similar to the work we're all invited to when facing our Passion. Focusing on the shape of the Passions only gives them more power. It's when we breathe into them with our whole selves that they are revealed for what they truly are. This helps us own them, integrate them, and make peace with them—finding the humor in the humility of our humanity. And once again, discovering how to find true belonging.

It seems the way most of us experience the Enneagram's Passions is triangulated in each of the three Intelligence Centers—a sort of cocktail merging the three distinct ways the Passions are internalized. I elect to scrutinize the Passions through the lens of the Intelligence Centers since our Centers are our primary modes of perceiving ourselves in reality. But we must remember, the Centers simply represent *organs of perception* or processes of translating experiences on an essential human level.

Integrating what's been disassociated from our three Intelligence Centers and confined to the soul's thirst for being, it seems the Passions take on a three-dimensional clarification when seen as an aggregate of a *carnal hunger* (held in the Body Center), an *emotional ache* (experienced in the Heart Center), and an *existential restlessness* (cerebralized in the Head Center).

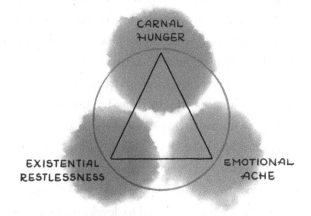

Any combination of two of these elements generates the third expression or attribute of the Passion.

Carnal Hunger (Body) + Emotional Ache (Heart) = Existential Restlessness (Head)
Emotional Ache (Heart) + Existential Restlessness (Head) = Carnal Hunger (Body)
Existential Restlessness (Head) + Carnal Hunger (Body) = Emotional Ache (Heart)
Carnal Hunger + Emotional Ache + Existential Restlessness = the Passion

Even more, the way we delude ourselves based on how our Passion creates addictive patterns for us is primarily experienced in our dominant

Intelligence Center. At the same time, our repressed Center is where our Passion hides itself from us, creating a blind spot of sorts and causing us our deepest pain and most dramatic struggles. The repressed Center, our most unconscious process of perception, then becomes the incubator of experience that gives the Passion its strongest grasp on the ego.

The challenge is to learn to recognize how we experience our Passion in each of our Centers so that when one driving force takes over, the other two can hold it accountable.

Overlaying the nine traditional Passions of the Enneagram with each of the Intelligence Centers offers accuracy, clarity, and candor. If we can truthfully admit to ourselves what we're contending with, then we know how to face, accept, and make peace with the sometimes painful layers of the Enneagram's Passions.

While exploring this theory, I called a friend who is dominant in type Five and asked him how he has related to his type's traditional Passion, *avarice*. He immediately protested the assumptions around its notions of greed and offered a detailed clarification of how he experiences this thirst to reconnect with his essential nature.

As I listened to others try to describe their type's Passions beyond the reductionist sin language, I started to develop a composite elucidation of the Passions as follows:

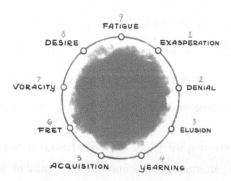

CARNAL HUNGER

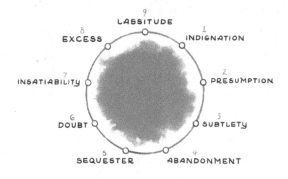

EMOTIONAL ACHE

9 LASSITUDE

8 EXCESS

1 INDIGNATION

7 INSATIABILITY

2 PRESUMPTION

6 DOUBT

3 SUBTLETY

5 SEQUESTER

4 ABANDONMENT

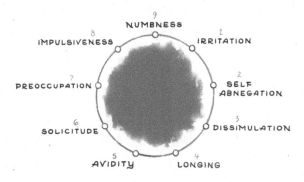

EXISTENTIAL RESTLESSNESS

9 NUMBNESS

8 IMPULSIVENESS

1 IRRITATION

7 PREOCCUPATION

2 SELF ABNEGATION

6 SOLICITUDE

3 DISSIMULATION

5 AVIDITY

4 LONGING

Let's explore these distinctions in each of the nine types.

Type One

	Traditional Passion	Carnal Hunger	Emotional Ache	Existential Restlessness
Type One	Anger	Exasperation	Indignation	Irritation

Traditionally, Óscar Ichazo assigned *anger* as the Passion for type One. This is perhaps better described in its relationship to the frustration of the Ones' Fixation (resentment).

For many Ones, the anger they experience is ironically located in feeling misunderstood that their Passion isn't merely unfathomable rage. It is better articulated as the exhausting *exasperation* carried in their bodies. When amalgamated with an emotional state of *indignation*, Ones' idealism begins to fade and turns in on themselves, creating deep and even sometimes somatic pain.

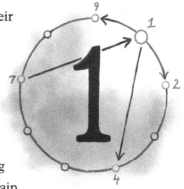

Having repressed their Head Center, the obscuring of this exasperated indignation leads to a persistent mental *irritability* or *irritation* expressed through fussiness and frustration, sometimes coming out as anger. But that is only a representation of what they are experiencing in their bodies.

Type Two

	Traditional Passion	Carnal Hunger	Emotional Ache	Existential Restlessness
Type Two	Pride	Denial	Presumption	Self-Abnegation

Pride is an unfortunate description of type Two's Passion, since people dominant in type Two rarely come across as arrogant, conceited, or any other overt form of pridefulness. False humility, a cousin of pride, gets closer to the meaning implied, though this still is inadequate.

Type Twos' *denial* of their own needs is held in their body as a way of diminishing wants or desires, yet they can't help but crave for these denied desires to be met. This leads to passive-aggressive presumption. *Presumption* that others would mirror back to Twos what they are offering of themselves is a common expression of the pain they feel. "You could have expressed your gratitude more explicitly," or, "Why didn't you think I would have liked to join you?" are emblematic ways Twos express their pain. Presuming is also commonly hidden in the assumption that if they did make their needs known—or even more difficult, if they actually asked that their needs be met—they would only experience rejection. The Two presumes initiative from those whom they most desire to meet their needs, all the while convincing themselves that when their needs aren't met, they'll be fine. *Self-abnegation* is the mental diminishment of the inner repression of these desires, convincing Twos to give away more of themselves at their own expense. And since the Twos' repressed Center is in their mind, self-abnegation shapes the notion of pride more than the other two aspects.

Type Three

	Traditional Passion	Carnal Hunger	Emotional Ache	Existential Restlessness
Type Three	Deceit	Elusion	Subtlety	Dissimulation

How shaming must it be for those dominant in type Three to have to reconcile the traditional Passion labeled as *deceit*. Their preoccupation with authenticity fortifies an internal dilemma that pendulum-swings between deception and integrity.

Type Threes metabolize this ever-present duplicity in their bodies by *eluding* its need to be faced and interrogated for what's instinctually behind it. On one hand, this elusion expresses itself as a playful parsing or evasion of truth, while on the other hand, there can be an obvious eluding or avoiding of those aspects of self they don't want to share or be seen by others. Their psychological ability to evade deception merely serves to give it more power over them. Aching because of this disconnect, Threes' repressed Heart Center can't bear to face yet another inner imperfection that could be viewed by others as a blemish. So type Threes' *subtlety*, or how they parse the full truth, refines their deceptions by over- or underexaggerating them in socially passable transmissions. In this way, they hope to be seen as more legitimized than they really are. Not entirely feeling the impact of their pretenses, type Threes *dissimulate* consequences by mentally dissembling or disguising the image projection of what they won't or can't be truthful about.

Type Four

	Traditional Passion	Carnal Hunger	Emotional Ache	Existential Restlessness
Type Four	Envy	Yearning	Abandonment	Longing

Among the most misunderstood of the Enneagram types, Fours suffer the marginalization of what's misunderstood by them and about them. This has given their traditional Passion's notion of *envy* a fraternal relationship to jealousy. But it's a much more delicately nuanced struggle than mere enviousness.

Like a hunger, the physical experience of envy may be more akin to a somatic *yearning* held in the bodies of those who feel more uniquely complex than simple personality descriptions can caricature. In repressing their Body Center, this yearning is felt as a hunger that their *abandoned* hearts sense must be starved, lest it become too strong of an internal driver. Type Four translates the world through an emotional sense of abandonment. Abandonment shows up as both self-abandonment and an unconscious attempt to be or feel abandoned. They look to people and circumstances in their lives as the confirmation bias of being abandoned. Those dominant in type Four mentally experience this convoluted sense of envy as ethereal *longing*. This is the gentler side of their impassioned longing for what they assume to be more significant than what their current quality of being offers.

Type Five

	Traditional Passion	Carnal Hunger	Emotional Ache	Existential Restlessness
Type Five	Avarice	Acquisition	Sequester	Avidity

The notion of avarice or greed is a poor grasp at the overdriven collecting tendency of those dominant in type Five. This drive is an overcorrection for an emptiness or hollowness of mental or material scarcity that they often experience.

This voracious need to *acquire* analysis, the correct questions, time and space for research, or a theoretical framework for understanding, is a substitute for a physical hunger felt in the bodies of Fives. Having repressed their Body Center, the experience of acquisition seems to get closer to what is typically meant by the traditional Passion, *avarice*. Feeding this acquisitive hunger supports the *sequestering* of the Five's heart by their mind, a handing over of their emotional self to their mental faculties as a way of managing their distrust of their feelings, which must be accountable to their cerebral aptitudes. Once their hearts are sequestered, the self-isolating tendency of Fives is given over to a voracious *avidity*, their eagerness to consume and connect all things.

Type Six

	Traditional Passion	Carnal Hunger	Emotional Ache	Existential Restlessness
Type Six	Fear	Fret	Questioning Doubt	Solicitude

Archetypal threat-forecasters, the overidentification of Sixes with fear fails to explain how doubling down on what they are concerned about is actually a way they care for people in their lives—as if they have to face *our* fears for us by internalizing all that could go wrong.

Carrying this burden in their body, those dominant in type Six experience a physical pull in two simultaneous directions: *suspicion* for all that is even microscopically off, and a visceral sense of *fret* that feels like an inner gnawing of unfortunate possibilities. The pain of all this gets parked in the Heart Center. They experience a repetitive compulsion for *self-doubting*, a form of questioning their own safety nets as a backup to their innate suspicion. Most keenly affected, however, is the repressed Head Center's *solicitude*—specifically the uneasiness of their anxious minds.

Type Seven

	Traditional Passion	Carnal Hunger	Emotional Ache	Existential Restlessness
Type Seven	Gluttony	Voracity	Insatiability	Preoccupation

Typically, the *gluttony* of type Seven is described as a form of overconsuming pleasurable options and opportunities as a way to distract them from facing their own inner pain or suffering.

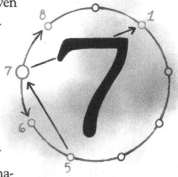

This Passion, once triggered, opens up a *voracious* appetite for experience, connection, and imagination. The Seven's inability to experience satiety, or being incapable of satisfaction, is the painful idealism of *insatiability* that characterizes the Seven's emotional ache. Their repressed Heart Center—and the fact that Sevens don't have a natural wing or Inner Flow path to their Heart Center—fuels this *insatiation* with very little responsibility to moderate it. Their voracious insatiability is wasted on the present. Yet, clever and savvy problem solvers, Sevens remain *preoccupied*, immersed in the daydream of what will voraciously consume their obsessions and fascinations next.

Type Eight

	Traditional Passion	Carnal Hunger	Emotional Ache	Existential Restlessness
Type Eight	Lust	Desire	Excess	Impulsiveness

Lust is a phrase that many Eights, even those who don't suppress or repress their sensuality and sexuality, experience as too personal of a descriptor to publicly identify with. The usual clarification that "lust in this case is more of a lust for intensity" helps, but this still doesn't describe what is experienced by those dominant in type Eight.

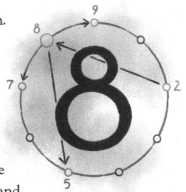

As the Passion is held in the body, it can be understood as the intensity of *desire* that grows and builds within, fueled by the frustration of its toomuchness. Having repressed their Heart Center, this desire is often unintegrated and unreconciled and so becomes unaccountable in its *excessiveness* or the overabundant surplus of energy that it produces. Though Eights are quick-thinking, their *impulsive* lack of reasoning regarding the consequences of excessive desire gives the Eight's lust more power than would ever be rationally intended. This creates the ensuing quandaries many Eights manufacture for themselves and others.

Type Nine

	Traditional Passion	Carnal Hunger	Emotional Ache	Existential Restlessness
Type Nine	Sloth	Fatigue	Lassitude	Numbness

Proclaiming *sloth* as the Nine's Passion can certainly be a blow to the composed, natural amicability of those dominant in type Nine.

The forgotten Body Center for those dominant in type Nine is less lifeless or lazy and more *fatigued*. Nines dispense a great deal of energy in their projection of the fragmentation of their inner lives in the proxy battles they arbitrate for their external lives. Often misunderstood as complacent (as if Nines are pleased with themselves) or apathetic (disinterested or unconcerned), Nines can quickly become worn out from projecting what has exhausted them internally. This exhaustion leads to an emotional lethargy that takes over their hearts and is experienced as *lassitude* or a strong sensitivity to their weariness. Exhausted from carrying unremitting fatigue in their

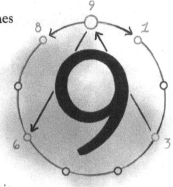

bodies and a tender languor in their hearts, Nines let their mind detach into a state of *numbness* to cope with all that overwhelms them.

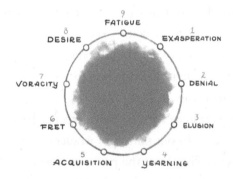

CARNAL HUNGER

9 FATIGUE
8 DESIRE   1 EXASPERATION
7 VORACITY   2 DENIAL
6 FRET   3 ELUSION
5 ACQUISITION   4 YEARNING

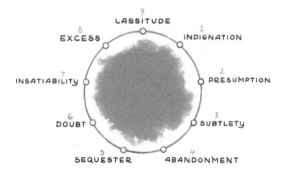

EMOTIONAL ACHE

9 LASSITUDE
8 EXCESS   1 INDIGNATION
7 INSATIABILITY   2 PRESUMPTION
6 DOUBT   3 SUBTLETY
5 SEQUESTER   4 ABANDONMENT

EXISTENTIAL RESTLESSNESS

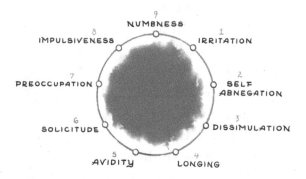

THE PASSIONS: Our Unlikely Friend

Needless to say, there's an urgent need to tighten the nuance of each of the nine Passions as they are wrapped around the color wheel of human character structure. As complex and sophisticated as the Enneagram's Passions are, the elaborateness of these emotional distresses requires thoughtful distinction to avoid the common caricatures one comes across.

With a compassionate lens, we can appreciate how very difficult it is to be each of us. In our pursuit of wholeness, the Passions are our unlikely friend. They have the power to alert us to the ways we are perpetuating our fragmentation. And if we can lean into deeper awareness of our self-defeating patterns, we can all the more empower ourselves to course-correct.

So, while traditionally the Passions are vilified, they offer us a powerful invitation. Rather than condemning our Passions and burying them, we can learn to listen to them and so better understand ourselves. Even our Passions belong. When we recognize this and seek to learn from our Passions instead of live in denial of them, we can press deeper into the journey of returning to our true selves.

PART

IV

BRINGING
OUR BODY
CENTER BACK
to BELONGING

10

Body Intelligence

Exploring the Nine Faces of the Instincts

Several years ago, three of my favorite people in Omaha started the coolest little bar I've ever been to. It has since shut down, but the House of Loom existed to weave the social fabric of our city together. Put simply, it was a place for all to belong.

You never knew what you were walking into on any given evening. Monday might feature someone spinning old Prince records. The first Tuesday night of each month centered on queer women of color. Wednesday could very possibly be hosted by a South Asian DJ spinning the best of Bollywood's latest hits. Thursday night salsa lessons were a blast. And then on the weekends the place would be packed out with some of the most diverse gatherings I've ever encountered in town.

Brent, Loom's in-house DJ, was a genius who always kept his cool. Jay was the hype-man, drawing a crowd with wild promotion. In fact, it was common to see him on the middle of the dance floor blowing a referee's whistle to wind the party up. Ethan, reserved and controlled while always aware of everything in his surroundings, was the business brains behind the operation.

The three of these guys couldn't be any different—at least on the surface, it seemed—Brent the epitome of social introversion, Jay clearly an extrovert, and Ethan definitely introverted.

Surprisingly though, they were all dominant in Enneagram type Three. Armchair Enneagram typing enthusiasts would have found it nearly impossible to land these guys on the same point around the circle, unless of course they were aware of their Subtypes or Instinctual Variants.

What's wild is how similar these men were because of their shared type Three traits, while still distinctly dissimilar in how they presented their Three identities.

Now that we've explored the four original Enneagons (the Holy Ideas, Fixations, Virtues, and Passions), the basic building blocks of the Enneagram of Personality and how they were used to define type, it's time to explore the current edge in Enneagram studies: the Subtypes or Instinctual Variants.[1] This is where things really start to come into focus.

As is true with nearly every aspect of type structure, Ichazo first introduced the three Instincts, though he didn't develop the Subtypes[2] (the twenty-seven ways personality presents based on the interplay of one of the Instincts with a type's Passion); that would come later through the work of Naranjo. When Ichazo named the Instincts, he referred to them as the Conservation Instinct, the Relations Instinct, and the Syntony Instinct. In today's parlance, the Instincts have been codified as Self-Preservation (abbreviated as SP), Sexual or One-to-One (abbreviated as SX), and Social (abbreviated as SO).

---

1. Don Riso originally called the type with its pronounced wing a "Subtype," only later to introduce the Instincts to his students and readers as "Instinctual Variants." As one might imagine, his use of "Subtype" correlated with the wings led to quite a bit of confusion.

2. It's important to note that the Instincts (the three unconscious drivers that serve as biological survival motivators) and Subtypes (the twenty-seven ways personality presents based on which Instinct is dominant) are not the same, though erroneously interchanged.

The three Instincts are the least conscious aspect of our personality structure. The Instincts are the more or less hidden impulses behind our compulsions—very, very powerful and yet almost completely unobserved. As Beatrice Chestnut[3] brilliantly explains in her own teachings on the Instincts, "If a thought moves at the speed of 'x' and an emotion moves at '10x,' then the Instincts are moving at '100x.'" These Instincts don't have the final say in terms of how we present personality, but they sure do create the "impulse tendencies" that produce the rails our personality uses to move forward. And they also account for why individuals who share the same type can present so dramatically differently.

Now knowing your type's Holy Idea and Fixation (housed in our Head Center) along with our Virtue and Passion (contained within our Heart Center) is a great start. But mere knowledge of type structure is only the beginning. The undramatic patient inner work of realigning with our Holy Idea and Virtue is the pathway to freedom from the stuckness our Fixations and Passions keep us trapped in. This is where one starts to experience the liberation from the limitations of type, as if mere awareness of the prison could free us from it.

So now that we've examined how the head and the heart lose contact with their Essence (Fixations and Passions), and how we can become free and find our way back again (Holy Ideas and Virtues), what about the body? This is where the Instincts come in.

Fundamentally, the Enneagram's Instincts are our species's intelligent biological survival tactics. If we attempt to locate the Enneagram's Instincts in one of the three brains of our Centers of Intelligence, then of course they would be located in our body.

---

3. Beatrice Chestnut's book *The Complete Enneagram: 27 Paths to Greater Self-Knowledge* (Berkeley, CA: She Writes Press, 2013) is the gold-standard, currently the most thorough explanation of the Subtypes as produced from the Instincts.

THREE LAYERS OF CONSCIOUSNESS

Fixations & Holy Ideas	Head Center	Conscious Level
Passions & Virtues	Heart Center	Subconscious Level
Subtypes	Body Center	Unconscious Level

The three dimensions of consciousness are namely: consciousness, subconsciousness, and unconsciousness.

Our consciousness (what we understand to reside in our mind) is what's floating around on the top of our heads; it's our basic talking points when asked mundane questions like, "How are you?" and the autopilot of response kicks in without much reflection. Our consciousness, when accessed, is what separates humanity from animals; it demonstrates our ability to be self-reflective. This is where we most acutely access the gifts of our Type's Holy Idea, but simultaneously this is where our Type's Fixation crystalizes.

Dropping from our conscious mind into our subconscious is the very difficult move from our heads into our hearts, our Emotional Center. Our subconscious is where our feelings and emotional triggers are located. There's a kind of *knowing* that happens on this level that often can't be rationally explained or justified, but we still know it's true—or at least genuine for us. When we explore the complex landscape of our subconscious, we breathe deeply into our hearts and allow a kind of trust to lead us. This, of course, is where we experience the elusive gifts of our Type's Virtue and also where we most painfully suffer the consequences and pain of our Type's Passion.

The move from our conscious mind to our subconscious heart is still an incomplete journey until we wade into the deep submerged waters of our unconsciousness—located in the belly or our Body Center. Now if we can agree that the Holy Ideas and Fixations are sorted out within the Head Center and the Virtues and Passions are in conflict within our Heart Center, then it only makes sense to understand that the jumbled Instincts must be stored (and, if we're honest, hidden from us) in our Body Center.

This invites us to consider what somatic intelligence has to say to us, what it has to teach us. But because this intelligence is stored away deep in our unconscious, it takes a kind of attunement that most of us have yet to develop. Attuning to the body's wisdom is awfully difficult but not impossible. The pain in our jaws from a night of grinding our teeth, for example, may be the indication that we're working out stress while sleeping. Or the butterflies in our stomach could be a sign of apprehension, inviting us into grounded self-confidence.

The keys to learning how to listen to these Instincts are on clear display throughout the animal kingdom. This is why I believe the Instincts are *the residue of evolution left over in our DNA.* The Enneagram's Instincts are our biological driving forces, our most honest and most undisguised compulsions, on a level that isn't self-reflective or emotionally engaged. Our unconscious Instincts are generally hidden from us. Hidden, but powerful. It's like how the majority of every iceberg is hidden under the surface of the water—while unseen, it is still the bulk of the mass. And our Instincts, though typically underexamined, may be the most impacting aspect of what shapes our type. Let's examine three Instincts that powerfully, though unconsciously, shape our lives.

What Is the Self-Preservation Instinct?

Our Self-Preservation Instinct is our compulsion for survival on a very practical level. Generally, people don't want to die. Our fear of spiders or heights is an unconscious reminder of our very real will to live. And who of us hasn't thrown their 1970s "seatbelt" arm across the person sitting in the passenger seat of their car when they unexpectedly slam on the brakes? We all have an aspect of self that wants to stay alive and keep our loved ones alive. We all have an inherent instinct to do what we can to ensure we're going to be okay.

What Is the Sexual Instinct?

The Sexual Instinct is about more than the sex act. It expresses something fundamental to the energy that pulsates through every living thing, also known as *eros*. Psychotherapist and relationship expert Esther Perel often describes *eros* less in terms of its sexual expression and more in terms of its zest for life. "Eros, also known as eroticism, is a quality of aliveness, vibrancy and vitality that is critical to both life and the clinical relationship. It's a sense of creativity, agency, and pleasure."[4]

If we think of the Sexual Instinct as *eros*, we find the Sexual Instinct playing out in all kinds of ways. The primal instinct in us to sexually procreate is but a wave in the spectrum of how this life energy shows up. Yes, this instinct can swell up physiologically with someone with whom we have what we might call natural chemistry.

Acknowledging this chemistry is the first step in becoming what Perel calls erotically intelligent. But the important thing to remember is that *eros* is activated in ways that can have nothing to do with another person. The Sexual Instinct is inherently about one's proficiency with their erotic energy, whether it's directed toward another person or toward a particular project like making music or art, writing a book, hiking in the woods, or swimming in the ocean.

---

4. Esther Perel, *Where Should We Begin?*, podcast, open.spotify.com/show/3fKOTwtnX5o ZLaiNntKWAV.

What Is the Social Instinct?

Our Social Instinct is what drives us to align ourselves with the various communities that incubate our sense of self. It's the part of us that needs to belong to a group. The Social Instinct is the part of our unconscious that finds a sense of safety, maybe even more fundamentally our sense of identity, in group affiliation. This doesn't necessarily imply that intimate connections will be made in groups; rather, the group gives meaning to the Social dominant individual's sense of identity.

DIFFERENT APPROACHES TO THE INSTINCTS

Instinctual Stacks

Just like all other teachings within the larger Enneagram community, those on the Instincts also have minor (and sometimes, not so minor . . .) nuanced controversies.

The first of these is the arrangement of how the three Instincts might be naturally stacked or originally ordered in nature.

There's one school of thought that lines them up as humanity's psychological development: Self-Preservation → Social → One-to-One.

This follows the cognitive development of children learning to survive by taking care of themselves (Self-Preservation), learning to fit into the structure of their familial birth order or their classroom or playground community (Social), and then eventually making deep and intimate connections through significant relationships (One-to-One). This arrangement seems to have more to do with psychological development than biological survival strategies.

The counterpoint to this ordering is less psychologically framed and more located in biological survival tactics ordered as: Self-Preservation → Sexual → Social.

I notice this in the ever-growing rabbit populations in the parks where we take Basil to play. I can't imagine how they survive our brutal winters (in Omaha we routinely suffer *negative* 40°–60° F wind chill temperatures every winter). Here on the great plains the snow can be merciless, and for these sweet little bunnies to attempt to endure the long winter months can't be easy. But somehow, year after year, after surviving the winter (Self-Preservation), springtime welcomes the possibility of new life and quickly becomes their most intense mating season—celebrating the unconscious sexual instinct that allows for the possibility of reproduction (Sexual). With a relatively quick gestation period of just four to five weeks, there are suddenly a slew of baby bunnies birthed into their underground warrens. Having to make room for all these tender new heartbeats requires a social instinct to include and incorporate into the life of their rabbit fluffles (Social).

Sexual or One-to-One?

The second controversy within the Enneagram conversation on the Instincts is the distinction or the hair-splitting between defining the *Sexual Instinct* and the *One-to-One Instinct*.

There are a few practical issues at stake here. Of course, in corporate or professional settings no one would feel comfortable having their boss referred to as a "Sexual Nine," when in fact you think they're more a "perverted Two" on an attractive scale of 1–10. Can you imagine all the harassment claims of an employer telling coworkers they're a "Sexual Four or Five"?

I get it; the language poses obvious problems.

But what's often tucked into the One-to-One description of that Instinct is the drive to connect on an intimate level with a friend, partner, or significant other (whether a sexual or nonsexual partner). This is tough for me since I'm convinced that our Instincts are the purest reptilian-brained aspects of us. Intimacy seems to be rooted in conscious connections and requires a choice in saying "yes" to a friend or a partner, when the Instincts are operating on a much more unconscious level.

Now the One-to-One school of thought doesn't restrict these connections or the desire of this Instinct to romantic partners, but if applied in that way it seems less instinctual and more consciously determined. Especially if one opts for monogamy. Because if we survey nature, we rarely observe any monogamous species out there, with the exception of some genuses of penguins and eagles. But even with humanity, most social scientists agree that humans are not instinctively monogamous; rather, it is a conscious choice.

Additionally, suggesting that animals are capable of making intimate bonds suggests that the One-to-One Instinct is a higher evolved expression of our unconscious that requires choice, decision making processes, and a highly developed sense of self-reflection. If the Instincts are raw and unobserved, then we have to consider the notion that One-to-One intimacy and bonding is more a function of our consciousness than our unconsciousness.

The counterpoint here, of course, is that the Sexual Instinct is simply the sexual drive in all forms of life to perpetuate life itself—a basic survival strategy for all species, equal to the Social and Self-Preservation Instinct.

So, before we convolute this any more than we might already have, let's offer some descriptions of what we mean by the Instincts.

As I've explored the nuances of these Instincts, I've determined that if I can't observe them expressed in my dog Basil, then they aren't Instincts but higher evolved expressions of our human subconscious or conscious minds. And this is crucial in our understanding of the Instincts—they are the unconscious *instinctive* part of us, just as animals rely on their instinctual intelligence to survive. And though the Instincts can be trained or their impact altered through awareness, if left alone and undisciplined, they lead to most of our personal drama, problems, and failures.

THE THREE FACES WITHIN EACH OF THE THREE INSTINCTS

I generally agree with the growing number of Enneagram experts who argue that there are three ways each of these three Instincts show up in our experience of them. This shouldn't surprise any of us if we believe (and I certainly do) the Enneagram to be a perpetual fractal of triads—continually proving itself over and over and over again in sets of three. So, let's set out to explore what I deem the three Faces of each of the Instincts and how our Intelligence Centers uniquely support them within our three Centers.

The Three Faces of the Self-Preservation Instinct
Self-Preservation for Regulation at Work in the Body/Instinctive Center

The body's intelligence for the Self-Preservation Instinct is the fundamental practice of self-care or **regulation**. Self-Preservation people generally exhibit a heightened need to ensure that they've gotten enough sleep, are exercising consistently, and are committing to a diet that serves their sense of well-being. Additionally, they tend to find practical ways of making sure their mental, emotional, biological, and spiritual needs are met. Now this doesn't imply that these needs are self-reflective or evolved; in fact, more often they are unconscious needs.

For example, bears show us how this facet of the Self-Preservation Instinct shows up in nature as they prepare to hibernate each winter. The weather triggers something instinctual in them, and they start to ensure they'll have enough body fat to make it through the drop in temperature and diminished access to food.

I recognize this face of the Self-Preservation Instinct in my dog Basil. The first thing Basil does every morning (*after* our singing, rolling over, and belly rubbing routine) is to groom himself. I joke around that he was raised by cats because he's sometimes obsessed with licking himself clean. And then, once he's tidied up, he jumps out of bed and scratches his itches. What's brilliant about this is that he scratches once he's *off* the bed—he's not smart enough to explain this to us, but what's happening is that he doesn't want to scratch potential fleas or other bugs onto the bed he sleeps in, so he relocates.

This self-preservation aspect is the first experience of health regulation, which in its simplest and purest expression is hygiene. Of course, in evolved human beings our Self-Preservation experienced as self-care regulation takes on a variety of forms.

In humanity we witness this play out in the person who's having a great time with friends or family, but at their routinely appointed bedtime stands up, says their goodbyes, and quietly heads off to bed, ensuring they secure adequate rest. Before I understood this as a Self-Preservation Instinct for regulation, I used to get frustrated with people who checked out too early in social settings. It seemed so out of touch or so self-centered, when actually it was fundamentally self-loving. Now, when someone dismisses themselves seemingly too early, I understand they may have a strong need to monitor their boundaries for self-care on an instinctual level—something I could actually learn from.

Self-Preservation for Preparation at Work in the Heart/Feeling Center

The second experience of Self-Preservation on an instinctual level arises from the heart and presents as **preparation**, distinct from regulation. Others have referred to this as a nesting instinct, a bias for domesticity, or homemaking. Instinctually, we observe this across all life—retreating to a cave or cavern or hiding in underground tunnels or holes. There's a self-preserving intelligence in hiding out or making a safe, clean, and comfortable home.

Nature is filled with examples of this. Consider a robin's nest. When I was a little kid I'd poke around the neighborhood after a thunderstorm looking for nests that had been blown out of trees. If you've seen one, they are stunning in their complexity. Think about it: a bird with a brain the size of a pebble searches out an array of materials (threads, strips of plastic, pliable branches) to weave together a durable nest. It's incredible. And this isn't something that a momma bird teaches her babies to build; it's intelligently hardwired in their instincts.

There are a couple ways this shows up in my sweet little dog. The first is when Basil feels threatened. For the good part of last fall there were roofers on the top of our office building tearing out the old covering and installing a new membrane. Whenever Basil heard the crew working on top of the building, he was terrified and immediately hid underneath one of our desks. Brilliant. I live in the Midwest, and when a tornado warning is issued, our meteorologists advise us to find a safe spot in our homes that will provide protection, usually a basement or a doorframe to brace the possible impact of the storm. Another way this shows up is when Basil hides in our closet during intermittent fireworks explosions leading up to the Fourth of July. Instinctively, he finds the safest place he can and waits out the danger.

Additionally, every time we make the bed at home (which includes carefully placing the extraneous pillows that we don't actually use but merely decorate our bed with), Basil jumps up onto the mattress, locates himself in the center of the stack of pillows, and begins to root around until he's pulled the down comforter loose with his paws and tussled the pillows all around him just right. Then, down he plops! The theory in dog behavior that explains this is when wolves were turning in for a good night's sleep, they'd have to dig around the grass or loose soil to make their resting place as comfy as possible.

In evolved humanity we observe this in the nesting instinct of a pregnant mother, whose heightened hormones don't simply nudge her to paint the expectant newborn's room because she's biding time, but because in all life there is a preparation aspect to self-preservation in allowing home to be not only a safe place for us but for those we welcome into it. Moreover, we notice this in the deep yearnings so many of us have to make our house a *home*, keeping it clean and hospitable for ourselves and loved ones.

Self-Preservation for Subsistence at Work in the Head/Thinking Center

Finally, the self-preserving intelligence of our instincts have to do with **subsistence**—sustaining a thoughtful sense of control, connection, and those things we are most concerned about.

Some popular Enneagram teachers have called this an obsession with the fundamentals, or the utilities of life, and point out how some Self-Preservation people may be really good at making money but terrible when it comes to taking care of their own health. This has often been clichéd out to the self-preservation tendency of people to make sure they've purchased enough life insurance or have their checkbooks balanced, but of course these types of behaviors operate on a more conscious level.

So, how does this show up on an instinctive level in nature? If you come over to our home, you'll notice that under our coffee table rests a half-chewed deer antler, two partially gnawed butcher bones, and an old rolled up salmon skin that's hardly been nibbled on. This is where Basil keeps *his things*. And if we move them when cleaning up for guests, you can be assured we're going to get a snarky side-eyed glance from Basil that feels like he's trying to say, "Those are mine; please put them back where I left them."

Now I'll bet if we had a backyard for him to play in, he might even bury a bone or two. Why? Because the Self-Preservation Instinct in all of us includes that lingering sense of storing up for the future, saving for our retirement, making sure we'll have enough to continue living the way we want and need to live. Nature is full of examples of this—squirrels saving nuts to get through the winter, for instance.

The ways we carry this Self-Preservation Instinct in our three Centers of Intelligence tell us something about ourselves. It shows us our unconscious drivers and compulsions to ensure our lives and livelihoods will go on as undisturbed as possible.

Basil's unconscious drives to regulate his self-preservation are obvious and remind me that my own self-care is important too.

When Basil jumps out of bed to scratch behind his ear (regulation), or when he retreats to his mat in our closet for some alone time or to find refuge from a thunderstorm (preparation), or when he hides his deer antler under the table (subsistence), he highlights his own instinctual intelligence.

And just as we all have instincts to preserve our life, we also have inherent drives to expand our life. Let's turn now to the Sexual Instinct.

The Three Faces of the Sexual Instinct
Sexual Enticement at Work in the Body/Instinctive Center

The first aspect of the Sexual Instinct is evidenced through **enticement**, which supports the body's basic drive for sex. This can be observed in someone's effortless charm and natural charisma. The Sexual Instinct is less obvious in Basil than in perhaps other animals. I attribute this to the consequence of him being neutered at a very young age, before we adopted him.

Luckily, we've not seen him attempt to mount another dog, an act that can be quite embarrassing to pet parents. And though mounting is sometimes a sign of dogs assuming dominance, it's more frequently a behavior associated with releasing sexual desire. Certainly, humping another dog isn't exactly an *enticing* play, but what triggers a mounting impulse *is* enticing. The potential mate is *alluring* the sexual behavior with their scents and signals. These scents are one of several ways a dog in heat will attract a potential sexual mate. Sexual enticement is fairly obvious when observed in dogs. And while certainly more complex in humans, this facet of the Sexual Instinct is just as present even if way less consciously observed.

Sex isn't always just about *the activity of sex*. It has layered impulses; sometimes it's about communication, power, connection, or a variety of other motivators.

Interestingly, bats demonstrate an aspect of this Sexual Instinct through sound waves. Now this isn't a deviation from the sexual edge of the Sexual Instinct but a further elaboration that what is meant by the Sexual Instinct doesn't exclusively have to do with sex. These furry little winged monsters know how to get around and how to attract a sexual partner by projecting sound waves. As they give off these signals, they navigate their way by the impressions of those sound waves bouncing off whatever or whomever is in their environment.

Likewise, there's something hidden in this natural phenomenon that shows up in our humanity. Just scroll through your Instagram feed and find a few friends whose photo galleries are disproportionately populated with selfies. Sure, some of those accounts might be owned by folks whose narcissism is clearly on display, but a more compassionate rendering reveals what may be motivating them instinctually. Perhaps, those accounts filled with selfies are people displaying a Sexual Instinct that puts itself out into the world to see what responses will come back to it—much like a bat's echolocation.

Sexual Exploration at Work in the Heart/Feeling Center

Exploration is yet another facet of the Sexual Instinct, less intuitive than the drive of this motivator and more affiliated with our feelings as an unconscious way of seeing what is possible. That's why the Sexual Instinct isn't a drive toward intimacy; rather, the Sexual Instinct may just want to explore possibilities.

It's remarkable how sensitive Basil's sense of smell is. We'll be on a walk when all of a sudden he starts pulling on the leash toward a stop sign post or a tree trunk where he's determined to smell whatever message another dog has left there. Urine and feces are one of the primary ways sexual pheromones are released in dogs. Certainly, there's a lot of sexual communication happening at these not-so-random stops around the neighborhood. So, Basil, being a good neighbor in his zip code, also leaves a message to perhaps say "Thanks for commenting" or "I hear you" or "I'll look for you in the park" or maybe even "This is my tree, stay away!" There's a purely animal instinct in all of us that explores—searching for possible mates and investigating messages that might have been left for us.

Exploring connections, possible partners, or even potential challengers to possible mates are all expressions of the exploration aspect of the Sexual Instinct. Sexual exploration is what drives many of us to be on constant alert, looking to make connections.

Sexual Opportunity at Work in the Head/Thinking Center

Finally, it appears there is a facet of the Sexual Instinct that is expressed in its relationship to **opportunity** and correlated to what we think about risk. We observe this in humanity with those who live on the edge, those who find themselves most alive when on the verge of risk or danger. Folks who struggle with gambling addictions are expressing this facet of their Sexual Instinct. It's as if they've unconsciously convinced themselves that the risk they are taking is worth it because of the possible opportunity it could provide. Again, this doesn't explicitly connect to the act of sex but originates in *sexual energy* required to secure a potential (opportunity) mate.

Since Basil's never been to a casino, I don't know the kinds of chances he'd be willing to take there. I do, however, observe the risks he takes when chasing bunnies. Several times a week I take him down to a local park that has an overgrown tangle of bushes and trees. It's a tiny urban forest where he can run free. Once I release him from the leash, it doesn't take long before Basil will catch the scent of a bunny. And once he does, his instinct for opportunity is on full display. At this point, he's not very responsive to my commands; instead, his instinctual drive takes over and he's determined to get a chase in. Lucky for the rabbits, he's very rarely caught one.

It's as if the mere *possibility* of catching a rabbit is more exciting than *actually* catching one. On those rare occasions when he's gotten one, Basil even appears fairly unsatisfied. It's as if he's disappointed the chase is over. When his hunting instinct sets in, he sets aside any Self-Preservation Instinct and will unthoughtfully put himself in harm's way. Once, when he was a puppy, he actually chased a rabbit across a busy street, nearly getting clipped by a truck. Nonetheless, when we do let him hunt rabbits within relatively safe boundaries, he inevitably comes home with a chest full of scrapes and minor scratches. The possibility of the hunt, the opportunity itself, becomes all that is important to him—even to his detriment.

This is also evidenced in the species of guppies who swim together in schools but occasionally have a rogue little fish who will leave the safety of their school to explore for possible predators. These random scoundrels who swim out ahead of the group are taking extraordinary risks on behalf of the others and, interestingly, end up becoming the most desirable mates. Clearly there's an aquatic sexual instinct at play.

Again, this bears out in humanity when a Sexual Instinct dominant person chronically dates around but never commits to a partner, or perhaps when someone lives for enthralling experiences that would normally seem entirely nonsensible to most people—things like cliff diving or bungee jumping or other activities that demonstrate the risk-taking nature of sexual energy.

What's important to understand, however, is while Sexual Instinct does allow for reproduction and the survival of species, it's not always about a sex drive but the energy that fuels one's sex drive in addition to the other life-forces that drive our experiences. Enticement, exploration, and opportunity may all have this energy about them without being explicitly sexualized. And this is what makes our Sexual Instinct so oblique and suggestive.

The Three Faces of the Social Instinct
Social Dominance at Work in the Body/Instinctive Center

Traditionally, the Social Instinct has to do with belonging. But the complexities of belonging also seem to show up in three distinct ways. We have unconscious attempts to regulate this aspect and compulsions behind how our personalities present themselves socially.

On a gut level, the Social Instinct shows up in how we navigate the various power dynamics at play in our social interactions—how we relate to the energies of **dominance**.

When I witness this in Basil, it's immediate. It's obvious within seconds of him meeting a new dog to discern who's the alpha and who's the subordinate. Rarely does Basil demonstrate aggression to take the alpha role when he's not naturally the dominant dog; he simply complies and adjusts to the power differential that's a natural part of canine hierarchy. Even more intelligent though, I've seen Basil try to reassure an alpha dog that Basil is cool with being submissive.

Sadly, this once led to Basil getting jumped in the park by an aggressive dog. I had taken Basil on a walk to one of the playgrounds where he'd meet up with a group of dogs he loved to play with, when a new dog owner and his pet asked if they could join the group. The ringleader dog mom, who more or less kept her eyes on all the puppies in this play-pack, asked, "Does your dog play well with others?" The unfamiliar dog owner replied, "He sure does!" After a few minutes the new dog was running around the park with Basil's group of friends. There were probably five or six dogs all chasing one red rubber ball when Basil caught it and started running with it securely held in his mouth. Now, Basil's a lean little guy and really, really fast. He also loves to get chased by other dogs and was outrunning them all. After a few laps around the park, it seemed as if Basil was sensing something from the new dog, so he went up to this unfamiliar animal, dropped the ball right in front of him, and then rolled over on his back exposing his heart as a sign of submission. It was amazing. Until the new dog bit Basil's stomach! Everyone was stunned, and poor little Basil was shocked. He ran and ran as fast as he could, as far away as he could. After I chased him down the street, I noticed wounds in his belly, and that night we took him to the pet hospital where he had emergency surgery to save his life.

This Social Instinct in all of us, as it relates to dominance, shows up in the ways we adjust to the alpha or how we handle unspoken power dynamics at work, in our families, social circles, and intimate relationships. Sometimes, we know that we can trust whoever is in authority. Other times, we find ourselves fighting to take over or gain control in situations where we don't feel safe.

Social Instinct for Association at Work in the Heart/Feeling Center

In addition to social dominance, the Social Instinct for belonging is demonstrated in the ways we feel about obtaining value through **association.**

When Phileena and I finally decided to adopt a dog, we agreed that we'd find a medium, brown, female puppy. Turns out we got an extra-medium, I've-seen-browner, male dog with an undetermined breed. People always ask, "What kind of dog is he?" And for a while all we could say was "mixed breed." But a few friends told us that Basil looked like a black-mouth cur, a dog that was crossbred in the southeastern part of the US to help herd farm animals. A working dog. This is why I jokingly suggest that Basil's Enneagram type is a Social Two with a One wing (the double compliant style), because he's such a good boy (the One wing) who was bred to help out (his dominant type Two) around the farm by steering herds (his Social Instinct).

Truthfully, he does have a super-pronounced herding instinct. It's remarkable when it shows up. If we're hiking with a group in the woods, or even walking down the hall in our condo or office building, Basil will trail back behind the last person in the group and gently nudge behind their knees urging them to catch up or keep up. If someone stops to take a phone call or tie their shoes Basil stops with them, waiting for them to find their way back to the group. It's amazing. But he can't help it. He wasn't *taught* to keep the group together; it was bred into his breed. His DNA was manipulated and altered over generations to enhance this instinct in him.

This facet of the Social Instinct for association is also rooted in belonging—satisfying our need for connection (though this doesn't imply intimacy).

We also observe it in Basil when he experiences deep relaxation. We know he's relaxed because he'll exhale a big belly breath and press his chin into the ground when he feels like he's finally at peace. But he only does this when he's with his pack. That's when he's the happiest. That's when he's the most relaxed. Of course, all dogs are pack animals, but this aspect of Basil's psyche seems highly attuned. He really does want his group *together*. It's kind of funny to watch. He loves it when all of us at the office gather together for a staff meeting. He'll jump in an empty chair and join us. Or when Phileena and I are home together, it's as though he finally can rest, assured that the family has been reunited and no one is leaving. I even experience it when I invite a few friends over to my library for a bottle of wine. He knows who's missing or who we're waiting for, and by the time my library night group is assembled and complete, he joins us in complete peace and lets himself rest as if he's one of the invited guests.

We're not much different as humans. Our need for association shows up in several ways—belonging to our neighborhood association, or our worshiping community, or even a club with a shared interest. Again, this doesn't require affectionate or intimate connections. It's more about the group identity and finding value in association with that group. Being a part of groups like this meets an unconscious need for belonging.

Social Cooperation at Work in the Head/Thinking Center

Finally, there is a facet of the Social Instinct that shows up in our considerable drive for **cooperation**. Practically speaking, this is about the betterment of the groups we're a part of. Some may argue this is actually evidence of an evolved consciousness, that this isn't animal in nature, but particularly human.

But again, if I can observe it in Basil, then it's got to be instinctual. And when Basil is around someone who is emotionally fragile or having a breakdown, he's instantly alerted to their emotional well-being and will do what he can to comfort them. It's beautiful to observe his sensitivity to someone's tears or broken heart, as if he knows they need a little care or attention. He'll gently climb up on the couch beside them or politely ask if he can set his chin on their leg or sit in their lap. He even offers tender little kisses, gentle licks on the faces of folks who express sadness. These attempts to offer consolation make me wonder what's going on in that small head of his. But that's when I remember he's not consciously reflecting on his responses to his environment, rather he's reacting out of his instinct to cooperate for the good of the group, just like we do.

Probably one of the most profound examples of the Social Instinct for cooperation is demonstrated in a story of the endangered killer whale who carried the corpse of her calf for seventeen days. In the summer of 2018, a pod of orca whales who had not successfully bred for over three years welcomed a new member to their pod, only to lose the baby just thirty minutes after it was born. In a sort of grieving ceremony, the mother floated the corpse of her baby in the Pacific Northwest waters, swimming with her more than 1,000 miles. If that's not moving enough, when the mother was too exhausted to carry her lost calf, other members of the pod took turns pushing the corpse to the surface of the water, allowing the mother to rest until she was able to return to this grieving ritual. It's stunning to learn of a pod of killer whales cooperating like this to contribute to the betterment of their own group, almost as if their compassion and need to care for each other was consciously considered.

I witness this facet of the Social Instinct in a lot of social activists. It's not like they didn't have a choice in their vocation. It's that they have a natural affinity for cooperating with others to help build a better world. On an instinctual level, many activists can intuit what their responses to suffering or injustice should be because it comes naturally to them—their unconscious intelligence at work.

HOLDING THESE FACES OF THE INSTINCTS IN OUR INTELLIGENCE CENTERS

Now, I've not come across anyone who has aligned these triads of Instinctual experiences, or what I'm calling the nine distinct *Faces of the Instincts*, with our Intelligence Centers. But if we don't support the three ways we experience these Instincts in each of our Centers, then we will miss the distinct ways the Instincts are at play within us.

This doesn't mean that those of us in the Body Center (types Eight, Nine, and One) will have a natural affinity toward a certain Face of an Instinct or a particular aspect of how that Instinct shows up. But if you are in your Body Center, then any one of the three Instincts (or any one of the subsequent three Faces within each Instinct) is fundamentally an unconscious attempt to gain or maintain *control*; just as those in the Heart Center (types Two, Three, and Four) will find their Instincts leading them to make *connections*; and those in the Head Center (types Five, Six, and Seven) will observe their Instincts driving their inner *concerns* as they relate to security and stability.

Just as there are two schools of thought in terms of how the Instincts are biologically ordered (Self-Preservation → Social → One-to-One versus Self-Preservation → Sexual → Social), similarly within each of the three Instincts there is an Intelligence Centered ordering of that Instinct's three distinct Faces or expressions:

- The Self-Preservation Instinct for **Regulation** is Body Centered Intelligence for Control.
- The Self-Preservation Instinct for **Preparation** is Heart Intelligence for Connection.
- The Self-Preservation Instinct for **Subsistence** is Head Intelligence for Concern.

- The Sexual Instinct for **Enticement** is Body Intelligence for Control.
- The Sexual Instinct for **Exploration** is Heart Intelligence for Connection.
- The Sexual Instinct for **Opportunity** is Head Intelligence for Concern.
- The Social Instinct for **Dominance** is Body Intelligence for Control.
- The Social Instinct for **Association** is Heart Intelligence for Connection.
- The Social Instinct for **Cooperation** is Head Intelligence for Concern.

APPLYING OUR INSTINCTS FOR SURVIVAL

Our Instincts are *our bodies' somatic impulses for survival.* Our Instincts are how we unconsciously organize our personality around our need to endure in the world. As simple as they may seem, our involuntary reflex drives for self-preservation, sex, and social belonging are intelligently designed through their triadic facets. I am convinced these instinctual motivators organize life around our biological needs for power and control (in our Body Center), affection and esteem (in our Heart Center), and security and survival (in our Head Center).[5]

5. Phileena Heuertz explains how Keating framed the biology of these compulsions as programs for happiness, "Trying to satisfy our desire for power and control, affection and esteem, and security and survival, we grow more and more dissatisfied with our self, God, and others. Father Thomas [Keating] refers to these desires as 'programs for happiness.' He says that these three programs emerge from very basic biological needs. It is a natural part of our human development to see a degree of power and control, affection and esteem, and security and survival. The problem is that, in time, we over identify with one by way of compensating for that basic need which may have gone largely unmet in our childhood. Then our need turns into an unconscious compulsion. We crave its gratification, unable to be happy or content when life fails to deliver the amount of power, affection, or security we desire. Our personality forms around this attachment. An overly emotional reaction to life exposes our vulnerable position." (*Mindful Silence: The Heart of Christian Contemplation*, 16–17.)

Instinct	Attuned Intelligence	Concentration
Self-Preservation Instinct	Body Intelligence	Regulation
Self-Preservation Instinct	Heart Intelligence	Preparation
Self-Preservation Instinct	Head Intelligence	Subsistence
Sexual Instinct	Body Intelligence	Enticement
Sexual Instinct	Heart Intelligence	Exploration
Sexual Instinct	Head Intelligence	Opportunity
Social Instinct	Body Intelligence	Dominance
Social Instinct	Heart Intelligence	Association
Social Instinct	Head Intelligence	Cooperation

But let's be clear, I'm not suggesting that only the Body Types lead with the regulation Face if they are Self-Preservation dominant, the enticement Face if they are Sexual dominant, or the dominance Face if they are Social dominant. What I'm suggesting is that whichever of the Faces from their dominant Instinct they lead with will be an unconscious focus for maintaining or gaining *control*. The same would be true for the Heart types, that whichever of the Faces most expresses their dominant Instinct would be for their desire for *connection*. Finally, the Head types would allow the Face of their Instinct to guide their mental *concern*.

What's exciting about this proposition is that it's one way to find access to aligning our three Centers of Intelligence by allowing for an instinctual intelligence to guide this critical integration.

For example, as someone dominant in type Eight, I am keenly aware of my repressed Heart Center. So, as someone who leads with the Social Instinct, it's actually the association Face of my Social Instinct that helps me connect with my heart.

Intelligence Center	Instinct	Concentration	8–9–1 Focus	2–3–4 Focus	5–6–7 Focus
Body Intelligence	Self-Preservation Instinctual	Regulation	Control	Connection	Concern
Body Intelligence	Sexual Instinctual	Enticement	Control	Connection	Concern
Body Intelligence	Social Instinctual	Dominance	Control	Connection	Concern
Heart Intelligence	Self-Preservation Instinctual	Preparation	Control	Connection	Concern
Heart Intelligence	Sexual Instinctual	Exploration	Control	Connection	Concern
Heart Intelligence	Social Instinctual	Cooperation	Control	Connection	Concern
Head Intelligence	Self-Preservation Instinctual	Subsistence	Control	Connection	Concern
Head Intelligence	Sexual Instinctual	Opportunity	Control	Connection	Concern
Head Intelligence	Social Instinctual	Association	Control	Connection	Concern

Or when my Self-Preservation wife, Phileena, who is dominant in type Two, needs to access her neglected Head Center, it's drawing attention to the subsistence Face of her Instinct.

Again, this validates that aligning and integrating all three Centers of Intelligence is what makes us whole, what makes us human, and what allows for us to have truly spiritual experiences.

Once we've established a basis for how each of the nine Faces of these Instincts expresses itself in three facets of the Intelligences, we then consider how they shape the nine Enneagram types into what are called Subtypes. The Subtypes are crucial to understanding the Enneagram of Personality because they explain the nuances of the different shades of types, what belongs and what is still becoming in each of us.

Subtypes or Instinctual Variants?

As always, there are a couple of versions of how this is explained in the Enneagram community.

Most commonly referenced is the language of Subtypes: the concoction of one of the three Instinct's interplay with an Enneagram Passion to present a personality style.

Of course, the notion of Subtypes is much more than personality. But generally speaking, Subtypes language usually references personality. This produces twenty-seven different renderings of type or the twenty-seven classic Subtypes. There's an implicit understanding that the Subtypes are derivatives of personalities presented by type.

On the other hand, there are others who describe a more complex and nuanced version of this by suggesting there's very little personality at play here. In fact, the Instincts are the basis for what shapes brain chemistry, ultimately suggesting that personality isn't a by-product of consciousness at all. Rather than suggesting this creates twenty-seven Subtypes, the Enneagram Institute goes as far as *stacking* or ordering the dominance of these Instincts into fifty-four Instinctual Variants. In this theory, the ordering of these Instincts matters as much as the dominant Instinct itself because inevitably there will be a third Instinct. Let's refer to the third one as the "back seat" Instinct because it is underutilized, underdeveloped, or neglected.

It's as if our leading Instinct is in the driver's seat of our unconscious, supported by a secondary Instinct in the passenger seat helping to navigate, and the third Instinct is still egoically an infant strapped in a car seat in the back.

Some believe the third or back seat Instinct may actually be the most important one to be aware of. Because it's hidden, it can be vulnerable. The back seat is typically the driver in our personality structure that creates our most pronounced weaknesses or shortcomings. The Instinct in the back seat is where most of us get into trouble.

I can personally attest to this. I self-identify as a Social dominant, Sexual supported, Self-Preservation neglected type Eight which means I lead with the Social Instinct, but I suffer the effects of not having easily brought my Self-Preservation Instinct into awareness. This shows up in my inconsistent sleep patterns, my fluctuations in prioritizing visits to the fitness center, and even in my lack of concern around maintaining a healthy, balanced diet.

Phileena, however, is a Self-Preservation, Sexual, Social type Two who does an incredible job of ensuring she lives a mindful, healthy lifestyle. But her Social back seat Instinct catches up to her in the ways she fails to recognize her impact on a group or the needs of the groups she's been a part of. Her awareness of this is outstanding and she's doing considerable work to grow in this area by frequently articulating, "I need to bring my Social Instinct into play by . . .," and then showing up for her community and in her friendships.

While the Instinct in the back seat may never become the dominant driver in our unconscious, we can develop this Instinct. We *can* make deliberate efforts to bring it into awareness and practice greater governance of this back seat Instinct.

I should also note that in all the Enneagram materials on relationships, especially material that suggests which types may be most or least compatible with other types, I've not seen much work around how the Instincts impact relationships. On a personal note, I can say that when your dominant Instinct mirrors the backseat Instinct of your partner, this may provide some of the most noticeable challenges in relationships. It's much easier to negotiate once it's been recognized for what it is.

But back to the word choice of Subtypes versus Instinctual Variants. Though these two schools of thought seem to have differentiated starting points, it appears they lead to a similar conclusion: that our principal Instinct produces primary features in our Enneagram type's personality.

What Are the Countertypes?

Not to complicate this further, but to offer some clarification, it's important to be aware of the anomaly personality style within the set of three Subtypes of each of the Enneagram's primary types. Claudio Naranjo called these irregular variances the *Countertypes*. They're called Countertypes because the intelligence of the Instinct makes a counter move against the type's Passion, almost as if the Instinct considers the Enneagram Passion as something that can't or shouldn't be permissible.

The Countertypes are the most commonly misunderstood Subtypes, and if you happen to be the Countertype of your Enneagram type then it may have taken more effort to determine what your dominant type is.

Another way to understand this might be recognizing the Countertypes as the Subtypes that generally lead with the Face of their Instinct that's supported by their *repressed* Intelligence Center.

For example, Phileena is the Countertype Two, that is, the

Self-Preservation Two. This is the Two whose drive for self-care supersedes their type's desire to care for others. And so, Self-Preservation Twos suffer an inner conflict of how to prioritize the expression of their nurturing concern. Should they nurture themselves or others first?

Let's consider these brief descriptions for each of the twenty-seven Subtypes (noting the Countertypes *italicized*):

Claudio Naranjo's Names for the 27 Subtypes

	Self-Preservation	Sexual	Social
Type One	Worry	*Zeal*	Non-Adaptability
Type Two	*Privilege*	Aggression	Ambition
Type Three	*Security*	Femininity/Masculinity	Prestige
Type Four	*Tenacity*	Competition	Shame
Type Five	Castle	*Confidence*	Totem
Type Six	Warmth	*Strength*	Duty
Type Seven	Keepers of the Castle	Fascination	*Sacrifice*
Type Eight	Survival	Possession	*Solidarity*
Type Nine	Appetite	Union	*Participation*

Self-Preservation One

This is the most perfect of the perfectionists, though their self-perception is that they are the most fundamentally flawed. They present as the most compassionate of the Ones because of their ability to control and repress

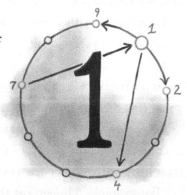

the externalized expressions of their anger. But inwardly, they are incredibly hard on themselves and attuned to the presence of their anger. All this managing of their inner lives is a subconscious way of structuring their controlled presence. But it also drums up a bit of frustrated unrest that fuels their inner unease. For this reason, it's common to mistype as a Six or sometimes a Self-Preservation Three. This explains why they were named "Worry" by Naranjo and "Anxiety" by Ichazo.

Sexual One (the Countertype)

This One Subtype projects their inner drive for perfection onto those closest to them, and their drive to fix others on the external world. This is where the name "Reformer" most aptly applies to the Ones. Of the three One Subtypes, Sexual Ones are the most assertive and the most comfortable allowing their anger to come out. Naranjo called this Subtype "Zeal" due to their determination to facilitate alignment with their standard of goodness. Perhaps the most "frustrated idealist" of the Ones, their notions of how the world should be fires the intensity of their ire and the strength of their energy. They will sometimes mistype as an Eight.

Social One

Social Ones best embody their vision of excellence through deeply held convictions. They alone know the correct way to heal the world. Their commitment to the highest of standards can be inspiring, but at times also intimidating. Driven and on the move, they can self-isolate, believing their image for what they've idealized is wasted on everyone else. This may lead to loneliness, which is why they sometimes may resemble a Five.

Self-Preservation Two (the Countertype)

Can you imagine a Two who doesn't put everyone else's needs first but tends to their own desire for self-care? The subtlety here is that this Countertype Two finds ways of utilizing others to get their needs met. People willingly oblige Self-Preservation Twos because there's a childlike innocence they present that

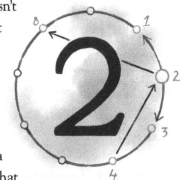

draws people toward them. Once they've won someone over, their natural ability to care for and nurture those closest to them can become a subconscious attempt to get their own needs met. This may be experienced as a kind of entitlement, a "trade" of sorts, presuming that their sacrifices for others will be reciprocated. When this presumption that others also instinctively know how to care for the Self-Preservation Two is exposed, they turn inward and suffer as "victims." Though still winsome and caring in relationships, of all Twos they are the most hesitant to fully open their hearts. They may mistype as a Four or a Self-Preservation Six.

Sexual Two

Captivating and enticing, they use their magnetic presence to attract whomever they desire attention from. Their enchanting passion projects an attractive self-confidence that is both determined and strong-willed. They will get what they want one way or another through their need for committed relationships. This often leads to making thoughtful sacrifices to make their bonds with others as healthy as possible. Sexual Twos are the most persuasive of all the Twos, sometimes coming across as a little too intrusive in relationships. They sometimes mistype as a Sexual Four.

Social Two

Naranjo called the Social Two "Ambition," due to the strength of their presence and their determination to ensure their accomplishments have some value to society, their community, or their most important relationships. They are more in their heads than other Twos, strategic and calculated about making their presence known in influential networks. Though less self-effacing than other Twos, they still appeal to subtlety to make an impact. This often takes place through the ways they support the groups or people they value, or the ways they broker connections to strengthen the causes they're most concerned about. Highly attuned to their environment, Social Twos know how to fine-tune their communication skills in efforts to bolster the image they carefully curate—an inspiring person aligned with important efforts. They may mistype as a Social Eight.

Self-Preservation Three (the Countertype)

Self-Preservation Threes are in-spiring through their hard work ethic, their devotion to being a reliable provider for those who depend on them, and their faithfulness to the service of their obligations. These Threes are the most self-deprecating about their own image consciousness, downplay-

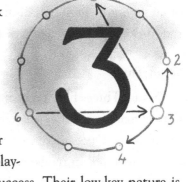

ing their focused efficiency and success. Their low-key nature is still rooted in their Passion of deceit, understating their own need for gratitude for all the ways they support those in their communities. Boundaries are important for them to cultivate, ensuring they don't work too hard or overdo the good they commit to. They are among the most reliable of all Enneagram Types, striving for excellence in all their endeavors. They may mistype as a Six or a Self-Preservation One.

Sexual Three

Image becomes overly important to Sexual Threes, who are driven by their subconscious efforts to *add* value to their work and in their relationships as an attempt to *earn* value. This allows these Threes to support others through mentoring, by championing others' work, and investing in the teams they're a part of. At times, they downplay the crucial roles they exercise in mentoring, their relationships, or their communities. Effortlessly charming, being "desirable" is a quiet driver and often is part of the natural charisma of the Sexual Three. They have a hidden or quiet competitive nature that is contagious. As they self-improve and self-perfect, they desire for those around them to join this quest. Their need for attention is often indirect, sometimes mistaken as shyness. Though viewed as coy and demure, Sexual Threes present with the most positive outlook or maintain the most optimism of the Three Subtypes. Sometimes they mistype as a Seven or a Sexual Two.

Social Three

Social Threes have no qualms about being the center of attention. In many cases, they actively pursue becoming the focus of their social groups. Once recognized, they internalize what is important to their community and embody what's valued by the group. It's a value for them to be seen as successful and significant. This is why Naranjo called the Social Three "Prestige." Much of their behind-the-scenes work is spent building a notable reputation by achieving professional or communal status; name-dropping or highlighting their impressive affiliations; assuming positions of leadership; and stretching the reach of their influence. Often overly confident, they are careful not to show their vulnerabilities and generally don't do well with critique. Perhaps the most competitive and aggressive of the Three Subtypes, they still strive for meaning through approval, primarily focusing on social standing as validation. Their highly skilled social intelligence allows them to be compelling communicators. They may mistype as a Seven.

Self-Preservation Four (the Countertype)

Quietly suffering their inner pain, Self-Preservation Fours hide their anguish through denial of the ways they hurt. They outwardly present with positivity and curiosity. By downplaying the spectrum of aches felt in their hearts, Self-Preservation Fours come to believe the real value in their emotional agony 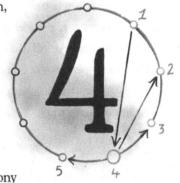 is their uncomplaining, enduring resilience. This is supported by their active lives, often driven through their inquisitive and tenacious efforts to help others. Like all Fours, they can still be incredibly sensitive, empathetic, and delicate. Exploring the contours of their feelings seems to be an unmerited extravagance, so they set high standards for themselves and think that compliance to these standards causes them to be more deserving of this luxury. Of all the Four Subtypes they can be the most private, but they are not the most withdrawn in their intimate relationships. They frequently mistype as a Two, Three, or Seven.

Sexual Four

Perhaps the most aggressive and intense of the Four Subtypes (in fact, of all twenty-seven Subtypes), Sexual Fours learn to express their needs in ways that may come across as overly demanding or indirectly punitive. They possess a strong competitive edge that drives them to ensure their needs will be satisfied, but this is often at their own expense. This only leads to isolation because others feel taken advantage of, pushed out of the Sexual Four's "inner circle," or forced to endure the same suffering the Sexual Four suffers. Typically very articulate and expressive, they will externalize their shame or anger without qualms. Shame and shamelessness are central themes behind which they hide their true feelings, but underneath it all is a tragic sense of deficiency. These feelings of inadequacy can be projected and frequently misunderstood as arrogance, snobbishness, or pomposity.

Their extreme range of emotional attunement allows for brilliance in creativity, curating aesthetics, and freedom, which ultimately is of utmost importance to them. They can mistype as an Eight.

Social Four

Astonishingly in touch with their feelings, the Social Four is the most sensitive of all Four Subtypes, conceivably suffering more than any other Enneagram Subtype. They are prone to internalizing an experience of victimization, blaming themselves for deep feelings of emotional disfigurement, of not fitting in or blaming themselves for why they feel they don't belong (even in their most intimate relationship). They suffer a hypersensitivity to their tragic and unreasonable experiences of inferiority. Presenting as shy or coy, they experience a degree of shame when expressing their desires or needs. So, if or when their needs go unmet, it just fuels their inner sense of being marginalized or unincluded in their social groups. Their intimate bond to their own anguish may lead them to assume a martyr-esque role in their relationships, pushing them deeper into their own emotional misery, which they believe is necessary for them to endure to become worthy of the love they desire.

Self-Preservation Five

No other Subtype is more withdrawn than Self-Preservation Fives, who fiercely protect their boundaries. They are the least emotionally expressive of all twenty-seven Subtypes. They are suspicious of extremes, though they themselves vacillate between austere minimalism or premeditated collecting and hoarding (usually of very practical items or experiences). Their utilitarianism typically is a mental attempt to control their deeply dug borders and boundaries. This keeps most people out so as not to be distracted from ensuring their basic needs are sufficiently met. Incredibly private, they may tend toward classic introversion, coming across as guarded, reluctant, or mistrustful of others' attempts to make personal connections with them. Their need for solitude minimizes disruptions to their routines by keeping people at a calculated distance.

Sexual Five (the Countertype)

Perpetually on the quest for deep connection, Sexual Fives have an intense need for tangible closeness to their idealized romantic partner or mental pursuit. Their carefully regulated eccentricity is largely hidden, seemingly secretive, but it is a passionate force of cerebral instigation connecting them to their emotional states. They can be determined, focused, and resolutely purposeful in their self-protective measures. Though still reserved like all Fives, the vibrancy of their inner landscapes is what makes them more sensitive than other Five Subtypes and one of the most mysterious of all Enneagram Subtypes. Surprisingly delicate and easily disappointed, they are attuned to rejection, often avoiding becoming dependent on others.

Social Five

If social introversion was an Enneagram Subtype, then the Social Five would utterly embody the experience of needing practical connection through affiliations while simultaneously insisting on boundaried seclusion. Holding these two desires in tension is a nuanced irony of their subtle brilliance. With an uncanny ability to discern life's most pressing and fundamental questions, they find meaning by offering solutions and pathways. They are remarkable problem solvers and generous with the outcomes of their analysis and research. Perhaps best exemplified through the technology of social media (a means of maintaining a controlled distance, at times even voyeuristic, in relationships that don't require actual time spent together), their desire for belonging is often privately expressed through observation. Transcendentalists at heart, they idealize alignment with their values as the only true way to live.

Self-Preservation Six

Prone to self-doubt, Self-Preservation Sixes lean into those closest to them for assurance. Their immediate holding environment needs to be a sanctuary where they can voice and vent their concerns, insecurities, and apprehensions. The perception of their indecision is one of the subconscious methods they appeal to in order to ensure that their most basic needs are met and their private lives are braced against intrusion. Like all Six Subtypes, they attempt to earn their desire for stability through doubling down on their fears. These fears lead to even more internalizing of their self-doubt, causing the Self-Preservation Six to be the most hesitant of them all. Affectionate, dependable, and steady in their unwavering support for those they love, they protect their social connections as an attempt to keep themselves out of harm's way. Sometimes Self-Preservation Sixes mistype as a Self-Preservation Two.

Sexual Six (the Countertype)

Prior to the relatively recent popularization of the Subtypes, the Sexual Six had been confused as the anomaly or deviation of the Enneagram's nine types, suggesting that the Six was the only type that had two "faces" or ways of expressing: phobic (what is generally considered the typical Six) and counter-phobic (what we now know to be the Sexual Six). The Sexual Six is a moving force to be reckoned with, asserting themselves and pressing into the very things that trigger their inner alarms and awaken their concealed concerns. Like all Sixes, fear still motivates much of how they relate to their environments, but they present stronger than they perceive themselves to be. They actually channel their unease into a substitute for courage, because a lingering edge of doubt still persists. Strong willed, often intimidating, and rebellious, the Sexual Six may be an instigator of mutiny as a means of overthrowing any threat to their need for security. Frequently they mistype as an Eight.

Social Six

Their adherence to group convictions, guidelines, or beliefs fortifies the inner insecurities of Social Sixes and orients their sense of belonging. More than the other Six Subtypes they are the attendants and defenders of their community's ideals, building consensus around their near-legalistic devotion to these shared principles. They maintain incredibly high standards and seek to enforce those standards to secure strength in groups. Unhindered to assume leadership roles, they serve as loyal guardians to shared values through a strong sense of efficient duty. They sometimes mistype as a One or Three.

Self-Preservation Seven

Pursuant of interior conservation, the Self-Preservation Seven forms functional coalitions to allay the typical restlessness that keeps all Sevens on the move. Often mistaken to be materialistic, Self-Preservation Sevens don't want to be trapped even in their own need for security. Their lavishness or gener-

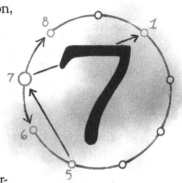

osity is an externalizing of their relationship with freedom. This may take on behaviors that appear to be over-celebratory of the mundane, untiring in their active expression, or, in extreme cases, hedonistic. Their natural ability to broker and facilitate connections may become an excessive pathway to safeguard what they fear they need most but may perpetually be unattainable. Full of positive energy and on the go, the Self-Preservation Seven's charm holds relationships together.

Sexual Seven

Could there be a more hope-filled and enthusiastic person than the Sexual Seven? That's highly doubtful since their idyllic view of reality tends toward novelty, innovation, and creativity. Versatile, flexible, and adaptable, they chase every dream within their grasp, exploring the most fascinating prospects of every possibility that piques their curiosity. Sometimes their naïve optimism gets them in trouble. But even their most desolate challenges are pregnant with favorable possibilities. Perpetual explorers and natural dreamers, the Sexual Sevens take everyone on extravagant escapades planned to provide risky and gratifying experiences.

Social Seven (the Countertype)

Turning their idealism into innocence, Social Sevens intentionally moderate their drive and desire for more, regulating this energy into a selflessness and thoughtfulness for others. Full of vision and imagination, they turn their creativity into acts of service, skillfully finding ways to help those closest to them. Like all Sevens, there is still a lifelong struggle with the fear of missing out, but Social Sevens even deny the possibility of exciting opportunities by repressing any self-centered tendency to distract themselves from their commitments (which they are strongly compelled to follow through on). More than the other Seven Subtypes, their long-view and long-term thinking helps them attain their audacious goals. Often abstemious and austere, their self-sacrificial generosity is inspiring. Yet they still require gratitude and recognition for all the good they foster in their communities. Sometimes they mistype as a Two.

Self-Preservation Eight

Sometimes mistaken as cold and distant, the Self-Preservation Eight's need for self-determination leads to intolerance for any imposition on their autonomy. Powerful, strong, direct, and hardworking, they are unintentionally intimidating. They have no reservations and skip the jargon, appealing to direct and effective communication tactics to get what they want. Excessive and demanding, they ensure that all their physical, mental, and emotional survival needs are ultimately met, which can cast them in a selfish light to those who don't understand their fundamental need for gratification.

Sexual Eight

Of all Enneagram types, the Sexual Eight is the most intense and volatile, possessing some of the biggest energy of all character structures. Their expansiveness takes over whatever environment they inhabit, their mood imposes itself on everyone around them, and their force of presence at times seems unstoppable. Obstinate and resistant to any attempt to muffle their obsessive drive, they provoke and fight back to entrench their dominance. They are the most rebellious, disruptive, and impulsive of the Eight Subtypes. Their brilliance lies in their fierce commitment to defend the causes or persons they feel may be exploited or taken advantage of. The strength of their impassioned assertations is often mistaken as being overly emotional. But like all Eights, they are still disconnected from the vulnerability in their own hearts. They can mistype as Sexual Four or Sexual Six.

Social Eight (the Countertype)

Moving against resistances that keep people disconnected is the countermove for the Social Eight, who Naranjo described as "Solidarity." The incongruence with other Eight Subtypes is seen in their relaxed, yet still driven, nature. They are highly motivated by service, dampening their aggression by channeling it into socially concerned efforts. This sometimes is a subtle projection of their attempt to protect their inner child and refrain from showing vulnerability. Their cause-driven disposition may also be a subconscious attempt to make sense of power dynamics, which they are highly attuned to. Relationships, though not always intimate, are of the utmost importance because of the social good they hope to foster. Sometimes they mistype as Sevens or Twos.

Self-Preservation Nine

With a steady focus on ensuring that their basic needs are met, Self-Preservation Nines often get lost in the essentials of fueling their reliable, calm, and low-key mentality. Inclined to retreat to their homes, they may fritter and fiddle away by overfocusing on the basics (specifically those things that

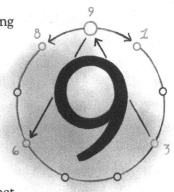

bring them the most pleasure) while procrastinating on life's more demanding responsibilities. In relationships, they may lose themselves in others, forgetting themselves and fusing their sense of self with their partner or community members. Their craving to satisfy their own needs (Naranjo described this as "Appetite") can be an ironic distraction from their tendency to self-forget and self-deny life's more fundamental gifts.

Sexual Nine

Losing themselves in others, Sexual Nines determine that what is missing within them can be discovered within another. This can lead to passive fusion in their most significant friendships or with a partner. Daydreaming and musing about their own sacrifices in relationships keeps them from finding their passions. Their receptivity to others has a subtle irresistibility and allows for effortless connections to happen. Relationships are key to their sense of self, so they often find it difficult to be alone. They also need to be aware of their own needs for boundaries. Affable, considerate, and tender, they are receptive and can be deeply spiritual beings who are in touch with their environments, especially nature. They may mistype as a Two.

Social Nine (the Countertype)

Driven to arbitrate harmony and social good, Social Nines compulsively work long and hard on the critical issues that are most paramount to their group's flourishing. Their need to unselfishly serve their group's cause is the sphere of life where they most commonly merge with the identity of others, putting participation and cooperation before their own need to admit their sense of self. Of all Nine Subtypes, they express the most levity and allow themselves occasional bursts of playfulness. Their unimpeded push to serve others, build consensus, mediate and broker divisions, and ensure inclusion often causes them to mistype as Ones or Threes. They may be the most difficult of the twenty-seven Subtypes to self-identify.

CONCLUSION

With these brief Subtype descriptions in hand, I'd recommend picking up a copy of Beatrice Chestnut's classic work *The Complete Enneagram* to go deeper and further. But don't forget, even Bea's thick descriptions of the twenty-seven Subtypes don't describe the fifty-four Instinctual Variants when all three Instincts are stacked. And even the Enneagram Institute's descriptions of the fifty-four Instinctual Variants don't offer explanations of how those fifty-four type renders change when adding a wing, which is how we find the 108 Enneagram types.

There are some people out there who think you don't really *know* your type until you've identified your Subtype or Instinctual Variant. I'm not so adamant as to go that far, but I will say that as we gain a new and compassionate understanding of ourselves in relationship to Enneagram types, we begin to become aware of the self-made and self-aggravated obstacles and challenges to the belonging we most long for. Here we use the Enneagram to make a deep dive into understanding our instinctual compulsions and addictive patterns. Left unchecked, these compulsions and patterns create our most serious personal, mental, emotional, spiritual, and communal obstacles to belonging.

And that's why this is important. If the nine Enneagram types are more than enough for you, there's plenty tucked away inside each unique type structure to begin tending to all that is beautiful and all that is forgotten in our human condition. If the twenty-seven Subtypes start to bring that human condition into compassionate focus, then you've taken another step toward clarity and acceptance of what makes you tick. But if the fifty-four Instinctual Variants bring these nine types under the microscope of introspection, then you've taken a leap toward what will be required to face inside yourself so that you can continue on your journey of radical self-acceptance for compassionate living.

Conclusion: Perfectly Imperfect

The Beauty of Being Human

S how me a dragon."
I frequently think about little Janae's prayer. Half the time the story still cracks me up. The rest of the time there's something about it that burrows deep into my soul and touches on a hope, a yearning to experience something buried inside me that's been hidden for a long, long time.

Unlike many dragons pictured in childhood stories, my favorite childhood dragon wasn't a scary monster that needed to be slayed. Rather, it was a sweet old companion to a little boy who was afraid of growing up.

In the spring of 1959, Lenny Lipton, still a teenager at Cornell University, spent an evening in the college library nostalgically musing over children's literature. He came across a poem about a dragon which he couldn't get off his mind. From the library he walked over to a buddy's apartment and let himself in. Lenny, inspired by that book of children's poetry, sat down at a typewriter and wrote a poem about a dragon named Puff.

Over the years, there's been quite a bit of controversy suggesting "Puff the Magic Dragon" is actually a reference to marijuana use, but Lenny adamantly denies all that (even still, the song has become an unofficially adopted anthem of stoners). In multiple interviews Lenny has emphatically stated that the poem is about the loss of childhood. As a university freshman he came to the painful realization that he needed to grow up—whether he was ready to or not. The poem is about the difficulties of becoming an adult, the hardships of leaving our childhood innocence behind.

That spring evening after penning his poem about a magic dragon, Lenny left his finished poem in the typewriter. As it turns out, the typewriter belonged to Peter Yarrow, an American folksinger who would later join a group called Peter, Paul, and Mary. They put Lenny's poem to music and in 1963 released the recording of this classic folk song.

As a little kid, I remember hearing that song softly playing on the radio and watching a feature-length cartoon about Puff in the late 1970s. It tells the story of a young boy named Jackie and his magical companion, a dragon called Puff. Puff lived by the sea in a mythical land called Honah Lee. Jackie and Puff would play together, sail the sea facing off with pirates—the best of friends whom it seemed nothing would ever separate.

But as the song goes, the day came when little Jackie Paper

stopped visiting Puff. Aching the loss of his companion, Puff's bravery dried up as he suffered the loss of his dear friend.

Back then and similarly today, that cartoon and song continue to break my heart, even when I don't always fully comprehend what it portrays.

You see, if Puff is a symbol of our unsophisticated purity, our inner child, or our deepest and realest selves, then why do we feel compelled to slay that dragon, or lose our innocence? Growing up doesn't mean leaving our Essence behind. But too often we believe that to become an adult we have to give up the wonder and innocence of our childhood, so we tragically end up parking the best of ourselves in our shadows. Just like Jackie Paper's dragon Puff, whose head hung low in sorrow and whose grief was so severe that his scales fell off, he eventually retreated to a cave to suffer his heartache alone.

Our Enneagram type—along with its fragmented components including our Holy Idea, Fixation, Virtue, and Passion—has to fill the emptiness of our loss of innocence. Our type takes over for our inner child when our ego determines it is time to "grow up." But actually, we're not growing up; we're merely falling asleep, stuck in a tragic state of arrested development. We're making unfortunate trade-offs that lead to a kind of forgetfulness of our truest selves. We're diminishing the power of our inner child and its potential to become a mighty dragon—not a monster, but a messenger of truth and freedom.

The truth our inner dragon has always told us, even when we've not listened, is we're perfect just as we are. Every bit of us belongs. And until we can fall into the grace of this affirmation, we'll continue to allow the fragments of our identity to lay claim to the whole of who we think we are. Until every aspect of who we are belongs, including the parts we find the most offensive or least desirable, then no part of ourselves can truly belong.

This is what it means to be human. To be seen and known. To be present to the good, the bad, and the ugly, thereby extending compassion and acceptance. By being present to it all, we open a portal for the good, true, and beautiful to really shine. We are perfectly imperfect. Instead of attempting to distance ourselves from the less attractive parts or the attractive parts that we have trouble believing are really us, we can boldly enter our shadowy caves, make peace with what we've otherwise abandoned, and discover the treasure hidden there. This is the process of integrating the whole of who we are and finding wholeness as a new way of being.

Belonging is a simple return, a remembering, a sacred journey back to our original innocence. Beyond type, beyond personality, belonging is a homecoming to our Essence.

Over the years, I've often said the Enneagram is a compassionate sketch of possibilities, showing us who we can become if we commit to the difficult soul work of learning to say "yes" to ourselves and our soul's created purpose. Today, I understand the Enneagram not as a teaching bursting with potential for who we might become but a gentle reminder of who we've always perfectly been. And here's the truth: it takes radical self-acceptance for us to live compassionately in the world, and that's the foundation for our collective belonging.

Radical compassion toward our self changes us. And when we are changed, the world is changed. When we can accept all that we are—even the parts that are more difficult to accept—we uncover a capacity to do the same for others. We find ourselves more aligned with love within, thereby becoming a source of love for others. When I accept all that I am, I can accept all that you are. In this posture of radical compassion, we become a powerful force of love in the world.

Here it's then possible to stand in line with all those who have gone before us in creating a new us—the beloved community where there's room for everyone just as we are. A community that we all long for, a community where everyone belongs.

Bibliography: Cited *and* Recommended Resources

Almaas, A. H. *Facets of Unity: The Enneagram of Holy Ideas.* Boston: Shambhala Publications, 1998.

Bakhtiar, Laleh. *The Sufi Enneagram: Sign of the Presence of God (Wajhullah): The Secrets of the Symbol Unveiled.* Chicago: Institute of Traditional Psychology, 2013.

Bartlett, Carolyn. *The Enneagram Field Guide: Notes on Using the Enneagram in Counseling, Therapy and Personal Growth.* Fort Collins, CO: Nine Gates, 2003.

Bennett, J. G. *Enneagram Studies.* Newburyport, MA: Red Wheel Weiser, 1983.

Blake, A.G.E. *The Intelligent Enneagram.* Boston, MA: Shambhala Publications, Inc., 1996.

Brown, Brené. *Braving the Wilderness: The Quest for True Belonging and the Courage to Stand Alone.* New York: Random House, 2017.

————. *Daring Greatly: How the Courage to Be Vulnerable Transforms the Way We Live, Love, Parent, and Lead.* New York: Avery, an imprint of Penguin Random House, 2012.

Calhoun, Adele, Doug Calhoun, Clare Loughrige, and Scott Loughrige. *Spiritual Rhythms for the Enneagram: A Handbook for Harmony and Transformation.* Downers Grove, IL: InterVarsity Press, 2019.

Chabreuil, Fabien and Patricia Chabreuil. "Passion and Counterpassion." *Enneagram Monthly,* October 2002, no. 87, 1, 21–22.

Chestnut, Beatrice. *The Enneagram System's 27 Personality Subtypes.* Self-published.

————. *The Nine Types of Leadership: Mastering the Art of People in the 21st Century Workplace.* Post Hill Press, 2017.

Comer, Kim (editor). *Wisdom of the Sadhu: Teachings of Sundar Singh.* Farmington, PA: Plough Publishing House, 2000.

Dostoyevsky, Fyodor. *Winter Notes on Summer Impressions*. Translated by David Patterson. Evanston, IL: Northwestern University Press, 1988.

Fernández Christlieb, Fátima. *Where on Earth Did the Enneagram Come From?* Ciudad de México: Editorial Pax México, 2016.

Goldberg, Michael J. "The Lines Are the Basic Building Blocks of the Enneagram, Not the Points." *IEA Ninepoints* online, October 1, 2014, https://ieaninepoints.com/2014/10/01/the-lines-are-the-basic-building-blocks-of-the-enneagram-not-the-points-by-michael-goldberg/.

—. *The Nine Ways of Working: How to Use the Enneagram to Discover Your Natural Strengths and Work More Effectively*. Philadelphia, PA: Da Capo Press a member of the Perseus Book Group, 1999.

—. "Inside the Enneagram Wars." *LA Weekly*, October 15–21, 1993, pp. 16–26.

—. *Travels with Odysseus: Uncommon Wisdom from Homer's Odyssey*. Tempe, AZ: Circe's Island Press, 2005.

Gurdjieff, G. I. *Meetings with Remarkable Men*. Mansfield Center, CT: Martino Publishing, 2010.

Heuertz, Christopher L. *The Sacred Enneagram: Finding Your Unique Path to Spiritual Growth*. Grand Rapids, MI: Zondervan, 2017.

Heuertz, Christopher L., with Estee Zandee. *The Sacred Enneagram Workbook: Finding Your Unique Path to Spiritual Growth*. Grand Rapids, MI: Zondervan, 2019.

—. *The Enneagram of Belonging Workbook: Mapping Your Compassionate Journey of Self-Acceptance*. Grand Rapids, MI: Zondervan, 2020.

Christopher L. Heuertz. "Interview with Richard Rohr." *Enneagram Mapmakers Podcast: Charting the Unexplored Interior Landscape of the Ego*. Podcast audio, March 24, 2020. http://chrisheuertz.com/podcast/enneagrammapmakers-interview-with-richardrohr.

—. "Interview with Marion Gilbert." *Enneagram Mapmakers Podcast: Charting the Unexplored Interior Landscape of the Ego*. Podcast audio, March 31, 2020. http://chrisheuertz.com/podcast/enneagrammapmakers-interview-with-mariongilbert.

—. "Interview with Sandra Maitri." *Enneagram Mapmakers Podcast: Charting the Unexplored Interior Landscape of the Ego*. Podcast audio, April 7, 2020. http://chrisheuertz.com/podcast/enneagrammapmakers-interview-with-sandramaitri.

—. "Interview with Ginger Lapid-Bogda." *Enneagram Mapmakers Podcast: Charting the Unexplored Interior Landscape of the Ego*. Podcast audio, April 14, 2020. http://chrisheuertz.com/podcast/enneagrammapmakers-interview-with-gingerlapidbogda.

—————— . "Interview with Jerry Wagner." *Enneagram Mapmakers Podcast: Charting the Unexplored Interior Landscape of the Ego.* Podcast audio, April 21, 2020. http://chrisheuertz.com/podcast/enneagrammap makers-interview-with-jerrywagner.

—————— . "Interview with Helen Palmer." *Enneagram Mapmakers Podcast: Charting the Unexplored Interior Landscape of the Ego.* Podcast audio, April 28, 2020. http://chrisheuertz.com/podcast/enneagrammap makers-interview-with-helenpalmer.

—————— . "Interview with Michael Goldberg." *Enneagram Mapmakers Podcast: Charting the Unexplored Interior Landscape of the Ego.* Podcast audio, May 5, 2020. http://chrisheuertz.com/podcast/enneagrammap makers-interview-with-michaelgoldberg.

—————— . "Interview with Jack Labanauskas." *Enneagram Mapmakers Podcast: Charting the Unexplored Interior Landscape of the Ego.* Podcast audio, May 12, 2020. http://chrisheuertz.com/podcast/enneagrammap makers-interview-with-jacklabanauskas.

—————— . "Interview with Beatrice Chestnut." *Enneagram Mapmakers Podcast: Charting the Unexplored Interior Landscape of the Ego.* Podcast audio, May 19, 2020. http://chrisheuertz.com/podcast/enneagrammap makers-interview-with-beatricechestnut.

—————— . "Interview with Russ Hudson." *Enneagram Mapmakers Podcast: Charting the Unexplored Interior Landscape of the Ego.* Podcast audio, May 26, 2020. http://chrisheuertz.com/podcast/enneagrammap makers-interview-with-russhudson.

Heuertz, Phileena. *Mindful Silence: The Heart of Christian Contemplation.* Downers Grove, IL: InterVarsity Press, 2018.

Hisham, Shaykh Muhammad. *The Naqshbandi Sufi Way: History and Guidebook of the Saints of the Golden Chain.* Chicago, IL: Kazi Publications, Inc., 1995.

Hurley, Kathleen, and Theodore Dobson. *My Best Self: Using the Enneagram to Free the Soul.* New York: HarperOne, 1993.

Ichazo, Óscar. *Between Metaphysics and Protoanalysis: A Theory for Analyzing the Human Psyche.* New York: Arica Institute Press, 1982.

——————. *The Human Process for Enlightenment and Freedom.* New York: Arica Institute Press, 1972.

——————. *Interviews with Oscar Ichazo.* New York: Arica Institute Press, 1982.

——————. *Letters to the School.* New York: Arica Institute Press, 1988.

Keating, Thomas. *The Human Condition.* New York: Paulist Press, 1999.

Keen, Sam. "'We Have No Desire to Strengthen the Ego or Make It Happy.' A Conversation about Ego Destruction with Óscar Ichazo." *Psychology Today,* July 1973, 64–65.

Labanauskas, Jack, and Antonio Barbato. "Inner Polarities: The Structure of Passion." *Enneagram Monthly* (March 2000, issue 59), 1, 18–20.

———. "Inner Polarities: The Structure of Passion (Part 2)." *Enneagram Monthly* (April 2000, issue 60), 8–9.

Labanauskas, Jack, and Andrea Isaacs. "Conversation with Don Riso." *Enneagram Monthly* 2, no. 9 (September 1996, issue 19), 1, 20–22.

Lapid-Bogda, Ginger. *The Art of Typing: Powerful Tools for Enneagram Typing.* Santa Monica, CA: The Enneagram in Business Press, 2018.

———. *Bringing Out the Best in Yourself at Work: How to Use the Enneagram System for Success.* New York: McGraw-Hill Education, 2004.

———. "Enneagram Theory: Soul Child; Maybe Not; Disowned Childlike Self; Perhaps." *The Enneagram in Business* online, December 12, 2010. https://theenneagraminbusiness.com/theory/enneagram-theory-soul-child-maybe-not-disowned-childlike-self-perhaps/.

MacLeod, Mike. "The Sufi Connection." *Enneagram Monthly* 1, no. 8 (October 1995), 8.

Maitri, Sandra. *The Enneagram of Passions and Virtues: Finding the Way Home.* New York: Penguin, 2005.

———. *The Spiritual Dimension of the Enneagram.* New York: Penguin Putnam, 2000.

Myers, Dick. "The Worlds of Óscar Ichazo." *The Gurdjieff Journal* 16, no. 61, 3–6, 16–21.

Naranjo, Claudio. "A Report to the 'First International Enneagram Conference' at Stanford University, 1994 [Transcript of the Video-taped Presentation]." *Enneagram Monthly* 2, no. 2 (February 1996), 1, 16–17.

———. *Character and Neurosis: An Integrative View.* Nevada City, CA: Gateways/IDHHB Publishers, 1994.

———. *Ennea-Type Structures: Self-Analysis for the Seeker.* Nevada City, CA: Gateways Books and Tapes, 1990.

———. *The Enneagram of Society: Healing the Soul to Heal the World.* Translated by Paul Barnes. Nevada City, CA: Gateways Books and Tapes, 2004.

O'Neal, Ryan. "'One' & The Enneagram." *The Sleeping at Last Podcast.* Podcast audio, October 9, 2017. https://sleepingatlast.podbean.com/e/episode-4-one-the-enneagram/.

———. "'Two' & The Enneagram." *The Sleeping at Last Podcast.* Podcast audio, November 17, 2017. https://sleepingatlast.podbean.com/e/episode-6-two-the-enneagram/.

———. "'Three' & The Enneagram." *The Sleeping at Last Podcast.* Podcast audio, February 9, 2018. https://sleepingatlast.podbean.com/e/episode-10-three-the-enneagram/.

————. "'Four' & The Enneagram." *The Sleeping at Last Podcast.* Podcast audio, April 13, 2018. https://sleepingatlast.podbean.com/e/episode-12-four-the-enneagram/.

————. "'Five' & The Enneagram." *The Sleeping at Last Podcast.* Podcast audio, June 8, 2018. https://sleepingatlast.podbean.com/e/episode-13-five-the-enneagram/.

————. "'Six' & The Enneagram." *The Sleeping at Last Podcast.* Podcast audio, August 3, 2018. https://sleepingatlast.podbean.com/e/episode-15-six-the-enneagram/.

————. "'Seven' & The Enneagram." *The Sleeping at Last Podcast.* Podcast audio, October 12, 2018. https://sleepingatlast.podbean.com/e/episode-16-seven-the-enneagram/.

————. "'Eight' & The Enneagram." *The Sleeping at Last Podcast.* Podcast audio, February 15, 2019. https://sleepingatlast.podbean.com/e/episode-17-eight-the-enneagram/.

————. "'Nine' & The Enneagram." *The Sleeping at Last Podcast.* Podcast audio, June 7, 2019. https://sleepingatlast.podbean.com/e/episode-18-nine-the-enneagram/.

Ouspensky, P. D. *In Search for the Miraculous.* New York: Harcourt, 1949.

Palmer, Helen. *The Enneagram in Love and Work.* New York: HarperOne, 1995.

————. *The Enneagram: Understanding Yourself and the Others in Your Life.* New York: HarperOne, 1988.

Parkin, OM C., and Boris Fittkau. "The Distorted Enneagram: The Gnosis Interview with Claudio Naranjo." *Gnosis: A Journal of the Western Inner Traditions* no. 41 (Fall 1996), 20–24.

Riso, Don Richard. *Discovering Your Personality Type: The Enneagram Questionnaire.* New York: Houghton Mifflin Company, 1992.

————. *Enneagram Transformations: Releases and Affirmations for Healing Your Personality Type.* New York: Houghton Mifflin Company, 1993.

————. *Personality Types: Using the Enneagram for Self-Discovery.* Boston: Houghton Mifflin Company, 1987.

Riso, Don Richard, and Russ Hudson. *Personality Types: Using the Enneagram for Self-Discovery.* New York: Houghton Mifflin, 1996.

————. *Understanding the Enneagram: The Practical Guide to Personality Types.* New York: Houghton Mifflin, 2000.

————. *The Wisdom of the Enneagram: The Complete Guide to Psychological and Spiritual Growth for the Nine Personality Types.* New York: Bantam, 1999.

Rohr, Richard, and Andreas Ebert. *Discovering the Enneagram: An Ancient Tool for a New Spiritual Journey.* Translated by Peter Heinegg. New York: Crossroad, 1990.

————. *The Enneagram: A Christian Perspective*. Translated by Peter Heinegg. New York: Crossroad, 2006.

Rohr, Richard, et al. *Experiencing the Enneagram*. Translated by Peter Heinegg. New York: Crossroad, 1992.

Schafer, William M. *Roaming Free Inside the Cage: A Daoist Approach to the Enneagram*. Bloomington, IN: iUniverse, 2009.

Smith, Pace, and Kyeli. "WCME 056: The 27 Subtypes with Beatrice Chestnut: 5, 6, and 7." *Wild Crazy Meaningful Enneagram*. Podcast audio, August 31, 2016. https://pacesmith.com/wcme-056/.

————. "WCME 057: The 27 Subtypes with Beatrice Chestnut: 8, 9, and 1." *Wild Crazy Meaningful Enneagram*. Podcast audio, September 14, 2016. https://pacesmith.com/wcme-057/.

————. "WCME 058: The 27 Subtypes with Beatrice Chestnut: 2, 3, and 4." *Wild Crazy Meaningful Enneagram*. Podcast audio, September 28, 2016. https://pacesmith.com/wcme-058/.

————. "Enneagram Countertypes with Beatrice Chestnut." *Dervish and the Mermaid*. Podcast audio, August 24, 2017. http://pacesmith.com /mervish-139/.

Tart, Charles T. (editor) *Transpersonal Psychologies: Perspectives on the Mind from Seven Great Spiritual Traditions*. New York: HarperCollins, 1975.

Theran, Rafael de J. Henriquez. "Enneatypes and Fingerprints." *Enneagram Monthly* 19, no. 3 (March/April 2013), 1, 15–22.

Waag, Torrey. "What Is the Enneagram?" *Enneagram Monthly* 1, no. 6 (August 1995), 8.

Wagner, Jerome. *The Enneagram Spectrum of Personality Styles: An Introductory Guide*. Evanston, IL: Enneagram Studies and Applications, 1996.

————. *Nine Lenses on the World: The Enneagram Perspective*. Evanston, IL: Enneagram Studies and Applications, 2010.

Wegner, Daniel M., David J. Schneider, Samuel R. Carter, and Teri L. White. "Paradoxical Effects of Thought Suppression." *Journal of Personality and Social Psychology* 53, no. 1 (July 1987), 5–13.

Acknowledgments

My Teachers

Beatrice Chestnut, the late David Daniels, Marion Gilbert, Craig Greenfield, Michael Goldberg, Russ Hudson, Jack Labanauskas, Ginger Lapid-Bogda, Sandra Maitri, Michael Naylor, Peter O'Hanrahan, Helen Palmer, Father Richard Rohr, Renée Rosario, Terry Saracino, Gayle Scott, N'Shama Sterling, and Jerry Wagner: Thank you showing us the gifts of this teaching through the embodied ways you've internalized the very things you teach. I honor you.

My Agent

Christopher Ferebee: Thank you for your friendship; it sure makes working together a true gift. You're a great man and a cherished brother.

My Publishing Team

The good folks at Zondervan—Robin Barnett, Greg Clouse, Tom Dean, Curt Diepenhorst, Alyssa Karhan, Alicia Kasen, Andrea Kelly, Kait Lamphere, David Morris, Stephanie Smith, Estee Zandee, and others who have worked on this project: Thank you for your attention to detail and all the thankless yet crucial contributions that go into bringing a project like this to life. I really do love working with you all.

My Editors

Greg Clouse and Stephanie Smith: I don't know how you do it; the early drafts of this probably pained you in ways I'll never imagine. Thank you for helping me to see the beauty beneath it all. You are truly experts at your craft, and I marvel at your skill.

My Illustrator

Elnora Turner: Thank you for bringing these pages to life with the beautiful art you generously share with the world. I can't imagine this book without your fingerprints throughout it.

My Review Readers

Brent Crampton, Denny Kolsch, Rob O'Callaghan, and Nhiên Vương: Thank you for the honest feedback at the earliest stages of working on this. I hope you each will find the nudges and direction you offered in the evolution of this project.

My Community

Gravity, a Center for Contemplative Activism—Angela Griner, Ying Guo, Mariah Houston, Melanie Kim, Vera Leung, Nikole Lim, Avon Manney, Betty McGuire, Cristina Mejía, George Mekhail, Alanah Nantell, Father Richard Rohr, Victoria Rosales, Anahí Salazar, Jared Spence, Oreon Trickey, Nhiên Vương, Eric Wilson, and Naisa Wong: Thank you for investing in the incubator of my vocational imagination by *being* the kind of community that is healing the world.

My Partner

Phileena, as we get older I'm less fixated on what you do or what you offer me and more enamored by the beautiful soul you continue to become. Thanks for being an amazing partner and a spectacular puppy co-parent. I love you so damn much.

Enneagram Consultations *and* Workshops

Chris Heuertz is an Accredited Professional with the International Enneagram Association and an internationally recognized Enneagram teacher. Chris presents and consults internationally introducing the Enneagram for personal and collective transformation with individuals, communities, universities, organizations, corporations, and small businesses.

To find an updated schedule for his Enneagram workshops, visit: www.sacredenneagram.org.

To schedule a one-on-one Enneagram consultation or a private or public workshop with Chris Heuertz, visit: http://gravitycenter.com /join/enneagram/.

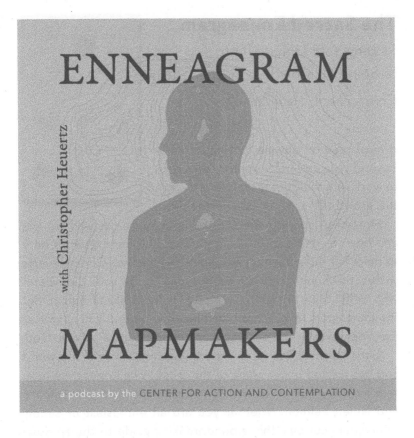

ENNEAGRAM

MAPMAKERS

with Christopher Heuertz

a podcast by the CENTER FOR ACTION AND CONTEMPLATION

ENNEAGRAM MAPMAKERS explores the interior landscapes of the ego through conversations with legacy teachers such as Richard Rohr, Helen Palmer, and Russ Hudson. Hosted by Christopher Heuertz, author of *The Sacred Enneagram* and *The Enneagram of Belonging*, this podcast journeys to the origins of an ancient and often misunderstood system designed to help us live a more embodied and integrated life. Transcend the temptation to fixate on a specific number and discover how to embrace all types within you.

The Sacred Enneagram

Finding Your Unique Path
to Spiritual Growth

Christopher L. Heuertz

A must-read for anyone looking to move beyond type as caricature and learn how to work with the Enneagram toward spiritual growth. Over 100,000 copies sold!

Most of us spend a lifetime trying to figure out who we are, and how we relate to others and God. The Enneagram is here to help. Far more than a personality test, author Chris Heuertz writes, the Enneagram is a sacred map to the soul. Lies about who we think we are keep us trapped in loops of self-defeat. But the Enneagram reveals both the nine ways we get lost, as well as the nine ways we find our way home to our True Self and to God.

Chris Heuertz has taught the Enneagram all over the world and has trained under some of the great living Enneagram masters, including Father Richard Rohr, Russ Hudson, Marion Gilbert, and Helen Palmer. Whether you are an enthusiast or simply Enneagram-curious, this groundbreaking guide to the spiritual depth of the Enneagram will help you:

- Understand the "why" behind your type, beyond caricatures and stereotypes
- Identify and find freedom from self-destructive patterns
- Learn how to work with your type toward spiritual growth
- Awaken your unique gifts to serve today's broken world

ALSO AVAILABLE: *The Sacred Enneagram Workbook*

Available in stores and online!